INTERNATIONAL TRADE AND INDUSTRIAL POLICIES

Government Intervention and an Open World Economy

Edited by
STEVEN J. WARNECKE

 HOLMES & MEIER PUBLISHERS, INC.

New York

First published in the United States of America 1978 by
HOLMES & MEIER PUBLISHERS, INC.
30 Irving Place, New York, N.Y. 10003

Library of Congress Cataloging in Publication Data
Main entry under title:

International trade and industrial policies.

    Includes index.
    1.   Commercial policy. 2.   Subsidies.
3. Industry and state. 4. Commerce.
I. Warnecke, Steven Joshua.
HF1411.15184   1978   338.9   78–611
ISBN 0–8419–0370–0

Printed in Great Britain.

Contents

Notes on the Contributors

STEVEN J. WARNECKE is Associate Professor of Political Science at the City University of New York, where he has been co-director at the Graduate School of the joint political economy program with Columbia University. He has also been a Visiting Professor at Columbia, the University of Pennsylvania and the College of Europe in Bruges and is currently a Visiting Scholar at the International Institute for Strategic Studies in London. Among his publications are *The European Community in the 1970s, Industrial Policies in Western Europe*, and articles on relations with the developing world. He is currently preparing a study on the strategic and economic implications of trade in uranium ores.

RICHARD N. COOPER is Frank Altschul Professor of International Economics and former Provost of Yale University. He has been an official in the US Department of State as well as on the staff of the President's Council of Economic Advisers. His numerous publications include *The Economics of Interdependence* (1968) and *Economic Mobility and National Economic Policy* (1974).

GUY DE CARMOY has been a French and later an international civil servant. He is teaching currently at the European Institute of Business Administration in Fontainebleau and the Institute of Political Science in Paris. His major fields of interest are international relations, European economics and energy policy.

WILLIAM DIEBOLD, JR. is Senior Research Fellow at the Council on Foreign Relations in New York where he has been since 1939 aside from government service from 1943 through 1947, first with the Office of Strategic Services and then with the Division of Commercial Policy of the State Department. Among his publications are *Trade and Payments in Western Europe: A Study in Economic Cooperation, 1947–51* (1952) and the *The United States and the Industrial World: American Foreign Economic Policy in the 1970s* (1972). He is currently working on a book on American foreign economic policy toward the communist countries.

SIDNEY GOLT was a United Kingdom civil servant 1941–70. He was Adviser on Commercial Policy at the Board of Trade 1964–68, and subsequently a Deputy Secretary of the Board and of the Department of Trade and Industry. Since leaving government service he has been a consultant on government relations and international commercial policy to a number of large firms and the UK member of the Commonwealth Experts Group on international economic affairs.

HARALD B. MALMGREN is head of an economic and business consulting firm, and also Professor of Business and Public Administration at George Washington University. He served under Presidents Johnson, Nixon and Ford in various capacities in international economic policy, most recently as Ambassador and Deputy Special Representative for Trade Negotiations, in which post he functioned as chief trade negotiator for the US Government. Among his publications are *International Economic Peacekeeping in Phase II*.

NOBUYOSHI NAMIKI, prior to service as First Secretary of the Japanese Embassy at Brussels 1963–7, was with the Ministry of International Trade and Industry and the Economic Planning Agency. From 1967 through 1975 he directed various divisions of MITI, and is now director and chief economist of the Japan Economic Research Center. Among his publications in Japanese are *International Economic Theory and Trade Policy* (1961), *On International Competitiveness* (1972) and *Japan in the Era of an International Economy* (1972).

SEAMUS O'CLEIREACAIN is Associate Professor of Economics at the State University of New York at Purchase, and Senior Research Associate at the Trade Policy Research Centre in London. He graduated from University College Dublin in 1963 and received his PhD from the University of Michigan in 1971. He is co-author with Geoffrey Denton and Sally Ash of *Trade Effects of Public Subsidies to Private Enterprise* (1975).

GORAN OHLIN is Professor of Economics at Uppsala University, Sweden. He has been Senior Economist of the Swedish Federation of Industries and has been associated with a number of international organizations, including the OECD Development Centre for which he edited *Adjustment for Trade*, a volume on industrial adjustment in various OECD countries.

CAROLINE PESTIEAU is Senior Economist with the C. D. Howe Research Institute in Montreal, where she specialises in international trade and payments and Canada's foreign trade and commercial policy. Among her publications are *The Canadian Textile Policy: A Sectoral Trade Adjustment Policy?* (1976), *Non-Tariff Barriers as a Problem in International Development*, with Jacques Henry (1972) and *Canada and Latin America: The Potential For Economic Partnership*, with Colin Bradford (1971).

Preface

This volume owes its origin to a concern with a policy issue. The effectiveness of GATT Articles VI and XVI on subsidies and counter-vailing duties has been considerably weakened by the proliferation of various kinds of defensive and offensive government supports to industry. These state aids have not only intensified the extent to which governments are resorting to unilateral and bilateral political solutions to trade conflicts such as voluntary export restraints and orderly marketing agreements, but have also added substantially to the politicization of international commercial relations. In light of the various forces which governments feel are pressing them to find nonmarket resolutions to trade problems, what are the prospects for maintaining multilateral rules on subsidies and countermeasures?

This is a particularly involved matter, since the restiveness with GATT regulations on subsidies is a manifestation of a profound change in the relationship of states to their economies, and hence to the international trade system. If the GATT is based on liberal rules for determining global industrial specialization, the interventionist policies of governments are a direct challenge to the political and economic principles upon which the trade system has rested for nearly thirty years. Additionally, the increasing use of countervailing duties by the United States has threatened Washington's traditional leadership role as the guarantor of an open global economic system.

The chapters in this volume are the result of a project which was designed to examine how, from the perspectives of the trade negotiator and policymaker, national subsidy policies have affected the GATT and what new rules and procedures might be necessary to deal with the conflicts that have arisen. With this practical goal in mind, specialists on trade and industrial policies from North America, Japan and Western Europe were brought together to assess what issues should be addressed and to prepare papers. Since it was intended that the results of the project should be relevant to the current trade negotiations, the various contributions were tailored to raise essential questions, provide basic information, analyze important issues, and in several cases make policy recommendations.

The first three chapters expand the discussion of subsidies beyond those subsumed under GATT Articles VI and XVI by examining them in the context of national industrial policies. This includes an analysis of the reasons for and nature of such policies, a survey of the sectors involved and the forms and levels of subsidization. As these chapters indicate, the multiplication of direct and indirect state aids has posed two major problems for interstate trade relations. It has not only become more difficult to determine which subsidies should be a source of international concern, but also to find methods for quantifying their effects.

The following chapters examine the impact such policies have had on the operation of the relevant GATT rules, the problems governments face in reconciling their domestic goals with their international commit- ments, and the difficulties states face in negotiating on subsidies. The contributions include an examination of the adequacy of existing GATT practices; the interests of the major members of the trade system, Japan, the EEC, the US and Canada; and the EEC experience with regulating subsidies among the Nine, since it sheds light on efforts to reform the GATT. Finally, policy recommendations are made both for relations among the industrialized states and between them and the developing world.

Chapter 9 examines the usefulness of existing methods for evaluating the trade effects of state aids and the extent to which policymakers can rely on presently available approaches when disputes occur. While such analyses are important for resolving trade conflicts, they are often inconclusive. Thus, as both the GATT and EEC experiences dem- onstrate, in the first instance, it is essential for governments to agree on the political framework and general rules for discussing the subsidy issue. The most elaborate framework, the European Economic Community's rules on subsidies, is examined in chapter 7. Chapters 2, 3 and 7 provide an overview of the EEC and its member states. The negotiating positions in the current MTN of specific nations and areas are presented in chapter 4 (US, Canada, Japan and the EEC), chapter 5 (US), and chapter 6 (Japan). The relationship between the developing and developed countries is dealt with in chapters 8 and 10. Sectoral arrangements in textiles, shipbuilding and potentially steel are covered in chapters 7 and 8. Finally, while many of the contributions reflect upon the desirability of increased government involvement in industry and trade, the most elaborate discussions of this theme are contained at the end of chapter 3, chapter 5 and chapter 10.

Several people were of great assistance in the course of the prepara- tion and conduct of this project, and I would like to express my appreciation to them. Guy de Carmoy, William Diebold and Harald Malmgren lent their support and encouragement from the outset, commented on successive drafts of the research proposal, and gen- erously made time available for discussions at various stages in the evolution of the work. Hugh Corbet not only played an important role in helping to refine the focus of the papers, but also very kindly made the facilities of the Trade Policy Research Centre available for a meeting held in London. I would like to thank Peter Kenen who was always available for advice, and Jan Tumlir whose extensive comments not only contributed to the direction of the project but are reflected in the introduction to this volume. Moreover, Caroline Pestiean graciously consented to prepare a revised version of a paper originally prepared for the C.D. Howe Institute. Appreciation is also due to Janet Strachan who organized the London meeting, Deborah Wilson who was responsible for the Washington meeting, and Annette Phillips who diligently prepared the manuscript for publication.

Finally, I would like to express my gratitude to the German Marshall Fund of the United States for providing the grant which made this project possible, and, in particular, to Robert Gerald Livingston, whose skilful and thoughtful involvement was a very important element in the course of the research. Of course, any omissions or shortcomings in the book are the responsibility of the editor.

London
October, 1977

S.J.W.

Introduction
Government Intervention
and an Open Global
Trading System

STEVEN J. WARNECKE

The current multilateral trade negotiations (MTN) are taking place under circumstances less promising and substantially different from those of the Kennedy Round. Not only have governments found it increasingly difficult to maintain their commitments to trade liberalization as a result of lower growth rates, but they have also called into question many of the rules which have been the basis for the international commercial system in operation since the late 1940s.

For three decades, the principles embodied in the General Agreement on Tariffs and Trade (GATT) have been the touchstones for moving toward and maintaining an open world economy based upon an international rule of law. They have provided some standards for exerting pressure on nations to use their resources efficiently and some limits to the protectionist and interventionist policy choices available to governments. In the last ten years, the conditions which produced a consensus on the legitimacy of these principles have been eroded. The fairness of the system has been challenged not only by Third World demands for a new international economic order, but by the less dramatic, although equally significant, conflicts among the OECD states. At issue now is whether existing rules can be modified or new ones drafted which can continue to contribute to world order and economic rationality in an increasingly diverse, complex and dynamic global economic system.

One of the major facets of this problem is the proliferation of government interventions to assist lead and declining industries, policies which often take forms which are incompatible with the GATT. Although the issue is not new, it has become more visible with successive rounds of trade liberalization as the reduction of tariffs and quotas has brought into prominence what are euphemistically called nontariff barriers. The significance of such policies as a source of conflict in interstate relations has been intensified as governments have subsidized an ever expanding range of industries. While the degree of efficiency enforced by the GATT rules has been far from perfect, subsidies have added to the concern about the extent to which the distribution of investments, the location of firms, and the direction of world trade are being influenced by nonmarket factors. In addition, they have not only increased the obstacles faced by governments and investors in calculating the risk in new investments if an industry depends for even a small part of its output on foreign demand, but also made it considerably more complicated to determine what is the most profitable investment in the first place. For those countries which feel justified in resorting to aids, the prospect of a countervailing duty is a source of uncertainty in the allocation of domestic resources. Since the regulation of state aids is one dimension of maintaining order among states, the frictions such aids cause potentially threaten the existing multilateral trade framework with its reciprocal obligations and agreed rules and procedures.

At least three avenues have been or are being pursued to deal with the traditional problem of the adverse effects of government intervention on other states' interests. Within the context of the current MTN, negotiations are under way to revise and expand Articles VI and XVI which deal with subsidies and countervailing duties. Parallel to the GATT round, discussions have been taking place in the OECD about drafting a code to regulate competition for investments. Finally, governments have resorted to the conclusion of bilateral 'voluntary' export restraints on a wide number of products and multilateral sectoral agreements in the particularly troublesome sectors of shipbuilding and textiles. Although sectoral accords represent an important shift in emphasis from dealing exclusively with the narrowly defined trade effects of subsidies to some of the causes of these conflicts, this entails two dangers. Since interest has been expressed in working out similar arrangements to allocate production on the basis of one formula or another for other sectors such as steel, political negotiations might be substituted for the play of market forces in more sectors. If this precluded state aids from being governed by a common set of rules such as those which might be contained in revised GATT articles, uncertainty and friction in international trade would certainly increase.

While criteria for determining what constitutes fair competition and acceptable government intervention are essential for maintaining an open global system and an international rule of law, the liberal model which has served as a guide in the past is no longer an entirely reliable basis for developing new criteria and procedures on subsidies. The GATT was designed to deal with the trade effects of a small group of direct export-oriented state aids. The relevant articles have been overtaken by the proliferation in number and type of subsidies, their use by governments to achieve goals not contemplated when the trade system was established, the rapid and complex evolution of industries, and the more complicated determinants of comparative advantage. Under these conditions, it is difficult to enforce rules based on the assumptions that comparative advantages change at politically and socially acceptable rates, that the distribution of production is easily determined and ratified by some notion of comparative advantage, and that governments should minimize their involvement in the market place. Moreover, a strict subordination of government interventions to GATT rules would not only infringe national sovereignty, but tip the balance· in favor of those states whose private sectors were the most competitive. Thus one of the central dilemmas which must be resolved before new rules can be established is how to reconcile national goals pursued through subsidy policies with multilateral commitments.

Before the revision or replacement of existing rules can be addressed, it is essential to determine why governments have been prepared to deviate from the ideal efficiency criteria as defined by GATT rules: that is, comparative advantages defined in terms of relative prices determined by firms competing in international markets. This means examining whether the principles which have legitimated the GATT for its members are still binding to the extent they were in the past, how effective liberal theories have been for organizing commercial relations among states, what factors allowed governments to support trade liberalization, how these factors have changed, and what implications this transformation has for negotiations on subsidies and countervailing duties. Without such a broad analysis, a technical revision of rules and procedures on the basis of existing assumptions about trade might end up being unenforceable, since many elements which have justified GATT practices on subsidies are no longer generally believed to be right or acceptable.

THE GATT SYSTEM

The international trade system which was re-established in the late 1940s was based on an intergovernmental agreement, the GATT, through which liberal principles could gradually be realized. In addition to the economic goals, the American proponents hoped that the GATT would lead to a depoliticization of trade in contrast to the national confrontations which marked the interwar period. In other words, the 'low politics' of commercial exchanges among private producers and consumers would replace the 'high politics' of interstate relations. Thus the attainment of the most efficient allocation and use of resources and the greatest degree of global welfare depended upon increasing the scope of international competition among firms by reducing tariff and quota

barriers separating national markets. Except for setting up and enforcing the rules, governments were to recede into the background. The
prospects for conflict would be minimized if there was no undue
resistance to structural changes dictated by changing patterns of
comparative costs, and if governments resisted the temptation to
intervene through subsidy policies. If they did not, it was hoped that
their treasuries would exert the necessary discipline.

Whatever limitations may have been inherent in this model were
overshadowed by the unparalleled economic growth of the 1950s and
1960s as well as the dominant role of the United States which allowed
Washington to set the agenda on international trade matters. For more
than twenty years attention was focused on lowering barriers, starting
from the first negotiations in Annecy and Torquay to the Kennedy
Round where the American belief that free trade was in everyone's
interest culminated in the optimistic formulation of the 1963 Trade
Expansion Act. Problems which had been kept below the surface began
to emerge with greater insistence after the completion of the Kennedy
Round.

One of the major weaknesses in the GATT was the discrepancy
between the desired and actual role of governments. Even before the
establishment of the Bretton Woods system, governments had begun to
intervene more forcefully and pervasively in their economies. The
change in the balance of public and private power was intensified after
1945, ironically partly in response to the major goal of the GATT-trade
liberalization. The source of this historical oversight was a US trade
policy which had clearly and inappropriately projected an idealized
domestic economic philosophy, market structure and industrial organization on to the international arena. The anomaly of this policy was its
being drafted at precisely the moment when the American economy
under the influence of the New Deal was undergoing substantial
modification through expanded government regulation and involvement in the private sector. If the Keynesian synthesis of demand
management, regulation of the private sector and distributive social
welfare policies had pointed the way on the national level to dealing with
some of the weaknesses of modern capitalism without replacing the
market mechanism as the most effective allocator of goods and
resources, internationally a new liberal trade system should also have
been counterbalanced by some rules which mitigated the competitive
inequalities among states.

A second omission in the GATT was the incorrect expectations
concerning the role of the various national private sectors. It was first
visible in the negotiations leading to the establishment of the postwar
financial system. As a result of wartime devastation, many states wanted
the monetary fund to participate in reconstruction and recovery as well
as assist in maintaining balance of payments equilibrium. The United

States took a particularly narrow and unrealistic view, seeming to expect that European recovery could be left to the market and revived private sector. When this did not happen, active intervention was necessary to restore the economies of the key member states in order for them to be able to participate in the Bretton Woods system. While the late 1940s was an exceptional period, the vitality and competitiveness of national private sectors have been a continuing source of concern for governments as reflected in the various Belgian economic expansion laws or the French and Japanese industrial policies. What this concern demonstrates is that private sectors have histories, and their capacities for regeneration may be impaired for reasons running from social and political ossification to the relative changes in economic power which constantly occur in the international system. In addition, two other significant conclusions should be drawn from the period of reconstruction and recovery. States with similar economic systems have most readily been able to accommodate themselves to the GATT. Even then, nations at the relatively same level of development with firms that are internationally competitive have been most comfortable with the operation of the international trade system. The prospect of having to accommodate states which fill few or none of these prerequisites, has faced the GATT with a difficult task.

These issues were raised by many of the smaller industrialized and developing world nations at the time of the negotiations on the Bretton Woods system. In fact, what was to become the GATT was to have been the commercial policy section of a more comprehensive charter for an International Trade Organization. The charter was to have included sections on employment and economic policy, economic development and reconstruction, restrictive business practices and intergovernmental commodity agreements. But the ITO was fated never to take effect, and rather than be left with a gap in the postwar system, the United States was able to get a number of states to accept the commercial policy section of the charter as the basis for trade negotiations. The failure to contain all significant trade issues within one political framework would later come home to roost with the establishment of particularistic and competitive fora such as UNCTAD or the EEC to represent those states whose interests could not be adequately dealt with in the GATT. This development has complicated negotiations on trade matters. However, what was lost in breadth and comprehensiveness in the transition from the ITO to the GATT was gained in the simplicity of the principles for organizing interstate commercial relations.

For the United States, imbued with a tradition which considered economics as low politics best left to the vagaries of the private sector and market, the GATT appeared to be an ideal mechanism, even if it was accepted with hesitation by many of the other participants. The seemingly apolitical approach to trade was in contrast to US policies in other areas where power politics and government intervention clearly dominated. Even though global welfare did increase and the participants in the system enjoyed reciprocal benefits, in time the US would be accused of hiding the special advantages it derived from trade liberalization behind a general economic theory, a criticism reminiscent of the 19th century view of British policy as free trade imperialism. The obvious source of this discontent was the overwhelming economic weight of America in the late 1940s. Since the US was the undisputed leader, specialization on the basis of the then prevailing distribution of industry and capital would inevitably reinforce American superiority. Frictions would increasingly arise as other states challenged this distribution as being politically and economically unacceptable. These challenges, which should have been expected, have increased as the Europeans and Japanese have become more concerned about their relative positions not only in regard to the United States and each other, but in reference to the pressures emanating from the Third World. These challenges are one of the sources of instability in trade relations today.

INTERSTATE RELATIONS AND THE LEGITIMACY OF TRADE RULES

Irrespective of how the benefits have been distributed, neither the reconstruction nor the stability of a new international commercial order would have been possible without US leadership and participation. But the preference for looking at trade through apolitical and ahistorical liberal rules has diverted attention from three crucial systemic features which are important for understanding how the GATT has functioned as well as what the prospects are for negotiations on revisions since these factors have been undergoing changes. These are: the relationship of the security framework to the economic rules which its members have been prepared to accept, the political structure supporting the GATT and the implementation of its rules, and the role of a hegemonic power in guaranteeing and managing the system. In spite of the ostensible 'low politics' approach Washington advocated for trade, there has been a considerable degree of government involvement necessary to maintain and stabilize the system.

One of the causes of the fragmentation of the international economic system after World War One was the failure to agree on a system for guaranteeing security. The security framework established after 1945 under American hegemony not only made it possible for a large number of states to accept a liberal trade order, but determined the geographic scope, continuity and stability of the rules. Throughout the 1950s and early 1960s, Europe and Japan were prepared to subordinate their trade, monetary and foreign policies to the US, not only because they were dependent, but because considerable benefits were obtained. They accepted the US lead in defining the inclusiveness of the system, the pace of negotiations and the implementation of the rules. A hidden lubricant was America's capacity to allow discrimination against itself when necessary through the European Payments Union, the European Economic Community, and the long delay before the Japanese were pressed to liberalize access to their markets.

Although the Europeans and Japanese still depend on the American security commitment, they have been confronted with the necessity for exercising greater independence in defining their external economic and political policies. The relative decline in America's power as symbolized by the new economic policy announced in August 1971, the weakening of its role as guarantor as it has no longer felt possible to continue to maintain a certain degree of aloofness from a competitive system it believed worked automatically in its favor, and the erosion of the internal consensus of the Atlantic Alliance, have all contributed to shaking the solidarity and consensus among the OECD states. This has led to the politicization of economic issues which previously were relegated to the level of 'low politics', and contributed to a competition for political and economic ties with the Third World, Comecon, the Soviet Union and even other industrialized countries. National foreign economic and political policies have been linked to concern about the evolution of industries, access to markets, and security of raw material supplies, areas which have in many cases required increased government intervention. An important effect of the manner in which states view their individual relations to the international economic system is the shifting of competition outside the GATT into areas where it either did not exist or if present before was relatively unimportant.

If these developments may hasten the transformation of the political relations which have supported the GATT, this transformation had already begun as early as 1957 with the establishment of the European Economic Community. American policy makers were divided about the implications of the EEC, but the view prevailed that it would be a way station before the Europeans could accept full trade liberalization. In historical perspective, it was a continuation in a new form of those interwar preferential systems through which France, Germany and Italy had attempted to overcome the economic limitations placed on them by their size. The EEC was constituted, in part, to counteract the existing distribution of power and economic advantage in the Atlantic Alliance. It was a catalyst both for its members and the Commission to intervene more deeply in the evolution of the industrial structure of that part of Europe which it covered. With the decline of the consensus which allowed the US to be the hegemonic center of a system, the EEC and Japan have felt compelled to press more forcefully for their interests in multilateral negotiations. The prospects of the industrialized countries reaching agreements among themselves on subsidies may become more complex with efforts to extend the GATT to include state trading countries as well as some of the demands of Third World nations.

GOVERNMENT SUBSIDY POLICIES

Although governments are tempted to influence the evolution of their industrial bases in response to a variety of domestic and international factors, the answers to several questions can assist in bringing more clarity to their diverse motives and goals. First, what would be the international division of labor and a nation's place in it, if governments did not intervene and relied entirely on private sector decisions? Second, what would be the economic, political and strategic implications? Third, under modern conditions which states can reasonably aspire to have which industrial capacities, whether they are attained strictly by the private sector or with some kind of government involvement? Stated somewhat differently, what are the efficiency criteria that should, if not bind governments, guide them when they decide to support or foster industries? Fourth, through which means and at what costs should they be attained? Fifth, what international effects of domestic policies should be a source of multilateral concern?

The responsibilities of governments and their time frames differ considerably from those of investors and managers. Efficient industries can be a source of current growth and jobs. But what may be the relevant geographic markets, criteria and patterns of operation for firms maximizing individual and corporate goals, do not necessarily include all of those objectives which are of immediate and long range importance to governments. There are a considerable number of externalities to the firm which have not been traditionally included in the calculation of production costs, although they are increasing. These include social security, lessening pollution, reducing regional disparities, improving the distribution of industries and easing social and class antagonisms. Extreme examples involve cases where national integration and industrial distribution are related to each other: for example, Canada, Belgium and Italy; or cases where industrial development and restructuring are part of a policy to reduce class conflicts: for example, France.

There is a similar discrepancy between the manner in which political leaders and firms view the relation of industries to the international economy. Governments are concerned about the conditions which foster their nations' present *and* future growth as well as those that affect the intensity and rate of change in declining sectors. Since the industries which contribute to growth today may not be those of tomorrow, when—if at all—are governments justified in trying to ensure that investments flow to the products and industries of tomorrow and that suitable reorganization and concentration take place in sectors where it is necessary? These are not idle matters, since there are innumerable domestic and international factors which continually affect the positions of states and their industries relative to those of other states. Since governments inevitably make comparisons with developments in other nations, the industries they wish to emulate at home are frequently those they believe enhance other nations' political and economic power. Thus many second level industrialized states aspire to be 'complete' economies. They refuse to accept international specialization by subsidizing lead sectors, often in the hope that they can obtain a domestic capacity before entry solidifies and the costs become too high.

Whether and if governments can achieve the goals they set themselves through industry is a politically volatile question. Some sectors may need a degree of government intervention, but what efficiency criteria should prevail, particularly when industries are also vehicles to achieve other goals set by the state? Governments are often prepared to temporarily curtail or subordinate efficiency criteria in the pursuit of political and social goals as well as in their efforts to maintain declining and foster expanding industries. Frequently, subsidy policies are pursued in the naive belief that losses will be short run until an industry is competitive, or that the long run costs of withdrawing certain firms or sectors from the market can and should be carried by other parts of the economy. Moreover, domestic preferences as to the types, degrees and duration of intervention vary, but governments of the Left have simply expanded on the extent to which those of the Right and Center were already involved in economic policy formulation. However, as numerous examples demonstrate, there are considerable limits to government officials and politicians effectively exercising entrepreneurial and managerial responsibility.

These economic anxieties can become exaggerated, as in the case of France, where the possession of certain industries has come to be equated with security, independence and power. Increased intervention is both a result of the effects the internationalization of capital and production have had on national monetary policy and the industrial base, as well as the pressures small states find they are under if they wish to improve their place in the global division of labor.

Although French concern about being overtaken economically reached its peak with de Gaulle's interventionist policies to improve French self-sufficiency and access to technology, it has not been an exclusive preserve of the Center parties. It has also been shared by the Socialists who, unlike the governments in power which have relied on indicative planning, are proponents of expanded state ownership of industries and central planning. Even then, the Gaullists, Independent Republicans and Socialists have not remained untouched by the

enormous costs the state had imposed upon itself through its entrepreneurial role and its efforts to determine the degree of specialization in French industry. The most interesting statement showing how a
variety of factors have contributed to the formation of a party program
has been made by Michel Rocard, a member of the executive committee
of the Partei Socialiste Francaise. While the French Left has had to
accept market forces for reasons of efficiency and an increased
international division of labor, this could not be done with reliance on
absolute free trade and non-intervention. First, since the end of the
1950s, the political significance of inflation and unemployment has
grown. No state, or for that matter political party, can be passive in the
face of these problems or in the face of accelerated change in the
structure of the economy. It cannot allow industries to adjust too
quickly, not only because of social considerations imposed by a
pluralist, democratic society, but because of the impact on the
distribution of power among the political parties. Conservatives fear a
drift toward the Left, and the Left has an obligation as the party of the
working class. Second, although increasing employment may be a
reason for intervention, it is not simply a matter of jobs, but jobs in
which industries. If as a result of entrepreneurial limitations that curtail
innovation and investment, can states with less able or less aggressive
private sectors abandon opportunities to keep options open through
subsidies. For countries with a huge investment in highly trained
managers, researchers, scientists and technicians, this is an important
consideration.

Japan's concerns, while similar, occur in a slightly different context. A
major pressure encouraging close relations between the government and
private sector is uncertainty about North American and European
responsiveness to Japanese economic interests. This is an enduring
problem predating the creation of the GATT, which indicates the extent
to which geopolitical and geoeconomic factors are constants which
influence foreign economic policy.

Before turning to a consideration of the GATT rules, one additional
dimension which is causing instability in international trade relations
must be examined.

THE DOMESTIC BASES OF SUPPORT FOR TRADE LIBERALIZATION

The consensus upon which liberal trade principles have rested has not
only been affected by increased government intervention in the economy, and the complex patterns of international competition, but also by
the transformation of the domestic sources of support. The cardinal
example is the American labor movement. Within a period of little more

than ten years, it has changed dramatically from being a supporter of trade liberalization to an adversary. Whether this is a temporary phenomenon in response to slower growth rates or a manifestation of a more long range one in response to profound domestic and international structural problems is still unclear. But it does parallel the relative change in the United States' position in the trade system, and is one manifestation of the unravelling of the domestic coalition in the US which has supported free trade. It makes clear that America's role as guarantor depended upon economic expansion, a high rate of employment and no undue resistance by key groups to structural changes at home. It also dramatizes the political and economic sociology which has allowed the liberal system to work, and raises the question of whether the conditions which have supported the GATT for thirty years were historically unique.

Examination of the sociopolitical dimensions of trade liberalization has generally tended to focus on the responses of specific groups, in isolation from those of other groups, to changing market relations. By judging these responses in terms of an equilibrium model drawn exclusively from economic analysis, a facile means is available for determining how groups should adjust their interests to the so-called dictates of the market. This not only makes interest groups a residual category in terms of re-establishing equilibrium in terms of a model with a narrow frame of reference, but also restricts what is to be considered as a legitimate determinant of comparative advantage. Such an approach is not only undesirable for social and political reasons (which should not be taken to imply that efficiency is to be subordinated to non-economic goals), but also because it obscures how comparative advantage is intertwined with group relations. The patterns of a country's comparative advantages depend not only on physical conditions and factor endowment, but also on socially acceptable group preferences as well. What is 'socially acceptable' at any particular moment is not the outcome of a rational process ratified by a democratically elected government, but the cumulative effects of rather complex processes. Groups view themselves both relatively and absolutely in reference to each other, and any change in the underlying conditions of technology, relative factor or material availability in foreign trade, which makes one group dissatisfied with its position can bring down the whole structure of what is deemed 'socially acceptable'. As Jan Tumlir has forcefully pointed out: 'We do not have a theory to explain how the structure of the "socially acceptable" can be self-equilibrating.' It is inherently unstable, and in a pluralistic democracy, this instability is very quickly transmitted to the legislature and executive. If subsidized imports were admitted as a matter of course, the domestic coalition that supports liberal trade would disintegrate in a short time; and if they were opposed out of hand, the multilateral trade framework would be severely weakened by the counter reaction of those states which feel their subsidies to be legitimate. As Tumlir has noted: 'After some more or less extensive upheaval a new structure of socially acceptable relations would be established. It would certainly require a new pattern of subsidization, protection and other forms of government intervention.'

If trade liberalization has depended on social, political and economic pluralism in the major members of the GATT system, then the causes and patterns of subsidization are symptoms of the serious impairment of the pluralistic model. While the relationship between inflation and domestic and international order has received extensive comment, little has been said about the implications for stability of the proliferation of subsidies in response to pluralism. As many governments have intervened, even over-committed themselves, they have moved from an organizational system essentially appropriate to an economy and to a framework of international trade rules based on the market as the dominant factor both internally and externally, toward one where the market, though still the principal factor, is much more susceptible to the political constraint of government manipulation or intervention. Such intervention has been initiated as much by political leaders as it has been by the readiness of governments in democratic systems to negotiate with all groups. The net results have been a loss of state power and the removal of important constraints on the granting of subsidies. Groups which have power positions on which to capitalize can contribute to inefficiency and inequality at home and conflict with unsubsidized producers in other states. A classic example of the adverse impact of subsidies is represented by Italy's 'dual economy' in which politically connected groups, often allied with the once innovative state holding companies, ENI and IRI, drain resources from the rest of the economy.

There is a limit to the economic inefficiency a democratic political system can tolerate as there is a limit to the inefficiency a multilateral trade system can tolerate as a result of such domestic policies. If sooner or later, governments feel the need to regain sufficient political power to protect themselves from groups not only politically, but also to exercise some constraints on subsidy policies, so too, the stability of multilateral trade rules will require not only some restraint domestically, but also principles for reconciling domestic goals with international commitments.

REFORMING INTERNATIONAL RULES ON SUBSIDIES

At present the global trade system is littered with retreats or near retreats from the GATT. Conflicts have arisen among states in declining and lead industries. Since expanding sectors show few signs of absorbing high unemployment, an increasing number of governments want to check imports in order to protect domestic industry and fend off higher unemployment rates. Advanced states are much less willing to give up to low wage countries the production of those labor intensive goods at which they have a comparative advantage. And in sectors like steel in which there is heavy government involvement, overcapacity has led to the search for political solutions. In general, too many states are intent upon controlling the rates of change in too many sectors. One particularly troublesome aspect is the degree to which the United States has resorted to countervailing duties to stem the flow of imports. The American countervailing duty law is a major irritant, since it does not require a determination of injury. Moreover, the delays possible in the administrative and judicial systems are also sources of concern.

It need not be emphasized that these developments introduce uncertainty in trade and, ultimately, in political relations. It is definitely not in the interests of the big powers to have unpredictability, and in their interests and those of the smaller states to have an orderly functioning and expansion of the global economic system. If the United States acts unpredictably, other nations, which are economically and politically less strong, are encouraged to go their own way without regard to rules and principles. But what should the rules and principles be? Which subsidies or dimensions of the subsidy issue should be regulated?

Articles VI and XVI of the GATT have provided some rules for dealing with the trade effects of national policies, but, as was mentioned, they cover a relatively small group of subsidies. Moreover, the remedy — the application of countervailing duties — is a device which in its present form is unsatisfactory. As in the case of the United States, it provides countries with large markets with disproportionate power to defend themselves against disturbances caused by changing trade patterns.

Procedural improvements alone in GATT rules would be insufficient. The GATT is based on the reduction of barriers to trade and the prohibition of certain government actions. In order to equalize the formal conditions under which firms and investors compete in global markets, the participants in negotiations have focused on finding nondiscriminatory rules for maximizing the sphere of action for the private sector and minimizing government intervention. If this were to be the major approach to subsidies, it is unrealistic. It would leave untouched the thorny problem of finding rules and procedures to reconcile the needs of a multilateral trade system with the domestic pressures and interstate inequalities which induce governments to intervene in their economies. Rules would have to balance the different interests of big and small states in regard to unilateralism and multilateralism. Small countries do not want the big states to have too much freedom of action, but they do want some degree of leeway for themselves. Is it possible to protect little states which need more intervention and ensure fairness in the system? Large states, while wishing to maintain freedom to protect themselves, are interested in rules on subsidies containing inducements for small states to adhere to a multilateral system.

Such general considerations can only be translated into operative rules, if there is agreement about the various dimensions of the subsidy issue to be regulated. Some commentators have expressed the hope that pressures on government to intervene in industry will be reduced or disappear as a result of the floating exchange rate system. If this were so, then an elaborate analysis of subsidies and government intervention would not be required. This view incorrectly assumes that subsidies can be dealt with entirely as a macroeconomic problem when, in fact, they are closely tied to microeconomic issues. In consequence, others have tried to define criteria [1] and priority areas [2] in which the economic effects of state aids can be assessed. Such criteria might assist governments in placing their policies on a firmer economic basis, serve as a guide to domestic action, and in improving the functioning of agreements such as the GATT because there would be an agreed basis for distinguishing between efficient and inefficient assistance, and thereby internationally legitimate and illegitimate forms of intervention. While economic evaluation of subsidies is essential, its usefulness for national policy makers and international organizations may be limited for a number of reasons.

1. Subsidies to industry take such diverse forms and are implemented in so many ways by diverse parts of governments, that the initial question is how to recognize them.
2. Measuring their effects in a coherent manner involves two difficult problems: finding ways to assess *ex ante*, policies whose goals are diverse and whose gains if they do exist, are far in the future or *ex post*, policies whose economic effects are either unclear or not entirely susceptible to cost analysis.
3. If the basic goal behind such calculations is the establishment of objective criteria for guiding national and multilateral decisions on industrial specialization, such figures alone do not necessarily lead to clear conclusions as to which policies should be pursued. There are two sets of reasons which influence governments to reject or resist the dictates of the market. In strictly social and political terms, changes in comparative advantage may be too rapid and technological innovation and diffusion too unsettling to permit the unimpeded operation of market forces. Even if adjustment were recognized as being desirable, domestic factor mobility is not always as easy as required by intra- and inter-sectoral changes, nor is it always clear to which sectors resources should be shifted.

However, if adjustment is possible, there are various policy options which may be available, with or without government assistance. Among them are the introduction of labor saving machinery and the substitution of capital for wage costs in the production of the same products, changes in the product mix in order to be less vulnerable to competition, or the relocation of some production abroad to low wage areas. Governments, for their part, can subsidize industries which have become uncompetitive, exert pressure to bring about greater concentration in a particular sector, or attempt to force the contraction of an industry. Which policies are chosen have different implications for the gravitation of industries to developing countries, or even their redistribution among developed nations. What is of importance is that economics does not always inevitably lead to the shift of apparently declining industrial capacities from one country to another. Political decisions are just as important in determining outcomes.

The second set of reasons is perhaps more serious than the first, since it involves a dilemma if reliance is placed on efficiency criteria to dictate the division of labor. If productivity outstrips demand and many countries are efficient or potentially efficient producers, how should production be allocated? Similar difficulties arise when several countries are potentially efficient producers and exporters of a product, but unable to realize their potentials because startup costs are prohibitive without government subsidies.

4. Finally, unlike tariff and quota negotiations, it is not possible to find a formula for determining reciprocity in negotiations on subsidies.

FUTURE AGREEMENTS ON SUBSIDIES

It is against this background that efforts to improve existing rules on subsidies must be understood. These rules have been applied to states whose different levels of development and disparate and conflicting economic and political aspirations encourage them to intervene in their economies. While this creates immense problems for maintaining a liberal trade framework, intervention, whether deplored or accepted, is a fact of international existence that cannot be denied. If states feel it imperative to regenerate their industries, whatever the reasons may be, it seems difficult to avoid an increasing number of sectors being withdrawn from markets. Even if in the long run it does not matter how much distortion governments introduce, because market forces have a way of reasserting themselves, the interim may be costly in terms of the international ramifications of national policies. Rules are necessary, since a multilateral recognition of the national right to inefficiency is unacceptable, both because of the global and domestic implications.

Politically, international commitments can constitute a strong defense against arbitrary and unilateral actions by individual states. But such commitments must be linked to the degree of commitment of other governments. To the extent that the United States wants others to behave in a defined manner, it must behave the same way and insist on adherence by others to negotiated obligations. However, when a state as economically significant as the US countervails, it raises the question whether such action is a mercantilist attempt to obstruct free trade by impeding specialization and encouraging continued dependence on American producers. The issue of specialization is the heart of the attempt to revise GATT rules on subsidies. What is an acceptable level of specialization? How is it to be achieved? And how is it to be distributed? The proliferation of solutions negotiated among governments outside the GATT such as voluntary export restraints, orderly marketing agreements and sectoral accords, or the establishment of a steel sub-group in the OECD are all indications of the reluctance to rely on markets.

The timing for developing new constraints is right, since the situation is in flux. The practices which have given rise to most international controversy at present are those of the United States; but the American position is now being reviewed in preparation for revision. The problems connected with exporting to the United States or competing with it in third markets are bound to become more serious, if no new international framework of rules and procedures is developed. In addition to a suitable reform of American practices, it might be possible to have all the major trading nations agree to sensible rules covering a sufficiently high percentage of international commerce that exceptions would not matter. It might be composed of a common framework with exceptions for weak states as well as incentives to eventually integrate them into the main system. The problems of reforming rules on subsidies are formidable, since they involve an area which has not been subject to sufficiently comprehensive multilateral agreement before. Whether adequate accords can be reached remains to be seen, but it will be easier to negotiate today, rather than tomorrow, since government intervention is generating and will generate more activism.

Notes and References

1. Geoffrey Denton and Seamus O'Cleireacain have suggested the following: (a) What is the estimated quantitative effect of the subsidy on the costs of firms? (b) How does this compare with the effect on the costs of firms of any domestic distortion which the subsidy may be intended to correct? (c) How significant is the effect of the subsidy on imports or exports? (d) How regular and predictable is the operation of the subsidy? (e) How do the effects of the subsidy in question compare with those of other distortions

affecting the same product, including tariffs? (f) How temporary and digressive is the subsidy intended to be? (g) Does the subsidy aim to promote structural changes such as will make its continuance unnecessary? (h) Is the subsidy genuinely intended for other than trade distorting purposes? See their *Subsidy Issues in International Commerce* (London: Trade Policy Research Centre, 1972), pp. 49–50.

2. In regard to priority areas the same authors have proposed: (a) subsidies appearing to have as their principal objective the curtailment of imports or the encouragement of exports; (b) subsidies to specific industries which cause substantial reduction in the costs of traded goods; and (c) subsidies on specific goods or services which enter into the costs of producing products that are exported or which compete with imports. Ibid., p. 50.

Part 1

National Policies towards Industry

1 Subsidies and other Industrial Aids

GORAN OHLIN

For some decades now, programs and agencies to aid industry in different ways have proliferated in industrial countries, *pari passu* with the liberalization of international trade. This is a source of concern to those who see in such practices the demise of the mixed economy, a new and covert protectionism, a source of international conflict, and an issue on which negotiated agreement may be difficult to come by.

Concern has focused on the extent to which increased state involvement in the private sector and the concomitant multiplication of direct and indirect forms of subsidization have contributed to the erosion of the validity and viability of the liberal economic concepts and assumptions upon which much of contemporary commercial diplomacy, such as takes place in the GATT, has been based. The changed relationship between governments and their private sectors has affected both the operation of firms and markets. The minimization of risk through subsidies has influenced the conditions under which international competition takes place. And active government industrial policies have challenged traditional notions of comparative advantage, thereby affecting the processes and rates at which the global distribution of industry advances.

Whether the role of subsidies has actually increased — say, as a share in the value added in manufacturing—is hard to say, although it seems highly probable. In the first place there are no such figures available. Governments are not anxious to compile them, and no major survey has yet been undertaken. Secondly, it is not all that clear what is meant by a subsidy. A tax rebate is the equivalent of a subsidy, but already in the case of privileged credit finance — a favored instrument of industrial policy — it is sometimes hard to assess the true element of subsidy, and the difficulty increases in the case of more recondite ways of supporting an industry.[1]

In all industrial countries agriculture is covered by a comprehensive system of regulations and subsidies, and agricultural protection in turn raises costs for the food processing industry which may then be helped through tariffs or quotas, but may also get large subsidies. Similarly, special situations often arise in energy, mining, shipbuilding, aviation, etc. Where the total volume of subsidies is heavily weighted by a few such cases, which may be temporary or subject to major fluctuations, an overall figure — if one existed — might be less interesting than the spread of subsidies and other forms of state support to new areas.

Before passing judgement on the subsidies that are now multiplying in mixed economies, it is necessary to take a closer look not only at their uses and effects, but also at the reasons why they are becoming ubiquitous.

This requires going beyond a discussion confined to the more purely economic aspects and relating these different forms of intervention to a variety of political, social and economic motives that now infuse government policy toward industry. By so doing the international discussion of subsidy policies will become more complex. This is already reflected in the effort within GATT to expand Articles VI and XVI to include production as well as export subsidies.

As will be demonstrated in the section of this chapter on the proliferation of types of subsidies, as state aids have increased in form and magnitude, it has not only become more difficult to reach agreement on just which ones should be included under existing international standards and practices, but whether this dilemma includes the obstacles to reaching a consensus on which aspects of state aids may be a source of multilateral concern, how their trade effects should be calculated, and what criteria should be applied in judging when the effects are adverse for the commercial interests of one or more nations.

By and large a substantial part of this issue is intertwined with administrative hearings, court cases and legislative processes, which means that the political and economic balances within states are as relevant to an analysis of international conflicts that arise from domestic subsidies, as are strictly economic considerations. Only through an understanding of the connection with internal domestic balances and group competition will it be possible to explain government behavior contrary to what might be dictated by economic calculations in reference to immediate market considerations.

POSITIVE INDUSTRIAL POLICY

A decade of fairly lively discussion of industrial policy has not produced any very sharply defined notion of what it embraces, partly because many traditional responsibilities of government, such as the maintenance and development of the legal framework of business, the regulation of public utilities, and above all the tariff, could obviously be called industrial policy although they never were in the past.

Talk about industrial policy began in the 1960s, at about the time when economic integration and GATT negotiations had made it more difficult and awkward to resort to trade restrictions to alleviate specific hardships or to further interests of special political importance, and at a time when the consequences of trade liberalization were making themselves felt. Nonetheless, it would be rash to regard the growth of industrial intervention as a mere substitute for traditional protectionism. Governments had also assumed very much greater responsibilities and the changing character of economic policy reflected the rise of new objectives requiring new instruments. In part, this has reflected a reluctance to accept the trends visible in market forces as well as efforts to compel outcomes other than what these forces might dictate. Among the reasons have been governments' concern about the manner in which the evolving global distribution of industry intersects with the structure of their own economies. This is not perceived as a development to be left entirely to outcomes determined by unhindered free trade. In addition, the whole issue of industrial growth has taken on a new character, as the corporatism of modern capitalism, with its powerful business and labor organizations, has led to new demands for participation and public control, imposing a new rigidity on industrial structure. Thus the political and economic sociology of the subsidy issue has become equally as important for understanding the confines within which governments define their policies, as it is for determining the pressures undermining multilateral obligations on subsidies such as Articles VI and XVI of the GATT.

It may be useful to distinguish between industrial policies that actively and positively seek to implement some strategy of industrial development, and others of a more defensive character which are the responses to more or less sudden and unanticipated crises.

Positive policies which rely heavily on subsidies and indirect taxes have everywhere been adopted for such purposes as regional development, the promotion of advanced industries, and the protection of the environment. Regional development policies use subsidies as incentives for firms to settle in lagging regions. Although regional considerations had always influenced public expenditure patterns, the deliberate regional development efforts which took shape in European countries in the fifties and sixties represented something new. The Cassa di Mezzogiorno, which sought to attract industry to southern Italy, was followed by a rash of agencies for physical planning and regional development in other countries, such as the Délégation à l'Amenagement du Territoire et à l'Action Regionale (DATAR), which in the mid-sixties drew up a long term plan to establish effective growth-poles and reduce the crushing predominance of the Parisian region in the French economy.

45423

Regional policies are usually launched in the hope of future take offs which will justify the social investment as a long term pump-priming operation. However, often they turn into quasi-permanent re-distribution schemes under which investors are compensated for the losses involved in locating in remote or otherwise ill-favored regions, in order to maintain incomes and employment in those parts. At the same time labor may be subsidized for moving out of depressed regions and for retraining, on the assumption that the social benefits of relocation will exceed the private ones, especially if regional income disparities are held to narrow limits, and private costs of moving exceed the social cost.

In energy and transportation, geopolitical considerations count heavily, as they always have done. Issues of strategy and security will sway political attitudes to the desirability of maintaining national capabilities. This is not to say that cost is of no account, but petroleum, coal, shipping, and aviation are industries which large and medium-sized industrial countries will not leave alone, and where heavy capital costs make for erratic market behavior in the absence of public intervention. With regard to science and technology, similar long term national objectives, though usually diffuse or confused, justify a good deal of support for R & D and innovation. However, it is also widely accepted that externalities and risk justify public support in order to avoid underinvestment in research. That still leaves a wide range of new uncertainty and risk in the choice of lines of research to encourage, but at least it justifies subsidies for a fairly straightforward reason, based on the characteristics of the market for knowledge.

The awakening to the need for environmental protection has in a remarkably short time produced extensive programs of regulation and research, and also a number of schemes for the taxing of emissions and some subsidies for investments in anti-pollution devices. A number of programs, most of them of rather old standing, provide services to small business and to exporters by supplying information and consultants, organizing fairs and trade missions, etc. Outright subsidies are also given to those groups in the form of cheap loans, export credit guarantees, etc.

Credit is often supplied at preferential terms for a wide variety of purposes which are considered socially or politically important but which, for one reason or another, are not sufficiently attractive to the private financial market. In France, the deposits of savings banks have, since the days of Napoleon, been pre-empted for such worthy uses outside the market. Housing is everywhere a priority sector for subsidized credit, but there are innumerable instances of public support of industrial activities which essentially amount to shading the interest rate, a practice to which legalistic auditors will not object and which the public is not likely to question as much as outright grants.

So-called structural problems have been handled by special agencies for industrial reorganization, such as the Industrial Reorganization Corporation (IRC) in England, with a mandate to intervene where major surgery is indicated and where it is thought that a government agency may facilitate mergers or other arrangements as broker, lender, or partner. But the IRC was shortlived, and structural problems of any magnitude tend to rise to a high political level where they are handled by the Ministry of Industry, and ultimately, when the public purse is involved, by the Ministry of Finance.

Very substantial subsidizing of investment in general is the result of the preferential treatment usually accorded capital goods in the imposition of value-added taxes, a practice that might be defended on the assumption that private risk aversion holds capital below the socially desirable level. Usually, however, it seems simply to be assumed that investment is a good thing of which there can hardly be too much, which in view of the trends to rising structural employment problems is surely questionable.

THE INDUSTRIAL CRISIS AND DEFENSIVE POLICY

Makers of industrial policy prefer to promote growth and expansion but they are soon brought to recognize that contraction is an equally important and far more complex-ridden aspect of economic growth. The special agencies sometimes set up to deal with structural problems usually do not prove adequate in the industrial crises that loom so large in modern industrial life.

The difficulties of a large company or a whole industry has come to be regarded as a matter of too great significance for the government to stand aside, and the industrial crisis has become a familiar phenomenon with a fairly standard scenario. It tends to escalate to a high political level, especially if there are no legitimate claims to public support under any of the special programs administered by various agencies, or if the amounts involved are very large. The government will be expected to do *something*—above all to protect employment, especially in one-company towns or in regions with persistent employment problems. Local governments that depend on the tax revenues from endangered companies will add their pressure to that of management and unions. Ideological conflicts and prospective inflation will add dramatic touches.

The justification actually given for public aid will usually be quite conventional. Wherever possible one refers to the need to match subsidies or offset trade obstacles resorted to by other governments. Inability to get finance from private sources or the high risk involved is often cited as sufficient ground for public support. Above all the crisis will be seen as temporary and requiring only some reorganization.

The outcome will be a deal in which a variety of instruments of state support is used to enable things to go on, although possibly with a measure of structural change in the form of mergers or technical cooperation, but with less disruption than if one or more large companies had closed down. Especially in the case of very large companies, the industrial crisis and the subsequent government entry on the scene has replaced traditional bankruptcy.[2]

Once a major government support operation has been undertaken to tide a company over its difficulties, this in itself creates a privileged relation which tends to make further relief seem natural and inescapable. This kind of industrial policy makes the government a financier of last resort, much as central banks function as lenders of last resort in the banking system, but experience with this practice is still rather limited.

The industrial crisis is not exclusively the hallmark of declining industries. Similar situations arise at the advanced end of the industrial spectrum where the government is often already a silent partner as a result of some promotional policy and where companies operate under very great risk and in especially intense international competition, as in electronics, atomic energy, or aviation. Here, as a number of well-known cases have shown, the government is easily sucked into a situation of mounting support, either because good money is thrown after bad for short term political reasons or because there is a sincere conviction that the long term operation will, in some sense or other that is not necessarily economic, be successful.

Defensive operations of this kind clearly play a very large part in the subsidization of modern industry. At any rate, the problems of declining industries seem to dominate it. According to Küster, two-thirds of German industrial aids were in 1970 directed to declining industries and only some 6 per cent to new industries.[3]

RESISTANCE TO INDUSTRIAL DECLINE

The mainspring of economic growth is innovation — the introduction of new processes, products, and ways of organizing economic life. But this is not a painless process — it makes old skills, old equipment and old resources obsolete and worthless. The 'creative destruction' has left the wrecks of countless farms and firms, individual fortunes and ghost towns along the path of progress. The cost of shifting resources into new uses is largely a non-market cost and almost impossible to assess. However, it is only reasonable to find it expressed in the political process.

In the early stages of modern economic growth, contraction was concentrated in agriculture, and to a lesser extent in traditional crafts displaced by mechanization. The contraction of the agricultural labor force created a social and political issue which to this day has isolated agriculture in the industrial countries from the world market. The relative and absolute size of the agricultural labor force did not therefore cease to decline. It declined rapidly but presumably nevertheless at a more measured pace than if agriculture had not been lavishly protected and subsidized.

Today manufacturing industry is replacing agriculture as the main source of contraction problems. It is easy to see a number of reasons for this. In the first place, population growth is slowing down and all structural change in the economy must be accompanied by more contraction, if more manpower is to be steered to the expansive sectors. Secondly, agriculture which has for so long been the 'reserve army' is far too small to make any significant contribution. Expansive industries must force other industries or services to relinquish some of their factors of production.

In the third place, the combination of productivity growth and income elasticities of demand makes for a diminishing role of manufacturing industry except for those escape valves offered by foreign trade to some countries with exceptional comparative advantage in manufacturing.

Finally, and perhaps most importantly, the response to a situation where market growth falls short of productivity growth is often a concentration by means of mergers and acquisitions, and a pursuit of real or fictitious economies of scale. The size of plants and companies increases to the point where failure will cause social disruption on such a large scale that political intervention is inevitable.

GENERALIZED ADJUSTMENT ASSISTANCE

Adjustment assistance has come to mean measures to relieve the hardships produced by trade liberalization. It is then understood that such assistance should not subvert the adjustment process but preferably accelerate it while at the same time identifying the factors of production which are harmed by a commercial policy pursued in the greater social interest.

Experience with adjustment assistance of this kind has not so far been very promising. In the US and Canada, special legislation has been passed to provide compensation in cases of proven injury. In England, the government has bought cotton textile plants to close them down. The organized closing of coal mines in the European Coal and Steel Community might also be cited.

By and large, however, the notion of adjustment assistance has suffered from an inherent contradiction. The support extended to distressed parties has usually weakened the market pressures making for adjustment and in the end made adjustment slower rather than faster.[4]

Though not all that was hoped for, this may not be entirely unreasonable. The lesson of agricultural protection in industrial countries, which is often wrongly regarded as quite irrelevant to the trade in manufactures, is that it has not prevented a very drastic contraction of the agricultural sector, although the pace has been held within politically acceptable limits. Some patience will undoubtedly be called for even in the case of industrial contraction. But seeing how easily any support to a declining industry is turned into a way of consolidating it rather than dismantling it, one may question whether ambitious adjustment assistance policies would really be preferable to a hands-off policy.

However, seen from the point of view of a ministry of industry, the striking thing about trade adjustment assistance is its irrelevance. To be sure, foreign trade is immensely important to industry, especially in smaller countries, but the displacement occasioned by foreign competition in connection with trade liberalization is trifling compared to the perpetual adjustment, displacement, and dislocation that characterizes industrial life. Even companies which suffer from foreign competition with or without trade liberalization will usually find themselves in acute distress because domestic producers in entirely different industries compete with them in factor markets and are able to meet substantially higher wage claims and offer higher returns to capital.

Technological change is a far more important source of industrial distress than trade liberalization. If factors of production were perfectly mobile they would flow into industries offering the highest rewards without much friction. But factors of production are not all that mobile, especially not in the case of stagnating industries, and that is what defensive industrial policy is largely about. It has emerged, in many cases unpremeditatedly or even reluctantly, as a way of mitigating the social and political impact of market forces.

Actually the degree of flexibility and adjustment of modern industrial countries is impressive, and the instances that develop into genuine crises have so far been few. The risk is that an irreversible process may turn an increasing share of industrial companies into public utilities which would be likely both to reduce their potential for innovation and to increase their resistance to decline.

TYPES OF SUBSIDIES

So far the emphasis has been on the objectives of the policies for industrial support rather than the forms they take, although these have been referred to. The forms are of great variety, and have contributed to the blurring of the boundary between government and the private sector. Although with increasingly indirect forms of subsidization, it has become more difficult to determine the subsidy element and its effect, as a rule, however, the thread that ties the various forms together is an effort to minimize the risk in private investments. Stated somewhat differently, it is a manifestation of the extent to which the private sector is still prepared to shoulder risk or prefers that it should be shared by or shifted to the state.

The mode of expenditure sometimes reflects a genuine purpose, as in the case of payroll subsidies to promote employment, but just as often one finds capital investments subsidized for the same purpose. And it often seems, reasonably enough, that the aid takes the form least likely to give offense. General export subsidies have also been resorted to temporarily for balance of payments reasons, but this is unlikely to be repeated now that exchange rates have become more flexible. They do, however, serve as a reminder that exchange rate policy is closely linked to the subject of subsidies or trade policy at large. Who could deny that a successful policy of undervaluation of the currency is an immensely effective policy of subsidization?

The textbook type of subsidy, reducing unit price below unit revenue to the producer, by some payment linked to the volume of sales or production, is probably the least interesting in the context of industrial policy although such subsidies are of course ubiquitous in agricultural trade. Thus tax relief has become more important than straight subsidies as far as manufactures are concerned, and the growth of indirect taxation has created the opportunity for full or partial exemptions—from excise, turnover taxes or value-added taxes. The border tax adjustments involving the restitution of such taxes on exports and their imposition on imports have occasioned well known resentment and been fully analyzed.[5] They are not to be regarded as subsidies, although they raise important problems about the impact of the tax system and the rationale for border adjustments which are only undertaken with regard to indirect taxation.

The most general use of subsidies in the form of tax relief does not apply to final output but involves the subsidization of capital goods and a number of other inputs. Similarly, utilities such as electricity and water can be supplied at privileged rates from publicly controlled companies. Payroll subsidies are not uncommon in regional policies in order to stimulate employment, and the subsidization of wages for special categories of labor — for example, elderly or disabled workers — is also practised.

Investment is subsidized in regional development policies by outright grants or low-cost credits, and such loans represent only one of the many ways in which finance is used as a vehicle for subsidization. The creation of public or semi-public financial institutions was in some cases prompted by the desire to channel funds already under public control, for example, in savings banks or pension funds, into the private sector in an approved manner. In other cases they were set up in response to post-war reconstruction needs or out of a desire to remedy real or imagined shortcomings of the private financial market, for example, the shortage of medium-term finance, the difficulties of financing small business, or the risk aversion of banks and other private financial intermediaries. The trade-related objective has been particularly clear in such cases as shipping and shipbuilding and most notably in export credits.

Many of these institutions provide finance on market terms but are enabled to take higher risks because of their public backing. Others have been used to bring the pattern of large investment projects into agreement with the intentions of public planners. This form of credit rationing need not involve any clear element of subsidy at all.

Taking risks that seem higher than those acceptable to other institutions would not be called subsidization if done by a venturesome private creditor. A steadily higher loss ratio without a correponding risk premium would however, seem a criterion of subsidization. It would involve lower rates of return or even deficits. Institutions which borrow at market rates and lend at lower rates will also operate at a loss and when this is covered out of the public purse there is of course a subsidy. But in many cases the books might not show a loss, as the institutions involved will in turn borrow at subsidized rates from central banks or some other publicly controlled source.

To identify and assess subsidies of this kind in countries with fragmented capital markets is therefore difficult. Even where it is hotly denied that the financing involves any subsidy, it will often be proudly presented as a valuable aid to industry. The question is then only how much it is worth. Whether financial subsidies distort the national or international allocation of resources is another difficult matter to decide, especially when reference is made to excessive private risk evaluation which can easily become an alibi for complete disregard of risk by public authorities.

In combination with the grants of regional policies, financial aids have undoubtedly come to affect the cost of industrial finance very greatly. Michalet estimates that in France about one half the investment in the private sector is directly or indirectly financed by the state, although it is not clear whether he means that the cost of finance is reduced by that amount or simply that public institutions serve as intermediaries.[6]

In crises and bail-out operations, the role of financial subsidies are even more obvious than in the regular operations of public financing agencies. In such cases it may be a matter of financing new capital expenditure, but more often than not the purpose is to consolidate the company or meet losses to stave off an imminent shut down. Such contributions may be regarded as *ex-post* subsidies.

Exemptions from corporate income taxes, tax holidays, or accelerated depreciation are used to encourage certain types of investment and again raise tricky problems of assessment. Marketing and sales are promoted in a number of ways. Government participation in export promotion and the provision of export credits and guarantees have already been mentioned. Restrictions on government procurement in favor of domestic firms are becoming increasingly important as the public sector grows to include a vast variety of new activities, making it a very big customer indeed. Where a specified preference is granted domestic suppliers, the effect may be assessed, but in many cases of unique tendering it is far more difficult.

The granting of overt or covert monopoly positions is becoming easier as the licensing powers provided in physical planning, environmental control, etc. confer considerable discretionary powers on government authorities. The government may take an equity interest in companies. It may pay an excessive price as one way of pumping public funds into a company, and once it is a partner the likelihood of privileged treatment in many contexts is greater. Where the government is a full or controlling owner, it may renounce dividends or meet sustained losses with new contributions, thus significantly reducing the cost of capital.

Public industries operating at a loss do not necessarily do so as part of a strategy in which this subsidization is a deliberate choice. They might well prefer not to, but the political pressures on such companies are often so strong as to preclude the adjustments that would be necessary, especially in times of rapid inflation. The report on the finances of British nationalized companies published by the National Economic Development Office in July 1976, found them in a state of hopeless confusion as the result of government intervention to find short term solutions to particular crises.[7]

INTERNATIONAL ASPECTS OF DOMESTIC AIDS

Subsidies used to aid industrial firms are in part meant to correct other distortions and market failures in order to promote developments considered desirable; in large part as we have seen, they are also used to mitigate the adjustment to changing technologies and markets. It is often highly disputable whether these policies are well advised. The objectives might be better attained by other means. Most of these policies must be considered on individual merit and they tend to be controversial.

Assuming, however, that the redistribution involved and the impact on allocation, growth, employment and welfare are all considered to be in the national interest of the country that adopts these policies, what will be the impact on other countries? Again one can make no sweeping statements about either reasons for complaints or their legitimacy. When, for example, one country introduces legislation for the protection of the environment stricter than that of its trading partners, they cannot legitimately complain if subsidies are offered to offset the incremental costs.

But the general impression must surely be that both positive and defensive industrial policies have a strong protectionist bias. In new industries of advanced technology, for instance, 'national champions' are fostered in intense competition with similar partnerships between state and business in other countries. Regional development policies, which were long considered to be the exclusive concern of each country, have grown to a size where their international impact cannot be ignored, and they have become the subject of difficult negotiations in such groupings as the EEC.

Obviously the effect of subsidies on other countries does not depend on what they are called or on the worthiness of the social and political motives behind them. If a foreign competitor is seen to survive or compete more effectively because he receives large favors from his government, the effect on world markets and the global allocation of resources will be the same regardless of whether they are called regional development subsidies or not. When regional aids have nevertheless seemed more acceptable than many others, it is partly because aids which only compensate producers for establishing themselves in lagging areas rather than others will not have outside effects. But this will not be true if the industries in the development regions are different from those that might otherwise have been established, and it is not true if firms are overcompensated or would in any case have invested in the development area, which is quite common.

It has perhaps been more pertinent that all industrial countries recognize that they themselves have a need for policy instruments to meet regional political demands. Politically speaking it is not unimportant that the protectionist or trade distorting effects of regional policy are incidental to its purpose — it is probably of secondary importance.

In the great number of *ad hoc* defensive measures in response to industrial crises or agonies of contraction, the problem may be even more delicate. Even when governments seek to promote some kind of trade adjustment with one hand while softening it with the other, the net effect will be to slow it down. Attempts to prevent or postpone contraction in one place will hold up expansion somewhere else. Some of these effects will be domestic. Factors of production will be in shorter supply in the rest of the economy, and companies in the same industry may be penalized and fail to expand or even lose customers to subsidized competitors. The same may happen to companies in other countries, at worst creating a new adjustment problem there.

Even when there are very strong social arguments for retarding the contraction in some sector of an economy, in an interdependent world economy it will thus tend to become an international issue, and this regardless of whether subsidies are used in preference to tariffs or quotas. But other industrial countries will have similar problems and use similar instruments of intervention. The prospects for some kind of understanding — implicit or explicit — about permissible types of intervention are not entirely bleak. As in the past when international agreement was reached on the GATT rules, it must of course be based on some shared view of the legitimacy of the policies to which industrial countries increasingly resort in order to meet pressing domestic problems, and which will, inevitably, affect others.

The preceding pages have raised a number of questions concerning the international dimensions of the subsidy issue which will be addressed in the ensuing chapters. These include how the various domestic developments which have been described affect existing standards and approaches such as those contained in the GATT, as well as what modifications of present concepts and methods might be desirable and possible. However, since much of industrial policy is based on resisting or challenging the drift of market forces for a wide number of domestically and internationally determined reasons, a strictly economic method for dealing with interstate conflicts which result from national subsidies is not entirely adequate. But this raises two additional problems. If modern states place all kinds of restraints on the domestic operation of market forces, what will this mean for the operation of global markets and the viability of rules to keep them functioning? Furthermore, with the pressures from Third World states for a new international economic order added to the trade conflicts that exist among the industrialized states, will it be possible to devise rules and standards that apply equally to all states? Or will there be differentiated treatment for the advanced and developing nations?

Notes and References

1. Donges *et. al.* found no trend in total non-tariff barrier protection in Germany in the 1960s. It was of about the same magnitude as tariff protection. However, they confined themselves to measures promoting or discriminating among specific industries and did not consider regional development programs or general support programs. Cf. Juergen B. Donges, Gerhard Fels, Axel D. Neu *et al. Protektion und Branchenstruktur der westdeutschen Wirtschaft* (Tübingen: J. C. B. Mohr, 1973).
2. The range of measures taken by the French Government in a number of industries in the 1960s is well described by Lionel Stoleru in *L'imperatif industriel* (Paris: Seuil, 1969).
3. In Raymond Vernon, ed., *Big Business and the State* (Cambridge, Mass: Harvard University Press, 1974), p. 74.

4. See OECD, *Adjustment for Trade* (Paris, 1975).
5. For example, by Robert E. Baldwin, in *Nontariff Distortions of International Trade* (Washington, D.C.: Brookings, 1970).
6. In Vernon, *op. cit.*, p. 106.
7. *Financial Times*, 27 July 1976.

2 Subsidy Policies in Britain, France and West Germany: An Overview

GUY DE CARMOY

In order to broaden and concretize the study of the subsidy issue, it is important that it be related to the policies of specific countries. This requires providing an overview and analysis of the various goals pursued, the instruments through which governments act, and the financial magnitudes involved. Britain, France and West Germany have been selected not only because of the differences in style which mark each country, but also because they allow a comparison of policies pursued by three advanced industrialized states at similar levels of development.

Two decades have elapsed since the signing of the Rome Treaty. During this period, the governments of the three major member states of the European Community have been eager to attain the basic goals of economic policy: overall economic growth, monetary stability, full employment and balance of payments equilibrium. They have considered the promotion of industrial growth as one of the most powerful means for achieving these goals. In so doing, they have been pursuing, in the words of the Organization for Economic Cooperation and Development, (OECD), a proliferation of objectives.[1] Rapid changes are taking place in industrial structure through intersectoral shifts, increased industrial concentration, and technological innovation. The three governments under consideration are, therefore, geared to adjusting industrial sectors to change while facing internal and external constraints, those of market forces as well as those of organized pressure groups. 'Faire aller' has become the motto instead of 'laissez faire'.[2]

All three countries consider that their industry should be present and competitive in every major branch. They aspire to excel both in the traditional and innovative branches. They invoke employment considerations for the defense of declining industries and prestige considerations for the launching and continuous support of high technology industries. As a consequence they have tried to prevent an international division of labor, either worldwide or within the Common Market, that runs contrary to their aspirations. [3] To this end, they have resorted to the same devices: subsidies, tax allowances, encouragement of mergers, procurement policies, and, in some cases nationalization. As time has gone by, the broadening of objectives has led to more integrated approaches in the formulation and implementation of industrial policies.

Under these circumstances, it is appropriate to sketch the institutional framework within which Britain, France and West Germany have developed their general economic and industrial policies before describing the various types of subsidies they grant to industries. Since all three are bound by Article 92 of the Rome Treaty which sets rules governing state aids, the discussion of subsidies in this chapter has been broken down into sectoral, regional and general aids in accordance with the classification of the EEC Competition Policy Directorate. According to the Commission, Article 92 is considered to include every type of allowance, regardless of the form, whether given directly or indirectly by the state to individual enterprises or sectors. Lastly, an attempt has been made to evaluate the scope of these national policies.

BRITAIN

GOALS AND INSTITUTIONAL FRAMEWORK

The interventions of British governments have been numerous and complex. The policies and devices have changed according to the party in power and to the state of the national economy. It is therefore difficult to find a set of guiding principles applied over the last two decades.

The most recent comprehensive statement is contained in a paper prepared by the Department of Industry and sent to Parliament on 12 Jan 1976. [4] This document observes that in the past financial assistance to industry has meant public money provided to the public sectors. Presently, the Department of Industry is concerned with allocation of resources to industry, public or private, operating in a market economy. The rationale for government intervention is that 'the process of resource allocation through the price mechanism does not ensure an adequate level of demand and employment nor produce an acceptable distribution of income, or cause resources to be set aside for public services'.

The correction of imbalance in employment and balance of payments considerations has been the most clearly evident reason for public assistance. The Industry Act of 1972 was the basic legislation on this subject until it was amended by the Industry Act of 1975. Section 7 of the Industry Act of 1972 supplied the essential criterion for the creation, maintenance or safeguarding of employment in assisted areas. Section 8 provided for 'national selective assistance' with no criterion for public assistance to individual industries or sectors.

The Industry Act of 1975 extended the powers to give selective financial assistance under the Industry Act of 1972. It also provided for 'voluntary planning agreements' which are arrangements between a company and any minister concerning the future development of the company. The main feature of the Industry Act of 1975 was the establishment of the National Enterprise Board, a major publicly owned industrial holding company with access to funds up to £1000 million. The Board could be a channel for indirectly subsidizing British industry if it aimed at lower rates of return than private investors do.[5]

The new Board may become an expanded version of the Industrial Reorganization Corporation, established in 1967 by a Labor government and terminated in 1971 by a Conservative government. The IRC was given the function of promoting or assisting the reorganization and development of any industry, through loans and investments drawn on its financial resources of £150 million.[6] Its main policy was to encourage mergers, especially in the automobile, computer and aircraft sectors. Thus the British government was also engaged in promoting 'national champions' in these branches. The penchant for merging in so called 'strategic sectors' was prompted by the need to avoid an undue reliance on foreign suppliers.

Financial assistance and encouragement to concentration were given, to quote again the Department of Industry, to 'sectors of industry identified as of special significance to the economy or designated in any strategic policy of government'. Under this broad definition the department had to make an assessment of viability, especially when it considered some problem cases known as rescue operations.[7] British industrial policy was not limited to regional and sectoral assistance. Another important feature was the granting of general incentives which were not linked to a specific sector or region. The main devices were investment incentives and the selective employment tax.

AID SYSTEMS FOR SPECIFIC INDUSTRIES OR SECTORS

Textile industry
The British cotton industry located principally in Lancashire faced a serious decline in the 1950s under the competition of low price imports from Commonwealth producers. The 1959 Cotton Industry Act provided for a major adjustment assistance program in the form of compensation for firms scrapping plant. The government also encouraged a re-equipment program through grants amounting to 25 per cent of the total costs of approved schemes. In the 1960s, further

adjustment measures took place. The first was the establishment of a global quota system in 1966, replaced in 1973 by specific quotas by countries. In 1970 the annual depreciation allowance was increased and a special loan to finance re-equipment was administered by the IRC.[8]

The adjustment measures performed a useful role in promoting the rapid contraction of the industry. But in isolation they were unable to solve the employment problems of Lancashire.

An aid scheme designed to promote rationalization of the British wool industry was established by the 1972 Industry Act, to be carried out during the four year 1973–7 period. Subsidies up to £15 million apply to re-equipment, rebuilding of plant and closure of firms or production units.[9]

Shipbuilding

Aid to British shipbuilding started in 1963 in the form of loans under the Shipbuilding Credit Act 1964. The concentration of the industry in development areas and especially along the Clyde made the majority of the firms eligible for various regional benefits. The Shipbuilding Industry Act 1967 empowered the government to make grants linked to regrouping schemes and loans at low interest rates to British shipowners purchasing from domestic yards. Though the shipbuilders had failed to make the adjustments prescribed by the Geddes Report, which was the source of the 1967 legislation, the Conservative government increased assistance to the shipbuilding industry. Its statutory powers derived from the 1972 Industry Act. The rate of operating subsidy varied from 2 per cent to 25 per cent according to the financial situation of each of the major merchant shipbuilding firms. Geoffrey Denton observes that 'the funds ostensibly intended for rationalization and modernization of the industry have in fact been given to the least efficient and least competitive firms threatened with bankruptcy'.[10] The Industry Act of 1975 increased the limit of credits from £1400 million (1972 Act) to £1800 million and renewed the guarantees given under the previous acts. The last step taken by the Labor government in 1976 was the decision to nationalize the shipbuilding and ship repair industries. The bill was finally passed in early 1977, although the ship repair industry was not included in the final version.

One should also stress the role of shipbuilding subsidies in promoting a better regional balance in Scotland.

Steel

The status of the industry has been plagued by the controversy between Labor and the Conservatives. Nationalized in 1951, denationalized in 1953, the steel industry was re-nationalized in 1967. The relations between the British Steel Corporation and the Department of Trade and Industry were tense until the Corporation faced a financial crisis in 1971.

After a review of the situation, a ten-year development strategy was agreed upon, involving a public outlay of some £3 billion.[11]

Aluminum smelting

Until 1967 Britain imported the greater part of its primary aluminum. The government encouraged the construction of three smelting plants in development areas. The building took place over the 1968–73 period with a subsidy cost of £60 million mainly in the form of a 40 per cent investment allowance. New power stations had to be built in conjunction with the smelters. Power costs were also subsidized. The purpose of the investment was essentially import saving. The employment benefits were small due to the capital intensive character of the industry.[12]

Aircraft

The aircraft industry has been the largest single recipient of financial assistance. Subsidies were estimated at £157.4 million for 1974–5.[13] These subsidies were made to maintain a national export-oriented industry in the face of overwhelming American competition and to sustain the employment of qualified manpower. The need for a defense aircraft industry was a supplementary reason for support.

In the 1950s, too many firms were competing on too many developments. A number of subsidized programs were started and stopped. The move toward consolidation took place only in 1960 and led to the constitution of two airframe enterprises, British Aircraft Corporation and Hawker-Siddeley, and one motor firm, Rolls-Royce.[14] The latter firm ran into financial difficulties and the aero-engine and gas turbine engine divisions of the company were nationalized in 1971.

Meanwhile in 1962 the British and French governments signed an agreement for the development of the Concorde supersonic airliner. The British government had to supply grants to cover its share of the full cost of development (which amounted to a total of £480 million in 1972) and loans or guarantees to cover the increased needs of the manufacturers for working capital.[15]

Subsidies to the aircraft industry amounted to 12.5 per cent of the value of output in 1970. Of the total exports of the industry during the 1960s, approximately three quarters were the products of government aided projects.[16]

Computers

The government support of the domestic computer industry was justified on the grounds of technological skills and of resistance to the dominant position of IBM. The emergence of International Computers Ltd. as a national champion took place in 1968 after a series of mergers. ICL is by far the largest European owned computer company. The government was empowered under the Industrial Expansion Act to provide research and development grants. These were estimated at a yearly average of $10 million in the 1966–70 period and of $25 million in the 1971–5 period.[17] Some support was also given to a selected number of academic centers. The major method of support to the industry has been preferences in public procurement. In 1970–1, 90 per cent of central government computer orders were directed to ICL. The procedure for single tenders was in current use.[18] The National Enterprise Board has recently acquired 24.5 per cent of ICL equity.

Automobiles
A succession of mergers in the British automobile industry culminated in the creation, initiated by the government and supported by the IRC, of British Leyland in 1968. When Chrysler took over Rootes in 1960, the government required of Chrysler a series of commitments to help the firm remain British, including an IRC share in the equity. IRC extended in 1970 a revolving credit to British Leyland for the purchase of machine tools.

The British motor industry was seriously affected by the world recession and the sharp increase in energy prices in 1973–4. In 1974 British Leyland went in the red. The government decided to devote a total sum of £900 million to assist the company to undertake a major restructuring program up to 1978. The financial support included a £200 million increase in equity capital so as to give the government a majority holding.

The government was also faced with the prospect of rescuing Chrysler (UK) which the American parent company intended to close down because of the heavy losses incurred. In view of the social and political effects of closing a major plant in Scotland, the government came to an agreement with the firm and the trade unions, involving a commitment of £162.5 million broken down into a grant, a guarantee and a low interest loan.[19]

Regional aid schemes
The aims of regional policy have been to create employment in areas affected by low activity rates, high outward migration and high unemployment rates.

The areas covered by regional policy have increased over time. They include (a) development areas (DAs) proper, substituted in 1966 for development districts, (b) special development areas (SDAs) entitled since 1967 to greater advantages, and (c) intermediate areas, benefiting from lesser advantages since 1970. More than half the total population lives in assisted areas. The regional aids consist of investment incentives and subsidies to labor. During 1966–70 firms benefited from investment grants at the rate of 40 per cent in DAs. In 1970, investment grants were abolished, but the buildings grants were increased from 25 to 35 per cent in DAs and from 35 to 45 per cent in SDAs. In 1967 a subsidy to labor in the form of a regional employment premium (REP) was introduced at a fixed rate per employee in manufacturing industries in the DAs.[20] The subsidy was available to all manufacturing firms regardless of its likely effects on employment. It was designed to benefit low paid labor intensive industries and also be a counterweight to capital grants which favored capital intensive industries. The cost of regional support has increased sharply from £218.2 million (at 1974 prices) in 1970–71 to an estimated £422.2 million in 1974.[21] Regional policy became ineffective after 1971 because of the high rates of unemployment. In times of low investment and general recession, regional incentives are unattractive.

GENERAL AID SCHEMES

British governments have used two basic methods as general investment incentives: tax allowances and cash grants for expenditure on plant and machinery. Under the Industrial Development Act of 1966, tax free cash grants were paid at the rate of 20 per cent, shortly after raised to 25 per cent. In 1970 the grants were abolished and tax allowances reinstated. Companies were authorized to write off for tax purposes 60 per cent of expenditures on plant and machinery in the year the expenditure was incurred. In 1972 the government introduced a free depreciation for plant and machinery and an initial allowance of 40 per cent for new industrial buildings.

As Geoffrey Denton observed, 'the effect of these measures was to give the whole country favorable treatment in respect to tax allowances on investment which had previously been confined to development areas.' In his opinion, 'the total value to firms of the tax allowances available to them over the years has been many times greater than the value of all the subsidies described above.' As they are available to all firms on equal terms, they should not be compared with subsidies which are discriminatory.[22]

In 1966 the government introduced the selective employment tax (SET) to be paid by all industries. But manufacturing industry was subsidized at the expense of the service industries since it receives a refund of 130 per cent of the tax. According to Geoffrey Denton 'the payroll subsidy to manufacturing firms encouraged wasteful use of labor in the sector which was receiving large incentives to install new machines'.[23]

ACCELERATED INVESTMENT SCHEME

In 1976 the British government launched a new project in the form of an interest relief grant. The purpose is to bring forward investment projects postponed because of the recession. The borrower can obtain a loan with a reduced rate of interest. The maximum subsidy is two years with no interest and four years with a 3 point reduction in the cost of the loan. The subsidy to investment is granted outside the assisted areas.

SCOPE AND EVALUATION

The following table summarizes the British government's expenditure on industry excluding nationalized industry, export subsidies and the functioning of the labor market:[24]

Table 2.1 Public support to British private industry by type (£m)

	1970–71	1974–5 estimate
Regional support	218.2	422.2
Industrial innovation (including aircraft)	269.2	259.2
General support for industry (including shipbuilding and investment grants)	703.7	305.2
Total including subsidies and also loans	1191.1	989.6

The above figures do not include tax allowances, the importance of which has been stressed above. Geoffrey Denton, in his assessment of British industrial policy, considers it has been incoherent in terms of objectives and uncertain as to the efficacy of methods.[25] In view of the Brussels Commission's criteria, permanent, general and nonquantifiable aids are not the best. In this respect several of the British devices for assistance to industry are open to criticism. Two examples are the regional employment premium and tax allowances.

A breakdown by industry of state subsidies was available for the fiscal year 1970–71 and is reproduced in Table 2.2. The net expenditure of public money to private industry represented 7 per cent of the national budget in that year.

The gross domestic product of Britain amounted to £56 billion in 1971 and £81 billion in 1974. The gross fixed capital formation in the same years amounted to £9.6 billion and £9.8 billion respectively.[26]

FRANCE

GOALS AND INSTITUTIONAL FRAMEWORK

The French state has a long tradition of economic interventionism and resistance to the free play of market forces. It is an accepted feature that

Table 2.2 Estimates of subsidies to British industry by branch—1970–71

(£m)

III	Food, drink, tobacco	59.005*	57.428†
IV	Coal and petroleum products	4.855	4.411
V	Chemicals and allied industries	138.528	135.637
VI	Metal Manufacture	93.693	79.969
VII	Mechanical Engineering	84.364	73.596
VIII	Instrument Engineering	9.849	9.289
IX	Electrical engineering	61.196	48.944
X	Shipbuilding	39.485	37.166
XI	Vehicles	219.462	209.879
XII	Metal goods not specified elsewhere	31.843	30.535
XIII	Textiles	61.300	53.833
XIV	Leather goods, furs	1.458	1.389
XV	Clothing and footwear	9.797	9.055
XVI	Bricks, cement	29.629	29.476
XVII	Timber, furniture	9.892	9.031
XVIII	Paper, printing, publishing	36.655	34.689
XIX	Other manufacturing industries	32.425	27.029
	Total	923.434	851.356

Source: W. M. Corden and Gerhard Fels, *Public Assistance to Industry* (The
          Macmillan Press Ltd. 1976), p. 123.
  * Government expenditure and indirect tax relief
  † Subsidy

in the last resort the state is the judge of the general economic interest. Its intervention is not confined to the formulation and implementation of macroeconomic policies in monetary and fiscal matters. It extends to a number of economic agents at the level of the branch, the firm or the region.

In accepting the principles of competition and free trade embodied in the statutes of the major postwar international organizations such as OEEC and GATT, the French authorities have been wary of keeping the maximum freedom of initiative by resorting to various forms of pressure through assistance to the industries which were considered essential to the strength and continued progress of the national economy. The major French preoccupation within the European Community has been to emulate Germany whose overall economic achievements were already impressive in the late 1950s. An effective industrial policy was also considered a means for fostering growth which in the minds of the governing elite was a priority goal over and above price stability.

The elaboration of a medium-term industrial policy is the responsibility of the Commissariat au Plan, a small task force which submits its recommendations to the Council of Ministers on the basis of a number of reports by specialized commissions covering the various segments of the economy.

Each industrial branch be it public, private or mixed falls under the 'tutelage' that is, the administrative and policy supervision, of a ministerial department. The Ministry of Industry and Research of course holds the largest responsibility in this respect. It has been recently reorganized in order to reinforce its action on those industries which fall within its province. But the Ministry of Economic Affairs and Finance is itself a tutor of sorts of the spending departments and often has the final say on the size and form of adjustment assistance to industry.

The Commissions of the Plan are a meeting ground for the representatives of enterprises, belonging both to the public and private sectors as well as representatives of the ministries concerned, which always includes one from Finance. Thus the stage is set for a continuous relationship between business and government. Cooperation is closer with large companies because of their active participation in policy formulation and their potential contribution to the goal of economic growth. [27]

Several specialized institutions should be mentioned at the operational level: (a) the Economic and Social Development Fund (FDES). Dependent on the Treasury, the FDES receives appropriations from the state budget and allocates low interest loans to individuals firms; (b) the Industrial Development Institute (IDI), modeled after the British IRC, is a combination of state capital and private management. IDI subscribes equity capital for a limited period of time in medium-size companies in order to help their development; it also promotes mergers: (c) the Directorate for Space Planning and Regional Action (DATAR), a division of the Ministry of Equipment, is in charge of proposing and implementing the various aspects of regional policy; (d) the Regional Development Companies (SDRs) sell cooperative bond issues in the financial market on behalf of selected small and medium-size firms.

The public sector has been considerably expanded by nationalization after the war. State enterprises occupy dominant monopolistic or oligopolistic positions in most of the branches of energy and transportation and also in banking.

A deliberate policy goal of the Vth Plan (1966–70) was to foster the creation of one or two firms of international scale in most industries. The policy of promoting and when necessary supporting 'national champions' through mergers was pursued both in the public sector (oil, chemicals, aircraft construction) and in the private sector (steel, computers, shipbuilding).

In the VIth Plan (1971–5) efforts tended to promote a faster overall growth and to encourage specifically four sectors: equipment goods, chemical, electronics, food and agricultural industries.

The preparation of the VII Plan (1976–80) took place during the world recession. The preliminary report expressed anxiety about employment. During this period manpower resources will increase by more than 1 per cent per year due to the age structure of the population and to the greater number of women attracted by the labor market. One third of industrial production is exported, but exports are concentrated in a small number of firms. Under these circumstances a high rate of industrial growth is required to fight unemployment and more attention must be given to medium size companies in selected sub-branches such as printing, peripherals, machine tools, measuring instruments and automobile equipment.[28] The anxiety about employment explains the steps taken to support a major ailing automobile company. This was an emergency measure outside the Plan.

To conclude this brief survey two basic observations are appropriate: the distinction between nationalized and private industries is somewhat blurred. Both are viewed as instruments of an ambitious economic policy and as partners deserving encouragement and guidance. Second, the French authorities combine an offensive strategy in favor of innovative industries in danger and a defensive strategy in favor of declining industries. The latter are generally labor intensive and the former capital intensive.

AID SYSTEMS FOR SPECIFIC INDUSTRIES OR SECTORS

Shipbuilding

Subsidies to the industry ranged from F300 million in 1963 to F650 million in 1972. They have been raised to F855 million in 1975.[29]

Steel

The French industry is under public control without public ownership. The government is the supplier of coal to the industry through nationalized coal mines. It is an important client through the state railways and exerts a direct control on steel prices. Since the early 1950s it encouraged a succession of mergers culminating in 1966 and 1967 in the creation of two national champions, Usinor and Wendel Sidelor. The duopolists are associated in a joint subsidiary, Solmer, which operates the steelworks at Fos near Marseilles.

A close cooperation has existed since the war between the trade organization Chambre Syndicale de la Sidérurgie Française and the government. In 1966 both parties concluded a steel agreement committing the industry to joint investment projects and to rationalization and specialization measures leading to a reduction of the number of firms and plants.[30] The counterpart was a sizeable financial aid in the form of low interest loans from the FDES covering about 60 per cent of the investment needs. Transfers to the steel industry have been estimated at F2363 million for the 1970–2 period.[31]

Oil
The French government levies special taxes on the sale prices of petroleum products which, in turn, are allocated to exploration and research. The appropriation spent on research amounted to F394 million in 1972 and F205 million in 1974.[32]

Aircraft industry
The government brought about a series of mergers of state owned companies, culminating in 1970 with the merger of Nord Aviation and Sud Aviation into Aerospatiale. In the private sector, Dassault merged with Bréguet in 1967.

With the decision to promote technological advance, the government decided to fund R and D for the civilian prototypes of Concorde, a joint venture with Britain, of Airbus, a joint venture with Germany and for a smaller short range plane, Mercure. In the case of Concorde the goal was not only to promote technological innovation but also national prestige. The cumulative R and D subsidies to the three projects amounted to F6 billion for the 1962–72 period.[33]

The government, aware that without substantial orders French industry would be faced with a dramatic reduction in activity, has pursued a consistent policy, but fast evolving technologies on the one hand and the American quasi-monopoly on sales in third markets on the other hand have made the industry more and more expensive to sustain.

Computers
The government did not take steps to prevent the take-over of Compagnie des Machines Bull by General Electric in 1964. It tried to promote a French solution by setting up a new venture in 1966, Compagnie Générale pour l'Informatique (CII) in which the state subscribed half of the equity. CII survived for some years thanks to government procurement and subsidies which amounted to F1280 million in the course of the Vth and VIth plans.[34] In view of competition in the European market, it could not expect to become a national champion to be reckoned with.

The government changed its tack in 1976. It promoted a joint venture of CII with Honeywell-Bull, the successor company to Bull-General Electric so as to pursue its national computer program. Honeywell-Bull is to merge the bulk of activities of CII into a new company in which French interests will hold a 53 per cent share. The government will subsidize this new company for four years in the order of F1200 million and will further guarantee important public contracts during this period.

Automobiles

Renault, the largest French car manufacturer, received subsidies of F1355 million over the 1962–72 period.[35] Their purpose was to provide the company with the equivalent of equity capital. In 1974 Citroën was unable to absorb the financial costs resulting from the replacement of a large part of its machinery. The losses of the company were estimated at F800 million. The government decided under these circumstances to foster the restructuring of the entire French automobile industry. Citroën was to merge its passenger car manufacturing activities with Peugeot under the aegis of the latter company. A concentration was also to take place in the heavy vehicles industry. Renault, the parent company of SAVIEM would take over Berliet, which was, like Citroën, under the control of the Michelin group. To this end, the government granted a loan of F1600 million to Citroën for the funding of its short-term liabilities and a loan of F450 million to Renault for the purchase of Berliet.[36] Both loans are managed by the Social and Economic Development Fund.

REGIONAL AID SCHEMES

Regional discrepancies in France derive from a number of causes: the congestion of the Paris area, the reduction in agricultural employment, the decline of traditional industries (coal mining, textiles), the difficulty in developing border regions (East and North). Many regions, especially in the West, have lost part of their active population. There is a need to correct imbalances among regions and also between urban and rural areas within each region.

The main instruments of regional policy are: (a) measures to deter the congestion of the Paris area in the form of taxes in the case of on the spot expansion and of decentralization subsidies to compensate for the costs in the case of transfer out of the area; (b) regional development premiums (PDR) in the form of a subsidy on employment with an investment ceiling, the rates varying from 12 to 25 per cent according to three types of zones and tending to favor medium-size industries. Some PDRs are granted preferably to selected industrial sectors so that the specific aid is linked to the regional aid; (c) tax allowances in the form of a reduction in the local tax on industry and of exceptional investment amortization of 25 per cent (only in the rural regions of the West); (d) low interest loans mostly through the regional development companies (SDRs) and exceptionally through the Economic and Social Development Fund (FDES).[37]

A calculation has been made of the global cost of these various measures in terms of subsidy equivalents. They amounted to F750 million in 1973.[38] Over the 1962–73 period, the various forms of regional aid have amounted to 6 per cent of the investments of the subsidized industries.[39] It is generally agreed in EEC circles that the French regime of regional aid is one of the less costly and most efficient. The OECD takes a somewhat more sober view and considers that the regional structure has changed less because of regional policy measures than because of the increase of total population and active population and the expansion of new branches of activity.[40]

GENERAL AID SCHEMES AND ECONOMIC RECOVERY MEASURES

France has no permanent general aid scheme comparable with that of Britain.

In May 1975 the government took a series of temporary measures aimed at fighting the recession by encouraging productive investment. A subsidy of 10 per cent of the value of orders for machinery was granted to all firms placing their orders between May and December 1975. Long-term finance in the form of a F5 billion loan was provided through state controlled credit institutions in order to help company investment programs geared to increasing production capacity, creating new jobs and saving energy. In September 1975, the funds allocated to FDES loans were increased by F3 billion.[41]

EXPORT AIDS

Short-term or medium-term loans to finance exports can be obtained from the Compagnie Française d'Assurance pour le Commerce Extérieur (COFACE). For large exports such as generators and plants, the guarantee of COFACE enables exporters to get advance financing from the banks.[42] The guarantee covers price increases during the period of the implementation of the contracts. The volume of contracts under COFACE guarantee has increased rapidly during the period 1962–72: from F3.7 billion to F16.3 billion for political risks and from F600 million to F5.9 billion for economic risks.[43]

SCOPE

The following table attempts to make an aggregate presentation of state aids to industry in both the public and the private sector in 1972.

To put these figures in perspective one should mention that gross domestic product of France in 1972 amounted to F978 billion at current prices and gross fixed capital formation amounted to F217 billion in the same year.[44]

Table 2.3 State aids to industry 1972 (Fm)

	Volume in million francs	*Percentage*
1. Subsidies to industry & transportation		
—public sector	11.912	81
—private sector	2.968	19
2. Loans by Development Fund (FDES)		
—to public sector	1.050	64.8
—to private sector	.670	35.2
3. Advance for Aircraft R&D	1.435	
Total	18.035	

Source: Anicet Le Pors et Jacques Prunet, 'Les transferts entre l'état et l'industrie,' *Economic et Statistique*, (April 1975), Tables 3, 4, 5.
Tax allowances to industry in 1972 are estimated at F3.4 billion.

WEST GERMANY

GOALS AND INSTITUTIONAL FRAMEWORK

Because of the decentralized structure of the country, the Federal Government shares a number of economic responsibilities with the Laender. The financial independence of the latter was reduced de jure but not de facto in 1967 by the Stability and Growth Act which gave federal authorities overall responsibility for maintaining macro-economic equilibrium and applying adequate measures to this end.

The concept of concerted action was a new wording of the liberal concept of social market economy which had prevailed in the 1950s and the early 1960s. It consisted of the participation of organized groups, that is, the labor unions and employer associations, in the discussions of economic policy with the various levels of government, the representatives of the Central Bank and the members of the Council of Economic Advisers.

Attempts were made in 1966 and 1968 to define the 'Principles of the Federal Government's Sectoral and Regional Economic Policy'. These principles included *inter alia* the stabilization of income in declining industries by helping the process of adaptation and the promotion of research and development in high technology industries.[45]

As in other countries, sectoral policy was largely protectionist. The first test case was coal which contrary to the situation in Britain and France had not been nationalized. Adjustment assistance was granted to shipbuilding and R and D subsidies to oil, aircraft and computers. The German industry was more concentrated than the French. Nonetheless mergers were encouraged in coal, oil and aircraft.

In the field of regional policy, the original feature was a close financial and policy cooperation between the Federal Government and the Laender. To conclude, the German authorities do not work out an overall medium-term plan, but they proceed to concerted planning in a number of sectors and regions leading to a series of voluntary agreements amounting to an industrial policy.

The major federal ministries concerned are the Ministry of Economics for subsidies to industry and to regional planning, the Ministry of Finance for tax allowances and the Ministry for Education and Science for research and development. The Ministry of Economics is for many practical purposes a ministry of industry. The Laender ministries of economics and finance also play an important role. Trade organizations and chambers of commerce are also active in the orientation of industry.

The Stability and Growth Act has committed the federal government to present a bi-annual report on financial assistance and tax allowances granted to nongovernmental institutions.

AID SYSTEMS FOR SPECIFIC INDUSTRIES OR SECTORS

Shipbuilding
German shipyards are protected by a comprehensive system of direct subsidies, sales promoting measures and investment supports. The direct subsidies of the Federal Government amounted to DM20 million in 1970. Capital investment may be depreciated over a shorter than normal time period. German shipping companies are granted a 10 per cent price reduction, low interest loans and depreciation facilities for orders placed with German shipbuilders.[46] The Laender of Hamburg, Bremen, Schleswig-Holstein and Niedersachsen also subsidize shipbuilding. The industry must conform to the 1975 directive of the EEC Council of Ministers specifying the conditions under which aid may be compatible with the Common Market.

Coal
The coal crisis in 1958 led the government to employ a combination of assistance measures ranging from subsidies for rationalizing and closing mines and for coal use in the steel industry and in power plants, to taxation on heating oil and a restraint agreement on oil imports.[47] The 1968 law on adjustment and restructuring of coal mining put strong pressure on mines to concentrate. Ruhrkohle A.G. was formed from twenty-six companies which turned over their mining assets and liabilities to the new Konzern and received in exchange interest yielding obligations guaranteed by the federal government and by the state of Nordrhein-Westphalia. Direct subsidies and tax allowances to coal mining amounted to DM1321 million in 1968, decreased to DM804 million in 1972 and reached a new high in 1974 at DM1721 million.[48]

Oil

While the merger in coal mining was expected to dampen the effects of the decline in that industry, the purpose of the mergers in the oil industry was to provide the country with more secure supplies of petroleum from a German owned company. In 1968 the government initiated a joint venture by seven oil firms. The new exploration company, Deminex, was granted state aid for the 1969–74 period in the amount of DM575 million broken down in loans for exploration projects repayable if the ventures were successful and grants to cover part of the cost of acquiring crude oil concessions. The scheme was renewed in 1975 for the 1975–78 period with an allocation of DM800 million. [49]

In 1975, Deminex was absorbed in a wider operation through the merger of the two largest German oil companies, Veba and Gelsenberg. As a result Germany at last had an integrated oil group playing the role of a national champion.

Aircraft

In terms of sales and manpower, the German aircraft industry is much less important than its British or French counterparts. A policy of merger was pursued, reducing the number of firms to three. Support for the development of new technology is provided by direct subsidies which amounted to DM170 million in 1970. In recent years the government has contributed to the financing of the R and D for the Franco-German aircraft, the Airbus. Joint direct assistance to aircraft and data processing industries amounted to DM351 million in 1974. [50]

Computers

Siemens and AEG the two major companies active in the heavy electrical communication industries, have engaged in the computer business. In spite of government support amounting to DM136 million, [51] AEG was unsuccessful in developing a large computer system. Siemens remains the main German producer in that field. A young company, Nixdorf, has made a breakthrough in the field of small computers without assistance. The government support to R and D in the 1971–5 period has averaged $44 million per year. [52]

Automobiles

The fall in the sales of motor cars in 1974 obliged Volkswagen to release a number of employees. These redundancies affected several regions, some of which were already suffering from economic difficulties. The German government embarked upon a three year program involving the expenditure of DM210 million, in order to encourage the creation of new activities in these regions. Thus the government approach was to solve the problem of a particular company through regional aid. [53]

REGIONAL AID SCHEMES

Through a 1969 amendment to the constitution, regional policy is an area of joint responsibility in which the Federal and Laender governments participate, the implementation being the responsibility of the Laender. A joint Federal-Laender planning committee formulates a series of framework plans for the twenty-one regional action programs covering all development areas except Berlin. Geographically these areas comprise the Eastern border (Zonenrandgebiet), the coal mining area of the Ruhr and Saar, and some rural areas with low income capacity from agriculture. All assistance is concentrated on about 300 so-called growth points (Schwerpunktorte) selected after a systematic review of the local labor markets on the basis of three criteria: regional income, employment deficit and infrastructural level.

The subsidy consists of investment grants ranging from 10 to 25 per cent of the investment. The growth points located in the zonal border area are entitled to the highest rate. The rates apply to the establishment of new plants as well as to the extension of existing plants. A distinctive feature is that entrepreneurs are free to make their own decisions about where to locate or to expand their plants.

In the opinion of the OECD, Germany has advanced further than many other countries towards a systematic approach to regional economic goals and to criteria for designating promotion areas.[54] The first plan 1972–5 provided for an annual average expenditure of DM850 million of which DM530 million were budgetary appropriations and DM320 million were in the form of tax free investment allowances. Both contributions were equally shared between the Bund and the Laender.[55]

The broad concept of town and country planning allows the Federal and Laender authorities to coordinate industrial, urban and infrastructure policies at local level. Therefore there is often a close correlation between regional aid and sectoral support, particularly when one sector is highly concentrated in one region.

SCOPE

The following table on direct assistance to German industry is derived from the official report the Federal government is obligated to publish according to the Stability and Growth Act. It is broken down into (a) subsidies (S) of the Federal government including grants, interest and amortisation support and public credit and (b) tax allowances (T) at the expense of the Federal government and the Laender.

Gross domestic product in Germany amounted to DM825 billion in 1972 and to DM982 billion in 1974. Gross fixed capital formation during the same years amounted to DM195 billion and DM180 billion respectively.[56]

Table 2.4 Direct assistance to German industrial sectors(in DM m)

	1972 realized		1974 planned	
	S	T	S	T
All sectors	1185	7031	2340	7357
Mining	458	346	1504	217
Mineral oil and raw material	78		87	
Aircraft and data processing	292		351	
Regional promoting measures	215	3753	232	4090
Others	458	847	665	942

Source: Bundesministerium der Finanzen, Vierter Subventionsbericht, Bundestagsdruchsach 7/1144, Bonn 1973, quoted by *PAI*, Gerhard Fels, Overall Assistance to German Industry, p. 100.

CONCLUSIONS

With important differences in scope and methods the three countries have been pursuing the broad goals of protection of declining industries and promotion of high technology industries.

The British industry was handicapped in its investments by the stop-go policy of the successive governments and curtailed in its outlets by the gradual erosion of the Commonwealth preference system. Some industrial branches did not adjust fast enough to the changing pattern of international trade. Therefore the defensive aspects of British industrial policy prevail over the offensive ones. France struggled to evolve from a highly protectionist and semi-autarchic economy to a more open one in the framework of the Common Market. Successive governments practised defensive action in favor of the branches which had difficulties in facing up to international competition and deliberately pursued a costly offensive policy in high technology branches. In Germany industry was largely willing and able to take care of itself. It successfully developed its sales in all the trading areas of the world. Therefore government subsidies to industry, defensive and offensive, were much more limited in scope than in Britain and France. In these two countries, policy makers do not consider the market system as an exclusive means of allocating resources. As Harald Malmgren writes in his chapter, adjustment assistance is in some cases a screen for adjustment resistance.

It should be mentioned that subsidies to industry as described in this chapter deal almost exclusively with aid to the private industrial sector. In the three countries, the public industrial sector also benefits from state subsidies. The content and size of the public sector as well as management practices and government rulings vary from country to country. The public sector is smaller in Germany than in Britain and France and is much less of a burden to the national budget.

There are dissimilarities in the regional aid dispensed in the three countries. A comparative study of the structure and cost of such aid in the nine Common Market countries has been made by the Commission. The major findings for Britain, France and Germany are condensed in tables 2.5 and 2.6. Germany and France rely primarily on capital subsidies and tax allowances. In the case of Britain, the regional employment premium substitutes for tax allowances. In money terms, British aid is the most expensive, amounting to twice that of German aid and about six times that of French. As to the origin of funds, the central budget alone is the provider of funds in France, while the regional authorities share the burden with the Federal government in Germany. In the three countries, but mostly in Germany, sectoral aid has strong regional undertones.

Table 2.5 Comparison of the regional aid in three countries
        Percentage Distribution by type of aid 1975

	Germany	France	Britain
Capital Subsidy	57.1	55.1	60.6
Interest allowance	—	—	2.1
Employment premium	—	—	36.9
Tax allowances	42.9	34.9	—
Aid for purchase of land, building		9.6	0.4
Aid in loans at reduced rates	—	0.4	—
	100	100	100

Source: Commission of the European Community, *Appraisal of Cost of Regional Aid in the Nine Member Countries*, DOC XVI/131/1/76, Brussels 1976

Table 2.6 Direct regional aid 1974

	Germany	France	Britain
Amount in Mil. units of account	435,8	124	864
Aid as percentage of GDP	0.14	0.06	0.57

Source: Ibid. as Table 2.5

General aid schemes are a permanent feature of British industrial policy. Germany and France have no comparable schemes, but have resorted to specific recovery measures in response to the 1974–5 crisis.

Changing energy costs have affected patterns of trade and industry in the three countries and are bound to influence national industrial policies. It was not possible in the present chapter to explore the latest policy reactions to higher energy costs and prices in any depth.

The three countries in spite of their EEC membership and the setting up of a customs union, have pursued policies with more or less mercantilist undercurrents favoring their national industry on a sectoral and regional basis. If similar devices are used, nonetheless the practice is deeply ingrained in the political cultures and bureaucratic traditions of each of them. Therefore government and business relations, including government subsidies to business, follow different patterns, the subsidies forming only a part of a wider national industrial policy. The European Community has not reached the stage of a common unified market and it seems difficult to introduce common rulings on subsidies in the present heterogeneous system. The prospects for accomplishing this are examined in the Warnecke contribution to this volume. Since the nine member states of the European Community have gone farthest of all the GATT signatories in removing barriers to trade among themselves, it is important to determine the extent to which they have been able to deal with the conflicts that have arisen as a result of their competitive subsidy and industrial policies. Their accomplishments in this regard may be instructive for similar efforts in the GATT and OECD.

Notes and References

1. Organization for Economic Cooperation and Development, *The Aims and Instruments of Industrial Policy: A Comparative Study* (Paris: 1975) Chap. 1.
2. Bertrand de Jouvenal, *La Civilisation de Puissance* (Paris: Fayard, 1976), p.165.
3. On this point see Steven J. Warnecke, 'Industrial Policy and the European Community' in Steven J. Warnecke and Ezra N. Suleiman, eds., *Industrial Policies in Western Europe* (New York: Praeger, 1975).
4. Department of Industry, 'Criteria for Assistance to Industry', Appendix A to Industry Act 1972, *Annual Report by Secretaries for Industry, Scotland and Wales* (London: HMSO, 1976) p. 35.
5. W. M. Corden, 'Conclusions on the Logic of Government Interventions', Chapter 8, in W. M. Corden and Gerhard Fels, *Public Assistance to Industry* (London: The Macmillan Press Limited, 1976), p. 225. Hereafter cited as *PAI*.
6. Geoffrey Denton, 'Financial Assistance to British Industry', *PAI*, p.132.
7. 'Criteria for Assistance to Industry', *op. cit.*, p. 36.
8. Caroline Miles, 'Protection of the British Textile Industry', *PAI*, pp.184–212.
9. Commission of the European Community, *Fourth Report on Competition Policy* (Brussels: 1975), p. 88.
10. *PAI*, pp. 146–150 and 154.

11. J. E. S. Hayward, on steel in Raymond Vernon, ed., *Big Business and The State*, (Cambridge, Mass: Harvard University Press, 1974), pp. 260–2.
12. Zuhayr Mikdashi on aluminum in Vernon, *op. cit.*, p. 177.
13. Denton, *PAI*, p. 124 (Table 5.2).
14. M. S. Hochmuth on aerospace in Vernon, *op. cit.*, p. 168.
15. Denton, *PAI*, p. 141.
16. Ibid., pp. 156, 157.
17. Nicolas Jequier on computers in Vernon, *op. cit.*, Table 3, p. 220.
18. Denton, *PAI*, p. 143.
19. Commission of the European Community, *Fifth Report on Competition Policy*, (Brussels-Luxembourg: 1976), p. 84.
20. Denton, *PAI*, pp. 134–9.
21. Ibid., Table 5.2, p. 124.
22. Denton, *PAI*, pp. 126–9, 150–51.
23. Ibid., pp. 129, 132.
24. Denton, Table 5.2, *PAI*, p. 124.
25. Ibid., p. 150.
26. Eurostat, National Accounts 1970–74, *Yearbook 2–1975*, pp. 345, 361.
27. Organization for Economic Cooperation and Development, *La politique industrielle de la France* (Paris: 1974), pp. 35–8.
28. *Rapport sur l'Orientation Préliminaire du VIIième Plan* (Paris, 1975).
29. *Fonds de développement économique et social; rapport pour 1974–75* (Paris: 1976), p. 86.
30. Hayward in Vernon, *op. cit.*, pp. 266–9.
31. Anicet Le Pors and Jacques Prunet, 'Les transferts entre l'état et l'industrie', *Economie et Statistique*, (April 1975), pp. 28, 34.
32. Comité professionnel du pétrole. *Éléments statistiques, pétrole 1974* (Paris: 1975), pp. 301, 303.
33. Le Pors and Prunet, *op. cit.*, p. 28.
34. Organisation for Economic Cooperation and Development, *La Politique industrielle de la France*, (Paris: 1974), p. 129.
35. Le Pors and Prunet, *op. cit.*, p. 26.
36. European Community, *Fifth Report on Competition Policy*, *op. cit.*, p. 83.
37. Organization for Economic Cooperation and Development, *Les Problèmes et et les politiques de développement régional dans les pays de l'OCDE, vol I, France*, (Paris: 1976), pp. 21–22.
38. Pierre Louis, 'Aide publique et développement économique régional', *Economie et Statistiques*, (July–August 1976), pp. 15, 16.
39. Ibid., p. 16.
40. OECD, *Politiques de développement régional, France, op. cit.*, p. 29.
41. European Community, *Fifth Report on Competition Policy, op. cit.*, pp. 96–7.
42. C.A. Michalet on France in Vernon, *op. cit.*, p. 108.
43. Le Pors and Brunet, *op. cit.*, pp. 24–5.
44. Eurostat, *op. cit.*, pp. 73, 77.
45. Georg H. Küster on Germany in Vernon, *op. cit.*, pp. 69–73.
46. Ulrich Hiemenz and Kurt v. Rabenau, 'Effective Protection of German Industry', *PAI, op. cit.*, p. 42.
47. Gerhard Fels, 'Overall assistance to German Industry', *PAI*, Ibid., p. 102.

48. Ibid., p. 104.
49. European Community, *Fifth Report on Competition Policy, op. cit.*, pp. 87, 88
50. *PAI, op. cit.*, pp. 42, 100.
51. Ibid., p. 104.
52. Vernon, *op. cit.*, p. 220.
53. European Community, *Fifth Report on Competitive Policy, op. cit.*, p. 85.
54. Organization for Economic Cooperation and Development, *Regional Development Policies, Part II, Germany*, (Paris: 1976), para 76.
55. Ibid., para 57.
56. Eurostat, *op. cit.*, p. 3.

3 Government Organization and Support for Private Industry: the United Kingdom Experience

SIDNEY GOLT

THE RESPONSIBILITIES OF GOVERNMENT DEPARTMENTS

It used to be an agreeable habit of some British participants in international commercial negotiations to try to enliven the tedium of the proceedings by contributing occasional light-hearted offerings for the amusement of their colleagues. As the Stockholm meetings at which the European Free Trade Association was established drew to a close, the British delegation circulated a draft 'Convention for the Frustration of Trade'. Its first Article declared the establishment of an 'Association for the Frustration of Trade', trade being defined as 'the benefits which it is feared may be conferred by the Convention'. And Article 3 read as follows:

> The objectives of the Association shall be:
> (a) to frustrate the normal tendency of trade to increase and to ensure its diminution.
> (b) to frustrate all measures that any Member State might attempt to introduce in pursuit of the first objective; and
> (c) to ensure, by use of subsidies, by the encouragement of dumping and by discrimination on all possible grounds, that the following provisions of the Convention, in so far as they may apply, shall be circumvented.

In November 1959, while the flood of enthusiasm for postwar international economic liberalism and cooperation was still flowing strong, this seemed quite funny. Nearly twenty years later, with the tide showing many signs of running the other way, the smile is rather a wry one.

It is perhaps not without interest that the authors of this 'Convention should have chosen to pick out the use of subsidies as primarily designed to frustrate trade, and clearly from the context specifically to prevent imports. The more general atmosphere of that time would have been more concerned with subsidies as illegitimate means of promoting exports. Certainly such energies as were expended during the 1950s in the GATT in relation to subsidies had been in that direction. But we may perhaps salute their prophetic vision of some of the tendencies in the development of national policies, in the wake of the removal of tariffs as the dominant instrument of protection.

This paper will be concerned almost entirely with the development of United Kingdom policy and the forms of administration of that policy, especially during recent years. It seems probable, from such material as I am familiar with on other countries' practices, that British theory, as expounded in official pronouncements, and recent practice, as worked out both in legislation and administration, has been carried further and exercised more intensively than in the other major industrial countries. Japan has been the exception, first in the early postwar period and perhaps also more recently. It is, however, a characteristic of this whole area of policy that there are many different and less direct routes to achieve broadly similar objectives; and it is certainly arguable that the French financial system, through the banks and especially the regional financing institutions, is at least as thorough-going a mechanism of government intervention as the more overt methods used in any other country.

The outstanding feature of United Kingdom administrative practice in the twenty years or so following 1945 was the central position of one department — the Board of Trade — under a single minister, the President of the Board of Trade. This was in relation to both domestic industry and international trade, as well as to the general interest of consumers, perhaps rather imperfectly recognized at that time. It is perhaps of some historic interest to note that with some exceptions, the great majority of the functions of modern government have in the British model been spun out of original responsibilities in embryonic form of what must now be called the 'old' Board of Trade. Early examples are the Ministry of Labor, now the Department of Employment, and the Ministry of Transport, which after a period of absorption into the new Department of the Environment — itself a fairly new creation — is now again a separate department. A more recent example is the Department of Prices and Consumer Protection, most of whose functions as recently as 1970, were the charge of a small division of the Board of Trade (by that time, however, about to be renamed the Department of Trade and Industry), and part of the responsibility, under the President, of a junior minister in the Department. The exceptions are the organization of law and order (the Home Office), the conduct of political relations with the outside world (the Foreign Office), defense (the Service Departments, now united in the Ministry of Defense) and national finance (the Treasury).

In the postwar period the President of the Board of Trade and his officials carried the central responsibility for both the government's relations with industry and the conduct of the country's external commercial relations. Two major qualifications, however, have to be made to this proposition. The first is that this responsibility was exercised within the overriding authority of the Chancellor of the Exchequer and the Treasury for general economic policy. Even this was of comparatively recent origin. Before 1939 the office of Chief Economic Adviser to the Government was located in the Board of Trade, though its holder reported to the President and the Chancellor jointly. The second was that already agriculture had been one of the earlier seceders. The Ministry of Agriculture, Fisheries and Food was firmly in the saddle on both the domestic and, with some blurring at the edges, the external aspects of agricultural policy. In this paper I shall not try to deal with the agricultural aspects. In addition, there were several further erosions of the domestic responsibility of the Board of Trade in relation to a few specific industries, for example, the Ministry of Health's concern with the pharmaceutical industry.

Subject to these qualifications, it is fair to say that the responsibility for determining the proper balance between the amount of protection against foreign competition given to domestic producers and the national interest in external trade rested firmly and solely on the President of the Board of Trade. This involved, on the one hand, any government action in relation to or in support of domestic industry, and, on the other hand, the promotion of competition through imports, the interests of importing firms, the interests of exporters in securing access to foreign markets, and the maintenance of good and friendly relations with other trading countries. Of course, the range and scale of government activity and intervention of the period up to the middle of the 1960s was far short of the development since that time. But it was clear that the British situation was different from that of the United States in the 1950s, where it seemed easy to say that the Department of Commerce was the mouthpiece in government for the interest of domestic industry, and that the State Department, with its external interest alone and without any domestic responsibility, was concerned only to secure agreement and goodwill abroad. No doubt the picture in both cases was a distortion of the truth. None the less, the necessity for coordination between domestic and external concerns was, in the United Kingdom, built centrally into the administrative machine. The United States structure was perhaps also brought somewhat nearer to this position by the creation, in 1963, of the office of the Special Representative for Trade Negotiations.

The change which has taken place in the extent and intensity of government activity has inevitably reflected itself in the mechanisms of administration. The lines of the future were perhaps foreshadowed by the first and ephemeral renaming of the President of the Board of Trade in 1964, still under a Conservative government, as Secretary of State for Trade, Industry and Regional Development and President of the Board of Trade. On this title base, the period since 1964 has seen a number of permutations of functions among different departments, including one period when responsibility for policy on monopolies and mergers lay with the Department of Employment. Over the period since 1964 the responsibility for government relations with and support to domestic industry has been sometimes partly removed from and partly still within the department concerned with trade. The so called 'technological industries' were under the Ministry of Technology, while the 'traditional' industries — clothing, footwear, films, miscellaneous consumer foods industries and services like tourism and insurance — remained in an enormously enlarged 'jumbo' Department of Trade and Industry. In the current (1976) manifestation, these are two separate ministries. On the one hand, there is the Department of Trade, which inherits the external responsibilities of the old Board of Trade. This includes a surviving interest in a few mainly service industries, publishing, tourism, films, insurance, shipping and civil aviation, as well as the distributive trades, and the general functions of commercial regulation, such as company law, insolvency, industrial property. On the other, there is the Department of Industry, covering the whole range of manufacturing industry and including the responsibility for regional development. It is also the supervizing department both for the work of the scientific establishments maintained by the government, the National Physical Laboratory, the National Engineering Laboratory, the Laboratory of the Government Chemist and others, and for the administration of government assistance to outside research and development organizations, which were formerly the charge of the separate Department of Scientific and Industrial Research.

Meanwhile, as a further offshoot from the Board of Trade, the Department of Prices and Consumer Protection now has the responsibility for policy in the field of monopolies, mergers and restrictive practices, and for the general interests of consumers, by now much more articulately formulated. The executive administration is exercised by the Office of Fair Trading.

The operations of government in relation to industry and, in particular, to the various support systems will be examined in more detail later. But some general comment might be made here. The effect of the departmental reorganizations of the last dozen years has certainly been to disperse the unified responsibility which resided in the President of the Board of Trade. Conflicts of interest between those of domestic producers and those arising out of international trade considerations therefore involve at least two departments and ministers, and in extreme cases might require to be resolved at Cabinet level. In the process, however, a substantial shift in the balance of influence has also taken place. The successive changes in the pattern of industrial policy from the middle of the 1960s have put more and more emphasis on the role of the government as the guarantor, not only of a high level of employment in general, but of the survival of particular types of production and even of particular enterprises. The balance has moved strongly from the 'trade' side of the equation to the 'industry' side. It has come to be increasingly the case that in the various periods, including the present one, when 'industry' and 'trade' are dealt with in different departments, the advantages of political weight and of seniority in the political spectrum are likely to be with the Minister for Industry rather than with the Minister of Trade. At the same time, and especially in the most recent period, the intense pre-occupation with the preservation of existing employment, even in the short term, has substantially increased the influence on the policy of the Department of Employment.

The British pattern has therefore moved not merely towards reproducing in the United Kingdom what was said above about the Department of Commerce/State Department relationship, but rather further in the same direction. The Secretary of State in a United States administration will certainly always carry more weight than the Secretary of Commerce; and a Secretary of State who wished to make international commerce policy an issue carries quite a lot of the big guns. Of course, international trade is very much less significant an element in the United States economy than in the British, and not many American Secretaries of State have interested themselves at all deeply in commercial policy questions. None the less, in spite of the weight of protectionist and sectionalist influence in United States policies, liberal international commercial policies have, in general prevailed. It is certainly too soon to say that this is no longer the case in Britain. But it must be recognized that the balance of forces, at least in the field of political organization, has shifted. This is not to say that the organizational changes have created a shift in policy. The organizational changes reflect underlying changes in circumstances and in attitudes. Over a period of time, the structure must adapt itself to the policies.

THE ADMINISTRATION OF GENERAL SCHEMES OF INDUSTRIAL SUPPORT BEFORE 1972

This section will describe in more detail the processes of administration of some of the successive schemes which have constituted British government policy toward industry since the 1960s. I shall not at this stage try to analyze the underlying philosophy of these schemes, partly because there have been different schemes operated by governments of different political conceptions, and partly because it will be more convenient to look later on at the most comprehensive philosophical presentation of the topic, which is contained in a Department of Industry paper of January 1976.

It has been said that the most notable feature of British industrial policy over this period has been its incoherence. Certainly, there have been many innovations, revisions and reversals. These have been dictated in part by the fluctuations of political fortunes, and occasionally by the urge to take 'initiatives' which is an occupational predilection of some politicians. Certainly, there has been a tendency to snatch at schemes which held out the promise of quick results, without adequate analysis; and a similar readiness to abandon them perhaps too soon for it to be demonstrable whether they have done good or harm, or have had little effect one way or the other. The complaint from industry itself has overwhelmingly been against this switchback process, which has made its own planning immensely difficult. On balance, over the years such changes must have had a tendency to reduce whatever advantages lay in any particular scheme. Since much of what is now being done by the Labor administration is based on the Conservative Industry Act of 1972 (with comparatively minor modifications, at any rate in the main operative provisions in regard to support of industry in the Labor Industry Act of 1975) we may perhaps have reached some degree of stability on the basic legislation. This is not to say that there could not be change in government attitudes and emphasis which could virtually amount to a change in basic policy. Perhaps one can take the charitable attitude that the shifts and turns were the innovations and experiments necessary to work out the right policy for so considerable a task as refashioning the structure, the attitudes, and the physical configuration of British industry.

It should be said at the outset that with the exception of shipbuilding, which is a worldwide special case, none of the British schemes of support for industry involves payments directly related to specific products. The thrust of the schemes is directed entirely at improvements in general efficiency, through encouragement of investment or modernization of equipment, or, in some special cases, by way of compensation for the scrapping of obsolete or redundant capacity. They thus take the form either of adaptation of the tax system to encourage investment, either generally or in particular areas, or of grants or loans, sometimes at advantageous interest rates, with the same purpose. It would be difficult to bring any of the schemes described here within any of the categories in the list of examples of 'export aids' for the purposes of the GATT Declaration on Export Aids of 1960. Much less, of course, could they in any way be held to produce lower prices for export than for home supplies. In any case, it would probably be extremely difficult to carry through the effect of the particular support, in any very precise way, into the unit end-cost of a specific item of the enterprise receiving it.

In the description which follows I have leaned heavily for the general schemes, on the material (with some updating) contained in a paper by G. M. Fields and P. V. Hills for the Department of Industry's conference on the economics of industrial subsidies in February 1975,[1] and have followed their classification.

Up to the middle 1960s the main incentives for industrial investment were operated through the tax system. They took the form of accelerated depreciation allowance and investment allowances. The acceleration was created by allowing a greater than normal writing down allowance in the first year, or under another scheme applicable to investment in industrial plant in development districts for a short period, 'free' depreciation, that is, depreciation at a rate chosen by the taxpayer. Investment allowances, which permitted an amount in excess of the total cost of the asset to be offset against tax otherwise due, were also used intermittently, and at varying rates, from 1954 until 1972. The investment allowance, which at its highest in 1963 provided an additional premium of 30 per cent of the cost of the investment, was virtually a grant towards the cost. However, since it was paid by way of deduction from tax liability, it was available only to firms making sufficient profit, therefore incurring enough tax, to absorb it. In 1970, a new differentiation between development areas and the rest of the country was introduced. Capital investment on new plant and machinery in the development areas qualified for 100 per cent first year allowance, while elsewhere the rate was first 60 per cent and later 80 per cent. Finally, at any rate so far, the 100 per cent first year allowance was extended to the whole country in 1972.

All these taxation systems were, and are, administered as part of the normal tax procedure by the Inland Revenue. They have, of course, presented a number of problems in supervision and enforcement. The tax allowance system, in particular, presented the real difficulty that it gave firms a substantial incentive to claim items which had normally been regarded as current — canteen cutlery is the example often quoted — as capital, and therefore qualifying for the additional allowance against tax. Similarly, all the arrangements which involved regional distinctions raised considerable enforcement difficulties. The position now reached has alleviated most of these problems.

The actual effects of variations, even differential variations, in tax rates on investment are extremely difficult to estimate — perhaps impossible. This is particularly so when both systems and rates are varied frequently and unsystematically. Investment decisions of any size are made on fairly long-term considerations. It is not feasible to base such decisions on so uncertain a foundation as the decisions of governments have seemed to be. Indeed, the general view of United Kingdom businessmen seems to be that they must decide their investment policy by their judgement of market prospects and prospective costs, disregarding taxation policies of the moment. However, there are no doubt marginal cases where the taxation arrangements may make a difference one way or another. It is fair to say that in the main incentive area, the regional development grant, it has been a conscious objective of policy to maintain continuity.

Outside the field of taxation incentives, there has again been a wide variety of forms of direct grant in aid of investment under a number of different acts passed by governments of both parties. These include the Industrial Development Act of 1966, which introduced investment grants, and the arrangements under which were terminated by the Investment and Building Grants Act of 1971; the Local Employment Act of 1960, 1963 and 1970 (consolidated in the Local Employment Act of 1972); the Industrial Expansion Act of 1968; and eventually the two Industry Acts of 1972 (Conservative) and 1975 (Labor) which have perhaps produced a more systematic general framework.

Each of the various general schemes operated under this clutch of legislation had special features of its own. The investment grant scheme, which ran under the Industrial Development Act of 1966, from 1966 until 1971 (but outstanding claims under which persisted for a good deal longer), offered cash grants towards capital expenditure on new plant and machinery in the manufacturing and construction industries, and on mining works, computers, ships and hovercraft. It also offered a grant to any firm in the United Kingdom for the purchase of computers and ships — a provision which had subsequently to be modified because of the golden opportunity it offered to foreign firms to buy foreign ships through United Kingdom based subsidiaries. This scheme was administered at its inception by the Board of Trade, but was part of the package of the Board's responsibilities which was transferred to the soon-to-be established Ministry of Technology. It was returned to the reunited Department of Trade and Industry on its creation in 1970. This was a scheme which raised most complex issues of administration for both the administering department and for industry, and contained almost all the problems that could be invented. It differentiated between development areas and elsewhere in the rate of grant. The rates varied from year to year. Eligibility was determined by the kind of process in which assets were used, so as to exclude all assets of service industries, and to some extent by the kind of asset. To enable these distinctions to be enforced, payment of the grant was made discretionary, not mandatory. All this made for a highly elaborate processing and examination procedure.

The headquarters staff was supplemented by five local offices, involving a total of 1000 at an estimated cost of some £2 million a year. This called for careful procedures to ensure uniformity of treatment.

There was elaborate certification, and rules to enable the grant to be recovered, for example in cases where an asset ceased to be used for a qualifying process or was disposed of. Enforcement of these rules, and of the scheme generally, required inspection teams in each local office.

More dangerously — especially from the point of view of the Treasury — the scheme was open ended, and threatened to become dangerously out of control. The original estimated expenditure for 1967–68 was £166 million; the out turn for that year was £315 million. By 1969–70, 140,000 applications were received in the year, and the amount paid out was £587 million. All these reasons reinforced the natural antagonism of the Conservative government, and its determination on its return to office in 1970, to bring this scheme to an end. In the event the termination problems proved hardly less intractable than those of operation.

Alongside the investment grant system, arrangements of longer standing for assistance on a regional basis existed under the Local Employment Acts. Assistance under these arrangements included access to loans on favorable terms, building grants, plant and machinery grants, removal grants and operational grants. Within certain standardized rules there was a considerable measure of individual case-by-case negotiation about the amount of grant; and grants were specifically linked to the provision of new employment, since this was the stated purpose of the legislation.

Here again administration was in the hands of the Board of Trade until the establishment of the Ministry of Technology, and subsequently in the Department of Trade and Industry. Subject to policy guidance from the headquarters the detailed inquiries and examination of proposals was the task of the departmental regional offices. But the appraisal of proposals, and the final advice to the responsible minister, was entrusted to an independent outside advisory committee, the Local Employment Acts Financial Advisory Committee. This consisted of individuals drawn from industry, banking, accounting and the trade unions, acting in their independent personal capacity and exercising expert independent judgement on the likely viability of the proposal, especially in relation to its employment forecast.

The combined action of the departmental inquiry organization through its regional office, and the advisory committee's appraisal, seems to have provided a perhaps unexpectedly strong safeguard for the financial soundness of the operation. The examinations were very thorough, and the committee, within the general policy conditions, was able to preserve its independence. Up to 1970, less than three quarters of 1 per cent of all loans advanced up to that time had had to be written off.

Building grants and the other ancillary grant operations, were dealt with similarly, and again the combined action of official inquiry and independent expert appraisal seems to have worked, in general, satisfactorily. The price of the care taken in processing of cases was a degree of slowness in taking decisions, which naturally irked applicants, and what was by some regarded as want of adventurousness in the committee's general approach.

Before turning to the new systems based on the Industry Act 1972, and to consideration of the more selective schemes and of some specific cases, a scheme of a rather different kind should be mentioned. This was the regional employment premium. By contrast with all previous attempts to provide an incentive to firms to take their activities to the development areas through advantages available there to capital, this was a direct incentive to labor. It was introduced in the Finance Act of 1967, and consisted of a payment at a weekly rate in respect to each employee. It was available for all employees in manufacturing industry without any criterion related to increased employment, and at the beginning a degree of security was included in its operation, since it was guaranteed to run for at least seven years — that is, up to 1974. It was in the event renewed beyond that date, but was eventually ended in January 1977. Unlike the capital loan and grant schemes, the administration in this case was put into the hands of the Department of Employment. The main problems of administration, however, were not dissimilar from those of some of the other schemes; the primary one was of eligibility. This arose in relation to the nature of the qualifying activity. It also arose even more acutely in relation to the number of employees in an establishment engaged in qualifying activities as against others, since the payment was for all the employees in the establishment provided that at least half of them qualified. Inspection and enforcement therefore involved building up a quite substantial bureaucratic machine, especially as the eligibility test had to be satisfied week by week.

THE 1972 WHITE PAPER

So far, the schemes described have been in the main those of the post 1964 Labor governments. However, the pattern of the Local Employment Acts schemes goes further back, and is basically a continuation of the assistance to the regions of high unemployment which dates from the early postwar period. One further measure of the late 1960s was the Industrial Expansion Act of 1968, which broke new ground in giving the government powers to give loans, grants, guarantees, the underwriting of losses or the subscription of share capital to projects designed to promote efficiency, to support technological advance, or to create, expand or sustain productive capacity. This meant that the government could now provide support to individual firms on a direct basis, rather than as part of a general scheme. The administration of this Act was the task of the Ministry of Technology. Its enactment was indeed clearly part of the same package of ideas which had led to the setting up of the ministry in 1966, under that particular name, to take over — on a very substantially enlarged scale and with a vastly more ambitious remit — some of the responsibilities of the Board of Trade. It was under this Act that the earlier more spectacular ventures of the United Kingdom Government into industrial support — Concorde, the construction of the *Queen Elizabeth II*, and the establishment of an aluminum smelting industry — have taken place. It will be more convenient to consider these separately, together with other selective schemes under the later legislation.

The Conservative government of 1970 had set out to try to wipe the slate clean of much of the structure of support schemes described above, and to return to incentives administered through the taxation system. But by 1972, they, too, found themselves moving back to the need to formulate a support policy. The White Paper on Industrial and Regional Development,[2] of March that year, sets out the objectives aimed at and also describes in a quite detailed way the administrative arrangements planned to carry it out.

The objectives of the 'new and comprehensive program to stimulate industrial and regional regeneration' were to be 'to promote and sustain faster economic growth; to secure the expansion and modernization of British Industry; to attack the continuing and serious problems of regional imbalance, and to assist industry to meet the challenge of Europe.' The program was presented within the context of successful negotiation of membership of the European Community, and as a means of improving the industrial base so as to seize the opportunities available in a wealthy and expanding market of 290 million people.

The measures proposed were to be both national and regional and both general, or 'basic', as the White Paper described them, and selective. The basic national incentive was the extension to the whole country of 100 per cent first year depreciation allowance on plant and machinery, which had previously been conferred on development areas, and some other taxation simplifications and ameliorations. It continues to be administered by the Inland Revenue. The basic regional incentive was the reintroduction of a regional development grant scheme. This was not completely dissimilar in concept from the investment grant scheme described above, and was to be administered in much the same way. But its more limited geographical coverage and a number of simplifications have enabled it to be run with a considerably smaller staff as the earlier scheme is wound up. Its qualifying definitions, however, are the same as for the regional employment premium. These raise the same kind of problems, though in a much less acute form, since there is not the complication here of the weekly test of eligibility. On the selective side, the proposals picked up again, in a slightly modified way, the ideas of the Industrial Expansion Act of 1968. It accepted the proposition that assistance was needed not only for projects providing additional employment, but also for modernization of industry. In operating such assistance, in the regions, a fuller part was to be played by the regional administrations. But in addition, the White Paper said, 'on occasion, particularly in view of our entry into Europe, it may be necessary to consider the wider structure of an industry or a major project beyond the boundaries of the assisted areas. The Government will seek new powers to provide selective assistance more widely in such cases.' As a *coup de chapeau* to more traditional Conservative attitudes, this fairly startling reversal of its earlier stance was accompanied by an affirmation that it would not be intended in any way to replace existing private sources of industrial finance.

The White Paper went on to describe the administrative machinery which was to be set up for these purposes. In the summer of 1970, the government had amalgamated the Board of Trade with the Ministry of Technology, and had also restored to the reunited department some of its other lost functions, such as the responsibility for monopolies and mergers. The reunited department was renamed the Department of Trade and Industry, under a Secretary of State with the same title. The historic 'Board of Trade' ceased to exist, though it seems that the Secretary of State continues to hold the title of President of the Board of Trade in order, under one of the odder British legal quirks, to qualify for a salary.

The Department of Trade and Industry had thus recovered the area of responsibility of the pre-1966 Board. But the development of 1966–70 meant that it was a vastly different department — enormously bigger, with a new and quite transformed vision of its role in the industrial scene, and with the balance of staff and of influence within it much different from what it had been in its previous incarnations. The department was now, in substance if not in name, two separate departments — Industry and Trade. The division was, of course, emphasized by the locational separation which had meanwhile taken place. The main industry divisions were housed in the magnificient Milbank Tower block, in its way the most advanced construction in London, where the Ministry had been originally placed so as to enhance its 'technological' image, and Trade still in its older and rather staid building.

The dual character of the department was now, by the White Paper proposals, to be further institutionalized. There was to be a Minister for Industrial Development, who would be 'under the broad direction' of the Secretary of State for Trade and Industry. He would have special responsibility for private sector industry generally and for industrial development in the assisted areas. He would also have what in effect would be an independent ministry, described as an Industrial Development Executive, headed jointly by a Permanent Secretary and a

'Director of Industrial Development', to be appointed from the private sector. A development unit was to be set up to help with the 'appraisal and implementation of industrial development needs'. The executive would recruit staff from the City and from industry as necessary to provide 'a full range of financial, industrial and administrative expertise'. There would be an Industrial Development Advisory Board of 'prominent persons in industry, banking, accounting and finance, and international industrial investment, with particular emphasis on relations with Europe', to advise generally on industrywide problems and priorities, and to consider specific major cases for selective assistance. Figure 3.1 shows the headquarters organization contemplated in detail. The headquarters was to be supplemented by a very much strengthened regional organization. It was to have a strong element of devolved authority, and would in effect provide in each region a simulacrum of the central organization, with a 'positive role in promoting industrial expansion and modernization, and in stimulating centers of growth'.

The proposals set out in this White Paper were duly embodied in the Conservative Industry Act of 1972,[3] the Minister of Industrial Development appointed, and the Industrial Development Executive was set up. But the beneficiaries of the legislation were, in the event, the Labor government of the following year. For once, there was no great break in the continuity of the legislative framework, and the schemes outlined by the Conservatives were taken over whole. Indeed, the legislation had been so broadly drafted, that the relevant sections of the 1972 Act, section 7 on regional development and section 8 on selective assistance, needed only minor adaptation to lend itself easily to greater use by Labor, and facilitated a more activist role by government than would probably have been contemplated by the Conservatives. Those removed limits that had been set on the power of the Secretary of State in relation to the acquisition of equity share in enterprises. The Act did, however, fall short of providing the powers to compel undertakings to accept government help which some of the incoming Labor politicians wanted, but for which they were unable to secure sufficient support to carry through.

The Labor government in its turn produced a White Paper — 'The Regeneration of British Industry' — in August 1974. In the field with which we are concerned, the only new development — apart from a further step in devolving responsibility to Scotland and Wales — was to propose the creation of a National Enterprise Board. The Board was to act in various ways as the government's instrument or operating channel in some of its assistance operations. In the event, the precise role to be played by the NEB has turned out in the Industry Act of 1975 less wide ranging than was envisaged, and it is still too early to say how powerful an institution it will be. The legislative system through all its develop-

Figure 3.1 INDUSTRIAL DEVELOPMENT EXECUTIVE—MAIN FEATURES
HEADQUARTERS ORGANIZATION

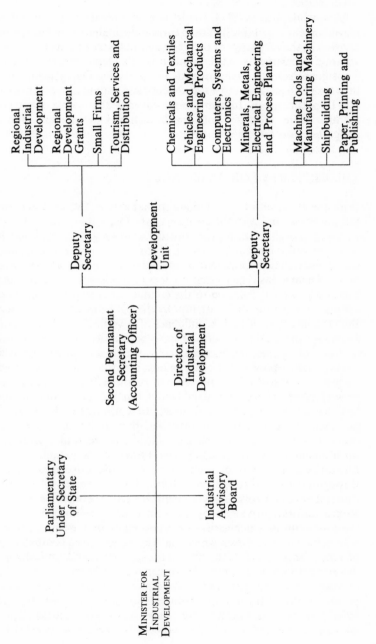

ment remains in essence a framework within which government reacts to circumstances.

Meanwhile also in 1974, the logic of the creation of the Industrial Development Executive had been carried through to a conclusion by the division of the Department of Trade and Industry into its two halves as separate departments. At the same time the Department of Prices and Consumer Protection was formed. The surviving Department of Trade thus shrank back again to a stature even less than in its 1966 form, since the Department of Industry now covered the whole spectrum of manufacturing industry, with the Industrial Development Unit fully integrated into the department.

THE CRITERIA FOR ASSISTANCE

With the 1972, and to a small additional extent, the 1975 acts on the Statute Book, and with the creation of the Department of Industry and its regional organizations, the United Kingdom government now has a very powerful mechanism to bring to bear on the operation and particularly the development of industry both inside and outside the development areas. The legislation does not endow the government with coercive powers in relation to the conduct of enterprises, and there is certainly no inclination or attempt by the government to act coercively. But certainly the role and the influence of government have been greatly enhanced and significant efforts have been made to equip its organization with the competence and skills which are needed to make an interventionist policy credible. The position now reached does perhaps suggest a new sort of counterpoise in relations between the state and private interests in the industrial field. Clearly, the developments of the last decade or so have done much to consolidate the role of the government as a strong, if invisible, participant in a great many decisions which companies have to take about size, timing and location of investment. More potently the power of government to give assistance is matched by its power to impose burdens on industry through taxation, through social legislation in a variety of forms, and through price controls. A government which does not see itself as willing to intervene as a provider of assistance may be more inhibited in creating the conditions in which assistance is needed, than one which is not only willing but eager to do so, which may regard itself as a competent judge of which firms should be the ones to prosper or expand, and which has a determined view of its own of a larger social interest.

Against such background considerations, it may be useful at this point — before returning to a detailed account of the use made of the 1972 powers — to examine the view which the United Kingdom government at present takes of its own role, and of the way in which it approaches the questions we are considering. This is set out in the document to which I referred earlier—a paper prepared by the Department of Industry and notified to Parliament in January 1976.

The paper aims to set out the conclusions reached by the government on the criteria for assistance to industry in the light of a stocktaking which takes account of the considerations affecting industry in general, of the problems involved in recent proposals for putting money into particular enterprises, as well as the similar problems in both existing publicly owned enterprises and extensions of the public sector. The same criteria, it is suggested, are applicable generally for assistance in all these areas.

The government's overriding objective 'must clearly be that British industry should compete more successfully in meeting the requirements of home and overseas markets'. Otherwise there can be no solution to our problems. The state has to establish the broad social and economic framework within which industry operates, through its macroeconomic and its social policies. Within this framework 'we are concerned with the allocation of resources to industries, public or private . . . operating in a market economy'.

Generally speaking, profitability and return on capital are the best prima facie indicators of where available resources should go. True, 'the process of resource allocation through the price mechanism does not ensure an adequate level of aggregate demand and employment, nor produce an acceptable distribution of income or cause resources to be set aside for public services. All these are mainly functions of government, not of the market.' But this 'in itself' does not invalidate the role of money as a measure for the market of relative costs and efficiency in production. Nor does state intervention in financing, either for private firms or through ownership, mean that benefit will be maximized by enterprises which give lower returns. However, company profits and losses are not in all cases a 'wholly accurate' measure of resource costs and benefits. The 'community' may strike a costs and benefits account different from that of the individual enterprise. In such cases, 'there are grounds for setting out to redress the divergence . . . whether by taxation, planning controls or subsidies'. The most clear cut instance of this is the provision for promoting employment in the development areas. 'The creation, maintenance or safeguarding of employment in the assisted areas,' for which section 7 of the Industry Act provides, in itself supplies the essential criterion for this 'regional selective assistance'. Section 8 of the Act, dealing with national selective assistance is less specific: it speaks in general terms of 'benefit to the United Kingdom economy and the national interest'. This reflects the difficulty in defining any other general class of case in which 'there is a pre-supposition that resource costs and benefits will diverge from money costs and benefits'. The balance of payments has provided the most clearly distinguishable reason for believing this to be the case, and has been the most common reason for assistance under section 8. Rationalization schemes have in some cases seemed to justify help, and so have industrial research programs.

Having set out these general principles, the paper goes on to discuss, on the one hand assessment of viability, and on the other, assessment of social costs and benefits. These are administered by the Department of Industry 'on the basis of such inter-departmental consultation as is appropriate', or by the regional organization within its agreed devolved limits, and in each case after receiving an opinion from the Industrial Development Advisory Board or its regional counterpart. Part of the process is to establish viability, which 'in this context is taken to refer to a company's ability, after receiving selective assistance on a once-for-all basis, to achieve and maintain profitability without continuing subsidies other than those available to all eligible enterprises.' Assessment of viability is a matter of facts, figures and commercial judgement, in which wider economic and social factors are not relevant.

In considering viability, it will be necessary to examine many aspects — financial and commercial data; the quality of management; the amount of non-governmental finance available; and other matters, including especially time scale. The keynote is realism. The concept of receivership — finding a means to revitalize faltering but still potentially viable undertakings — has an important part to play.

Side by side with viability, the government has to consider what social benefits can properly be taken into account, 'quantified as far as possible, for example, as regards employment effects or balance of payments gains and resources required to achieve them'. Other factors — the importance of a particular firm in its area — may also arise. The cost of achieving viability has to be set against the value of these benefits, and the public expenditure implications must be 'an important element in the total valuation'. Job security is important, but 'if we are to break through the balance of payments constraint and thus achieve more room for manoeuvre . . . more and not less emphasis will be required . . . Failure to achieve this would in the end be the enemy of job security.'

After saying that workers' cooperatives must be judged by the same basic criteria of viability and social benefit, that on balance proposals should be given the benefit of the doubt where the social cost of refusal would be particularly high — for example, in areas of persistent high unemployment — and emphasizing the importance of consultation with both workers and management, the paper discusses at some length the question of cases which amount to rescue operations. On this, three points are made. First, 'there is a limited number of cases where it is immediately clear that the government will wish to intervene to ensure that the capability and as much of the employment as is economically possible are retained. . . . In these exceptional cases . . . the special features are not merely the scale of the social cost which would otherwise be incurred, but the strong presumption that it must be possible to reconstruct the enterprise on a viable basis'. But, once emergency holding action has been taken, 'the basic principles should apply in determining . . . longer term support'. The second class of cases where help may be justifiable is where it may be possible to avert bankruptcy and restore viability by a reasonable amount of assistance. The third class is the limited number of cases where some comparatively small provision of assistance would make possible some sort of reconstruction to salvage the enterprise as a going concern when otherwise, perhaps because of the pressure of time, it would founder.

I have summarized this paper at some length. The original is considerably longer still, since it is a good deal more explicit about the motivation of government thinking than most material that is available, and throws a good deal of light on the administrative process and problems involved. It is, however, possible to expand a little more on this latter point.

The administrative structure for assistance to industry does now look reasonably coherent. There are, of course, still vestigial survivals of operations under the earlier legislation; the investment grants under the 1966 act are still being phased out, and the same applies to some operations under the Local Employment Acts. But, generally speaking, operations are now based on sections 7 and 8 of the Industry Act of 1972. These are administered by the Department of Industry (or, for section 7, by the Secretaries of State for Scotland and for Wales in their countries) with the help, and in some cases, through the regional organizations. Essential elements in the administration are the Industrial Development Board and the Industrial Development Unit. The former, like its predecessors under earlier legislation, is independent, strong minded, and highly competent. The latter has also built up a substantial degree of competence and expertise since its establishment following the 1972 White Paper. It is now situated within the department, but staffed largely from outside the Civil Service.

OPERATIONS SINCE 1972

As has been said in the discussion of the 1972 White Paper, the structure of the general schemes was much simplified by the introduction of the 'basic' national incentive of 100 per cent first year depreciation allowance, and the 'basic' regional incentive of the regional development grant. These need not be discussed further.

There have been two outstanding features of developments since

1973—in effect since the incoming Labor government of that year inherited the machinery of the 1972 Act. They are: the continuously broadening range of 'selective' operations, within the criteria set out above, and the extent to which use has increasingly been made of the act beyond the geographical limits of the special regions which had traditionally been the target of assistance. The number of cases where the Government has offered loans or grants under the 1972 Act, and the amounts involved, up to 31 March, 1976, are shown in table 3.1:

Table 3.1 Loans and Grants under the 1972 Act

	Pre-Apr 1974		1 Apr 1974 to 31 Mar 1975		1975–6	
	Number	£m	Number	£m	Number	£m
'Regional' assistance (section 7)	1013	135.8	910	96.9	766	75.5
Other (section 8)	2	6.3	295	33.3	250	228.8
Total	1015	142.1	1205	130.2	1016	204.3

A series of schemes have now been set in train, and it must be expected that the selective operations will increasingly become part of a more general industrial strategy rather than the earlier drive to correct regional disadvantage and imbalance.

The first schemes were in the wool textile industry, the clothing industry, the ferrous foundry industry and the machine tool industry. Their general underlying objectives in each case are broadly similar but the formulations have varied. The aim is to ascertain industries homogeneous in character, and for the industry itself to diagnose its own problems, and formulate the incentive appropriate to its own circumstances.

The wool textile scheme was based on studies and surveys carried out by the economic development committee for the wool textile industry. At its commencement in July 1973, the government provided £15 million, later increased to £18 million. The scheme was intended, on the one hand, to encourage firms to modernize and rationalize their production processes, and on the other to reduce the number of firms and eliminate 'uneconomic' surplus capacity. Firms could apply for assistance under one of four heads. Firms which re-equipped were eligible for capital grants of 15 per cent (later 20 per cent) of costs incurred. Secondly, projects combining re-equipment and rebuilding could receive 20 per cent (later 30 per cent) of the new building cost. Thirdly, additional concessionary loans or interest relief grants were available for more comprehensive projects involving, in particular structural change through mergers, takeovers or concentration on a single site of production units previously separate. The form in which the assistance might be given could be adapted to the needs of the particular case. The avowed aim was to give a 'real incentive towards major restructuring in the industry leading to stronger and more efficient units.' Finally, grants were available to encourage the elimination of marginal capacity. The scheme included safeguards against the recurrence of over capacity in the industry by requiring, as a precondition of any assistance, the scrapping of replaced equipment equivalent to at least 90 per cent and in some cases 100 per cent of the new equipment's capacity, and the demolition of vacated buildings. There was also a 'code of manpower practice'. Its objective was to ensure that any employees who lost their existing jobs as a result of the scheme would whenever possible be retained in the industry 'after retraining, and redeployment where necessary'. A time limit (31 December, 1975) was set on applications. However, a further continuing scheme, aimed mainly at rationalization and restructuring, will now run to 31 March 1979.

The clothing industry scheme set as its objectives to encourage concentration of activity in more efficient units, and restructuring and reorganization within firms without an overall increase in the capacity of the industry. Applicants for assistance had to show that their project was commercially and technically viable, was 'appropriate to the managerial and financial resources of the applicant firm' and would significantly improve productivity and efficiency. Assistance was available for consultancy within very modest limits and for investment aimed at improving productivity and efficiency which was eligible for a grant of up to 20 per cent. Priority was to be given to projects in areas faced with particularly pressing social problems or sectors facing serious problems of adjustment: and for restructuring and reorganization, which also covered common service ventures and mergers, and might include working capital, in the form either of loans at concessionary rates or interest relief grants. However, the scheme in this original form does not seem to have seized the imagination of the industry. In December 1976, the government, disappointed that it was 'unlikely that grants of more than £4 million will have been authorized by the current closing date', announced improvements in the scheme and an extension of the closing date.

The ferrous foundry industry scheme, for which £4 million has been made available, and the machine tool industry scheme, for which there is £20 million, have similar aims and patterns of operation. They are the encouragement of investment in new production and buildings and improvements in production facilities and management techniques, with grants or concessionary loans, and additional inducements for rationalization or resiting within a company or following mergers. In each case the Department of Industry has to be satisfied as to the viability of the project and of the applicant company. It must also consider whether the 'project will make a contribution towards the objectives of modernizing and redeveloping the industry and improving its general ability to meet the needs of users' (the ferrous foundry scheme). Finally, it must ensure it forms an integral part of a realistic business plan covering a reasonable period ahead, and that it will enable the applicant to establish a significant share in a substantial market, preferably on an international scale (the machine tool scheme).

Schemes of a similar character for other industries will no doubt follow. Some have already been announced or foreshadowed in outline. All of them are covered by the administrative arrangements already described. Clearly, these envisage a very high degree of expertise, and competence inside the Department of Industry machine, and, if the objectives and conditions set out by the government are to come anywhere near fruition, they involve technical and commercial decisions of great complexity.

In these developments, it becomes clearer that what is emerging is a substantial supplementation of the market process. There is a clear assumption, on the part of the framers of United Kingdom policy, that a centrally controlled decision making process will produce better results than would be produced by the market, even though there is still pressure in the private sector to produce the bulk of the money required. To this end, the government must, necessarily, equip itself with an administrative machine far more closely involved in the operations of industry than it ever previously had. To a considerable extent this is achieved through the advisory bodies referred to above, by systems of consultation in the National Economic Development Council and the individual industry Economic Development Councils, and by direct consultation with the Trades Union Congress and the Confederation of British Industry and with the relevant trade unions and trade associations. At the end of the day, however, the decisions are made by the Secretary of State for Industry (especially, of course, the textile industry; and the wool textiles scheme has some rather ghostly echoes of the pre-1939 cotton industry reorganization acts). But his department, even during the development of 'sponsoring' divisions for industries during the 1939–45 war and the period of controls, did not have and did not need the function in relation to their industries which present policy implies. A senior UK civil servant has described this as being, in contrast with earlier periods, 'much more positive and active now; concerned with analysing critically the performance of industry, and the factors which could improve that performance, including structural change within the industry itself (this last factor being something which is largely beyond the capabilities of a trade association) . . . All this has been given renewed emphasis in the context of the new approach to industrial strategy.'[4]

In these respects, the 'selective' schemes under the 1972 Act may be a more significant development of policy than either the great technological forays of the earlier period — Concorde, the *Queen Elizabeth II*, or even the aluminum smelting industry episode — or the more widely publicized 'rescue' operations — Meriden, Rolls Royce, or even Chrysler and British Leyland. In the last analysis, none of these was a policy. They were reactions to events, sometimes vigorous or innovative, more often reluctant and almost despairing—expedients, rather than policy. Nor do they have much to add to the discussion of administrative structure which is the topic of this chapter. The decision making in these cases has been political rather than bureaucratic, and virtually every case has faced the politicians in power at the time with options all almost equally repugnant. The situation seemed to the governments concerned to show a real deficiency in the private enterprise system's ability to cope with social situations which demanded solutions. For the Conservative administration, the Rolls Royce decision marked a change which was really a turning point in that government's history, and which went much beyond the narrow area of assistance to industry or even industrial policy in the wider sense. For the Labor administration which succeeded it, the Chrysler case, with the crosscurrents involving attitudes to multinational firms and arousing the latent anti-Americanism of its supporters, presented perhaps less traumatic, but not much less difficult, problems. As for British Leyland, the underlying philosophical approach of the government clearly made it impossible to withhold support, and not to snatch at the opportunity to nationalize; but the sheer scale of that operation, the uneasiness of the company's internal labor relations situation, and the timing of the crisis in relation to the development of what the government was just beginning to describe as an 'industrial strategy' designed to 'pick the winners', made this case also one of enormous difficulty.

It is not to be supposed that the last of such cases has been seen. To some extent, however, 'rescue' cases have been brought within a more manageable administrative framework through the operation of the criteria described above. The government itself, at any rate, sees the 'rescue' cases as minimal in relation to the total operation. Of the pre-April 1974 total of 1015 cases and £142.1 million, rescue represented 15 cases and £12.9 million of loans and grants; in the two years to 31 March 1976, there were 54 cases out of the total of 2420.

In terms of administrative structure, the long history of assistance to the shipbuilding industry can equally be regarded as not significantly affecting the picture which has emerged so far. There has also been detailed analysis of the UK shipbuilding story elsewhere.[5] But shipbuilding assistance is so much part of the international complex[6] that, without rehearsing a detailed account of its operation in the United Kingdom, it will be convenient to set it in the context of the next section of this chapter.

The selective sectoral schemes, however, do not by any means exhaust the range of activity. The 1972 Act has also been the basis of an effort to promote counter cyclical expenditure on investment, through the accelerated projects scheme. This scheme, inaugurated in the budget of 1975, was based on the low rate of new investment during the trough of world trade and the belief that an early recovery in trade and in the economy might come before firms felt sufficiently strong financially to expand production resources in anticipation of expansion of their potential market. According to studies made by industry — as well as by government — there was the likelihood that production capacity, in some sectors at all events, would in these circumstances be inadequate to cope with demand; but that while firms wanted in principle to go ahead with investment, 'cool appraisal of the cost' often meant that projects were shelved. The scheme offered firms government assistance in the form of loans or interest relief grant to bring forward investment projects which would otherwise have been deferred. The objective was to ensure that assistance would be given to genuine projects which were viable, which would involve a substantial benefit to the UK balance of payments, and which would be begun before a deadline, originally March 1976, later extended to September 1976. At first the scheme was confined to projects involving a capital cost, including working capital, not less than £2.5 million; but the government was encouraged by the response to reduce this minimum to £0.5 million, and to enlarge the total funds available to £120 million. It was a further objective to provide the least amount, in each case, required to bring the project forward. By the close of the scheme out of the 350 applications received, 114 had been rejected: 120 had had offers amounting to some £84 million and it was estimated that the total capital investment initiated by these offers amounted to £640 million. The Chancellor's December statement on economic measures in connection with the newly-agreed IMF loan included provision for further funds for a replacement of the scheme. As with all the other 1972 Act schemes, the administration of this followed the pattern already described — responsibility in the Department of Industry — or the Scottish or Welsh Office with the advice and cooperation of the Industrial Development Advisory Boards and the regional machinery of the department.

A variety of other schemes of more limited application and similarly administered, have been set in train or foreshadowed. All in all, a quite substantial structure of government financing with some concessional elements has thus become an established feature in the scene. It is no doubt still a very small part of the total annual investment outlay, and a minuscule part of the total working capital of industry. But it is by no means insignificant in some sectors and for an increasing number of firms. In the comparatively short period since the 1972 Act, it has become an increasingly acceptable factor in firms' assessments of their financing. The client relationship of firms to government has correspondingly become much more pervasive, so that industry becomes acclimatized to the belief that government is the fountain of health. In the extreme case, the risk factor in maintaining a firm in being for primarily social, rather than commercial profitability reasons, may be borne to a considerable extent by the government rather than by the firm. For the most part however, the British pattern has still been to try to throw on to industry—either collectively for the firms in a particular sector or for individual firms—the responsibility, and a substantial share of the risk, of working out their own salvation. None the less, over a long period of the atmosphere of client relationship, it seems inevitable that both the lure of high rewards for the efficient and for the speculative innovator, and the danger of failure for the inefficient and the plodder, must tend to lose their efficacy. In shifting from the wealth of the nation to the National Enterprise Board as a source of action and innovation, we would move a long way indeed from the splendidly sturdy answer which the merchants of France gave—'laissons *nous* faire'—when Colbert asked what the government could do for them.

THE INTERNATIONAL DIMENSION

It will certainly not have escaped notice that throughout this description and discussion of United Kingdom industrial policy and assistance to industry, there has been very little reference to the consideration of international commitments or indeed to the international aspect of these operations at all. There appears to be a deficiency in the whole system of administration on this score. This is, in fact, not quite so glaring an omission as appears on the surface.

The international obligations which might be relevant for the United Kingdom are those which arise from her membership of the GATT throughout the whole period under discussion, of EFTA from 1959 to 1969, and now of the European Community.

As far as GATT is concerned, it has never been seriously suggested that any of the various schemes, which (in spite of the many revisions and reversals) all conform to much the same spirit, have been in contravention of Article XVI.

However, it is certainly the case that during the 1950s and 1960s, when these schemes were being evolved, there would always have been, as a matter of course, consultation among all the divisions of the Board of Trade concerned whenever a new variation was introduced, to clear the ground on this point. This was one of the aspects of the concentration of responsibility for both domestic industry and international relations under one minister which I discussed in the opening section of the chapter. Moreover, in the many discussions of export subsidy policy which took place in the GATT, especially in the discussions leading up to the 1960 Declaration, assistance to industry of the kind exercized in the United Kingdom, which at no point related to exports, was never under attack.

However, it is no doubt true that the awareness of the GATT as a factor to be taken into account in framing domestic policies would be much less present to the minds of the general body of the United Kingdom civil servants in the mid-1970s than it was twenty or even ten years earlier; and this would no doubt also be emphasized by the change in the departmental pattern of responsibility. It seems highly probable that there is much less automatic coordination on this aspect now, even though a conscious and deliberate effort is made to maintain this. Meanwhile, however, the role of the United Kingdom in relation to the GATT has been somewhat modified by accession to the Community, even though her individual obligations remain unchanged. I shall come back to this point later.

The EFTA obligation is a somewhat different matter. Again, however, it is fair to say that during the period of United Kingdom membership of EFTA, the considerations arising from membership would always have been present automatically in the minds of those concerned with any act of domestic policy on which the Stockholm Convention might bear. There were throughout the period standing interdepartmental committees, and within the Board of Trade well established liaison arrangements, to ensure adequate consultation. This does not by any means imply that no decision was ever taken which would be unwelcome to the other members of the Association, or even which might be assailed by them as in breach of the Convention. The imposition of the import surcharge in 1964 was one such decision, and the assistance given to the establishment of an aluminum smelting industry was another—both, of course, decisions of the highest importance. It does, however, mean that no such decision was made in ignorance of the likely reaction, or without the EFTA aspect having been taken into consideration.

There remains the question of the European Community. Here we have to recognize that a relationship of an entirely new kind has come to exist between national civil services and the central international organization, in this case the Commission. There is, of course, still within the United Kingdom organization the same kind of coordination procedure as I have described above. This is exercised partly through the interdepartmental committee structure, now normally under Cabinet Office chairmanship, where any major proposal would be considered, but also, and much more generally, through the normal processes of informal consultation. In this case there would be in the ordinary course regular contact between those responsible for the conduct of industrial policy—whether, as they were in the early stages of membership, in the

Department of Trade and Industry, or as now, in the Department of Industry—and the division which has been set up precisely to deal with general questions of Community industrial policy, the European industry and technology division. The latter, now somewhat eccentrically in view of other changes, is located in the Department of Trade. In fact, however, though this internal liaison goes on, the close and continuous relationship with the Commission means that there will be constant direct communication between the operative division in London—often the industrial development unit—and officers of the Commission. Thus it can be reasonably assumed that United Kingdom policy and its implementation in quite considerable detail has been accepted by the Community.

Insofar as any policy measures were to be criticized in the GATT, the United Kingdom (as also any other Community member) would no doubt look for support and defense to the Commission, as the custodian and spokesman of common Community policy.

All this said, there remains the question whether, leaving aside the formal obligations of existing international instruments, there is a wider international dimension to a policy of assistance to industry as well articulated and, potentially at any rate, as far reaching and effective as the United Kingdom has now formulated. It is clear from the references to balance of payments considerations in the Department of Industry paper on criteria that in some at least, perhaps in most cases, under section 8 of the Industry Act, it will be a decisive factor in making assistance available that the resultant output will tend either to reduce imports or to increase exports, or both. It may never be possible to quantify the actual price effect of assistance; that it will have some price effect, and therefore some trade effect, is none the less **a** datum in the discussion.

Taken only so far, it looks as if there is here a prima facie case to enlarge the international discussion to take in operations of this kind. But is this really far enough to take the inquiry? Should it not go further and ask why it becomes necessary in a particular country for government intervention in the operations of private industry to be carried so far? Is it a case of the government merely giving back with one hand what it has, excessively, taken away with the other? Can policies on one such aspect of the whole complex of relations between government and industry be abstracted from the totality of the conditions in which industry operates?

It is at least doubtful whether the United Kingdom organization for the formulation of policy and consultation on it is, in its present form, inclined to include consideration of such wider ranging questions in relation to its industrial assistance policies. But it would be mistaken to suppose that such changes as have taken place in the administrative system, or in the allocation of responsibility between departments, have been a cause of weakness in policy or have contributed to insufficient weight being given to international considerations. On the contrary, it seems probable that consciously or unconsciously, the organizational developments have only too accurately reflected the underlying trend of attitudes and policies.

This is certainly not to say, however, as other papers in this study demonstrate—that Britain is alone in treading these paths. It is indeed probably the case that Britain was a slow, and on the whole reluctant, starter in the field. This was at least partly due to the long surviving and widely accepted view that Britain had most to gain from trying to secure international adherence, not only to the letter of the GATT, but to the underlying spirit of the search for freer international trade without government intervention or distortion. This in its turn does not, of course, mean that British policies even in the heyday of the fifties and sixties were without peccadillo. It was perhaps due even more to the fact that in Britain the unwritten assumption which the framers of the GATT relied on to put some muscle into the otherwise essentially feeble provisions of Article XVI of the General Agreement had really worked more potently than in many other countries. This assumption was, in effect, that in normal circumstances, and always excepting agriculture, national Treasuries would be strong enough to exercise adequate checks on the desires of governments, to give assistance to industry, and to keep expenditure to this end within reasonable bounds. When, as in Britain during recent years, the Treasury's influence is blunted by the pressures of the politico-economic situation, the most powerful internal reinforcement of the international restraint system is removed. And, like many late starters, once on the move, Britain has travelled perhaps farther and certainly faster than most other industrial countries.

It is against the background of these general reflections that it may be instructive to consider briefly the shipbuilding cautionary tale. The OECD's study of the measures operating in fourteen member countries mentions several in addition to customs duties and import restrictions. They are: government purchasing; direct subsidies (Belgium, France, Canada, Italy and USA); fiscal assistance through tax exemption or rebates; finance for activities of yards and public ownership or participation; credits on favorable terms (all 14 countries); home credit schemes (all except the Netherlands and Sweden); demolition and/or modernization subsidies; and operating subsidies. Not all countries use all the methods listed, though all use several. The consequence has been that over the now fairly long period during which this situation has been building up, there has been continuously increasing distortion of all 'normal' market conditions. The factors which have determined the placing of contracts have been increasingly influenced by the terms which yards have been enabled to offer through government intervention. At first this meant that it was almost invariably advantageous for buyers—of any nationality—to place their contracts in foreign countries. Successive expedients by one government after another—each chasing any new innovation in the battery of devices—has in effect amounted to a subsidy war.

Meanwhile, there have certainly been efforts to moderate the conflict, which have taken place chiefly inside the OECD. By now the floor is littered with arrangements and understandings which for one reason or another have had extremely limited effects. In 1969, with amendments in 1974, the OECD Understanding on Export Credits for ships aimed to limit the best terms of credit which might be offered with state support. In 1972 the OECD General Arrangement required subscribing countries to remove progressively aids to shipbuilding which constituted an obstacle to normal competitive conditions. Some aids and barriers were removed, but the renewed crisis in shipbuilding and the entry of newcomers outside the Arrangement has virtually put it into abeyance. In 1975, a joint forecasting team of European and Japanese shipbuilders agreed on the level of orders to be expected up to 1980–5. It is perhaps indicative of the scale of the problem to realize that what was foreseen was an average of between 10.5 and 13 million gross tons annually, compared with a total theoretical world capacity of 39 million.

The subsequent discussions have moved towards pressures from the countries who see themselves as losers in the conflict for a formal OECD arrangement to ensure what they regard as a 'fair distribution' of new orders, and what the winners regard as iniquitous 'market sharing'. The sort of proposals under discussion seem to involve an agreement for monthly international discussion of order book positions, and to imply a distribution of orders by agreement.

Clearly, if something of this sort does occur, the industrial world will have moved into an entirely new area of administrative machinery in the relations between government and industry. It will also, in this industry at any rate, have gone very far toward implementing Article 3 of the Stockholm Convention for the Frustration of Trade.

Shipbuilding is an advanced stage of this development, at least in the industrial sphere. We must remember that in agricultural trade for a long time there have been equally advanced cases which similarly exemplify the progression from support or intervention by one or a few governments to a situation in which the combined interventions of many governments in relation to the same commodity can eventually be resolved only by intergovernmental attempts to share out the markets. 'Resolved' is, of course, much too emollient a word. The situations which result are indeed never resolved in any wholly satisfactory way, but remain as continuing causes of international contention.

Yet this seems to be the unmistakable trend underlying much current discussion in Britain and elsewhere about the proper role of government in relation to industrial development, restructuring and regeneration. This is especially true about industries which appear to have fallen behind in the international technological race. The progressive reshaping of the British administrative structure is, in essence, the adaptation of the organization of government to what is certainly seen as the fulfillment of a positive and inescapable task. Even when it appeared to result from other factors, it no doubt reflects the constraints and pressures on government and the attitudes which are thereby produced. There is, moreover, a ratchet effect. By assuming a larger function, government has to equip itself, especially in terms of information, to try to perform the function efficiently. In so doing it is led further and further into involvement in the day to day affairs of industry. It will always be a matter for controversy, how well and efficiently such involvements can be discharged, and whether government can consistently and with certainty beneficially influence the shape and structure of a firm or an industry. More fundamentally, it will be questioned whether it is right, in a free society, that the prosperity of one firm rather than another and one set of workers rather than another should be determined by the favor of governments.

None of this should be exaggerated into a picture of government in Britain in 1977 imposing an iron hand on every aspect of industrial activity through regimentation or control or even persuasion and incentive. This would be very far from the matter. As I have said, the legislative framework and the organization stemming from it are reactive, not coercive. None the less, we have surely moved from an organizational system essentially appropriate to an economy, and to a framework of international trade rules, based on the market as the dominant factor both internally and externally, towards one where the market, though still the principal factor over far and away the greater part of economic activity, is much more susceptible to the political constraint of government manipulation or intervention.

In this development, Britain has in some respects followed and mirrored what has existed, or has been thought to exist, in some other countries. She has also participated in a process which, in one form or another is a characteristic of developments in many, if not most, industrialized countries in this decade. It is difficult to avoid the uncomfortable conclusion that a widespread continuation of these trends, without some kind of international constraint, will produce an increasing number of sectors—following agriculture and shipbuilding—where the full concept of international rules based on the international competition of market economies, and the operation of comparative advantage as a basis for the international division of labor, becomes increasingly less relevant. In such a situation, it will be the weaker members of the international trading community, not the strongest, who will suffer from the failure of the concept and the potential breakdown of the system.

Notes and References
1. Published in Alan Whiting, ed., *Economics of Industrial Subsidies* (London: HMSO 1976).
2. *Industrial and Regional Development*, Cmnd 4942 (London: HMSO March 1972).
3. 'Industry Act 1972' in *Annual Report by Secretaries of State for Industry, Scotland and Wales*, Appendix A (London: HMSO July 1976).
4. In a letter to the writer of this paper.
5. See G. Denton, S. O'Cleireacain and S. Ash, *Trade Effects of Public Subsidies to Private Enterprise* (London: Macmillan 1975).
6. Organization for Economic Cooperation and Development, *Measures of Assistance to Shipbuilding* (Paris: 1976).

Part 2

The International Trade System

4 Revising the GATT Approach to Subsidies: A Canadian View

CAROLINE PESTIEAU

INTRODUCTION

The issues raised by the widespread recourse to industrial policies illustrate some of the essential weaknesses of the General Agreement on Tariffs and Trade (GATT). The regulatory power of the General Agreement reposed, for the first 25 years of its existence, on a tacit international consensus that the United States should take the lead in, and assume responsibility for, world trade liberalization. Not surprisingly, given the traditional US insistence on the contrast between market and government decision-making, the distinction between the two spheres was endorsed by the GATT. As a result, many GATT articles are based on the premise that governmental activity in the market place leads to discriminatory and unfair competition and, indeed, is abnormal and should be strongly discouraged if not eliminated.

However, both the international economic leadership of the United States and the *a priori* assumption that governmental interference in trade is undesirable have been seriously challenged in the last ten years. As national governments have come to play an increasing role in international exchange of goods and services, several GATT rules have been severely challenged. Consequently, the Agreement's credibility will diminish considerably, even among those nations that have hitherto observed its rulings, unless its articles can be reformed to take account of new realities. The discussion of the subsidy/countervail question in the following pages is but one example of this need for reform.

Subsidies and countermeasures taken to offset the effects of subsidization are priority issues in the current round of Multilateral Trade Negotiations (MTN). Subsidies are enjoying a high profile in the trade talks for two main reasons—they tend to nullify trade liberalization agreements, and they are likely to multiply in number rather than to disappear.

First, subsidies can effectively undermine or, in the language of trade negotiators, 'frustrate the benefits of' tariff or other trade concessions obtained through multilateral bargaining. A fundamental principle of negotiating procedure adopted by the GATT has been the 'binding' of tariff concessions. Binding gives countries making concessions a guarantee that the reciprocal offers on the basis of which they negotiated will actually be implemented and maintained by their trading partners. However, in the years following the negotiation of substantial tariff cuts in the Kennedy Round, exporters in several countries, especially the United States, have complained that the freer access to foreign markets that they believed they had obtained from the trade negotiations has been impaired or nullified by foreign government subsidization. The subsidies in question may take the form either of assistance to import-competing producers or of assistance to domestic exporters competing in third markets. To the extent that these grievances are real, such subsidization sabotages trade liberalization agreements and hence threatens the usefulness of the whole MTN exercise.

Second, there is every likelihood of subsidies multiplying as the responsibilities assumed by governments widen. In accepting new and unprecedented responsibilities and deciding to influence resource allocation in accordance with them, many governments have implicitly relegated efficiency in the use of their countries' resources, in a strictly economic sense, to second place. This implies that one cannot discount the possibility of a government subsidy being used to respond to almost any domestic problem that may arise. Looked at in the context of international trade talks, this propensity to subsidize may cause dismay to those who desire effective trade liberalization, or simply want to prevent the existing system from moving backwards.

Countervailing duties (CVDs) are the accepted means of offsetting subsidies within the GATT framework. CVDs are special import duties levied by individual governments to cancel out the effects of foreign subsidies on the levying countries' trade. They may equal, but not exceed, the value of the original subsidy. The United States has traditionally made the most use of countervailing duties, and in the last few years both the total number of US CVD cases and the number of countries cited in them have increased dramatically.[1]

Unlike the United States, which has to date been able to rely on its political and economic power, Canada is concerned about both the subsidy and the countervail aspects of the issue. As a major agricultural exporter, Canada suffers from the effects of agricultural subsidies accorded less efficient producers, particularly in Europe. At the same time, both the federal and the provincial governments in Canada use a wide range of assistance measures to promote balanced regional and industrial growth. Some of these measures can be interpreted as subsidies. Thus when goods from production facilities benefiting from government assistance are exported, they may be subjected to countervailing duties in the importing country. Until 1972 this danger seemed remote, but when the US government imposed CVDs on imports of tires produced by the Michelin plant at Bridgewater in Nova Scotia, the future of industrial assistance measures in Canada was called into question. Since nearly three quarters of Canadian trade is with the United States, the intensification of US countervailing action represents a serious threat to Canadian investors and exporters.

The Michelin case, which was widely reported and discussed in Canada, is an example of the difficulties entailed in attempting to fit elements of a national industrial strategy into a legal and technical framework drawn up at a time when such strategies were assumed to be the exception rather than the rule. If one country, in this case Canada, is no longer satisfied with the international distribution of industry, its government can be expected to attempt to influence market signals so that investment and production opportunities will open up in sectors or areas previously regarded as unattractive. If, in addition, the country that wishes to change its industrial structure has a relatively small domestic market, the incentives offered by its government may lead directly or indirectly to increased exports and thus be labelled export subsidies. At the same time, firms already well-established in the industry concerned are likely to view negatively competition from new sources and to take whatever legal, as well as competitive measures they can to prevent it—including strong demands for tough countervail action. Hence a national government's decision to try to improve its country's regional or industrial structure becomes, on a micro-economic level, an infringement of another country's trade rules. As we will see, the GATT is at present of little assistance in dealing with this problem.

Canada is far from being alone in feeling that its domestic policies are threatened by the increase in US countervailing action. Many other countries—both developed and less developed—consider that regulation of the right to impose CVDs is important enough to constitute a separate negotiating item in the MTN. Some of them have proposed the adoption of a countervail code similar to the Anti-Dumping Code adopted at the end of the Kennedy Round. But the US delegation in Geneva, supported in this by Canada, believes that agreement on offsetting action can be reached only in conjunction with agreement on the use of subsidies that affect international trade and thereby spark off CVDs.

In this context, there is a distinction to be made between the way the GATT deals with anti-dumping duties and the way it is suggested it should deal with countervailing duties. It is true that in the General Agreement both anti-dumping and countervailing duties are dealt with in Article VI (while subsidies are discussed quite separately in Article XVI), but the two kinds of special import duty need not be treated identically. Anti-dumping duties are levied to offset unfair pricing by private exporters, whereas CVDs are intended to offset the damaging effects of government actions. Since private exporters are not signatories of the GATT, there can be no procedure for making their market decisions conform to its rules other than by imposing compensatory duties on exports 'unfairly' priced. In the case of CVDs, however, the GATT could regulate the measures that give rise to special duties as well as regulating the countervailing action when the initial decision to subsidize, which provokes a CVD, is taken by a government that is a party to the GATT. When both the government levying the duty and the government subsidizing are contracting parties, both elements of the situation can, theoretically, be dealt with within the General Agreement, although in practice, any attempt to regulate the subsidy decisions of sovereign governments is viewed with suspicion by many GATT members.

In this context, the subgroup set up in Geneva (within the Non-Tariff Barrier Group) has been given a broad mandate—to deal with both countervailing action and subsidies. Despite, or more probably because of, the importance major trading nations attach to these joint issues, agreement on the basic problems has not yet been reached.

SUBSIDIES AND COUNTERVAIL IN THE GENERAL AGREEMENT

The difficulty of negotiating an international agreement on subsidy/countervail issues can be attributed to the ambiguous way in which they have been treated in the General Agreement on Tariffs and Trade as well as to changes affecting the shared basis of legitimacy on which multilateral trade rules have traditionally rested. Inevitably, ambiguity has held up application of the relevant articles and allowed some of the contracting parties to build up interests in conflicting interpretations of the Agreement. Existing provisions dealing with subsidization and offsetting action are examined briefly in the following paragraphs.

GATT PROVISIONS

The GATT is known to be more tolerant of subsidies than of other obstacles to international free market competition, such as quotas or even tariffs. In 1947 the contracting parties declared their intention to eliminate quotas and hoped for an eventual phasing out of most tariffs. But when discussing subsidies, they merely required each contracting party to notify the others of any subsidies it was granting which could be expected to affect trade. If such subsidies were causing serious prejudice to another party, the subsidizing government was to consult its trading partners with a view to limiting the subsidization (Article XVI.1).

In 1955, Additional Provisions on Export Subsidies (Section B) were added to Article XVI. These took a harder line with respect to export subsidies as opposed to other types of subsidy and, within the category of export subsidies, dealt more strictly with subsidies on non-primary products than with those granted to the producers of primary commodities. Since 1955 a contracting party has been required not to subsidize primary production in a manner that would lead its country's exporters to obtain more than an equitable share of world trade in any primary commodity (Article XVI.3). Export subsidization of non-primary products is prohibited if it results in sales for export at prices lower than those charged in the domestic market (Article XVI. 4). This last prohibition applies, however, only to the seventeen countries which have accepted a declaration putting it into effect.

A GATT contracting party has the right to impose unilaterally a countervailing duty on imports of subsidized products (whatever the nature of the subsidy) equal to the margin of subsidy once it has determined that the effects of this subsidy are causing, or threatening to cause, material injury to one of its domestic industries. But under the 'grandfather clause' of the Protocol of Provisional Application, the United States is exempt from this injury requirement because mandatory countervail legislation, which did not specify an injury finding, was in force in the United States when the Protocol was signed.

WEAKNESSES OF THE GENERAL AGREEMENT

Despite repeated attempts to clarify and tighten up these provisions regarding subsidies and countervailing action,[2] there is no clear, enforceable set of GATT rules governing the use of either measure. The problem is partly one of definition. First, the GATT nowhere defines subsidy. One generally accepted indication of the presence of subsidization is that a particular assistance measure entails a net cost to government, but this leaves open a number of questions such as tax deferral, donation of government research and development, privileged advertizing, and tendering. Failure to define the basic concept is significant, since a country's trading partners may levy CVDs against any 'subsidy' they have found causing injury (which is also undefined).

Second, and more important, there is no GATT definition of what constitutes an export subsidy. Article XVI.4 appears to rely on the dual pricing criterion to define a prohibited export subsidy on non-primary products. But a 1960 GATT Working Party which drew up a list of such subsidies did not refer to dual pricing at all. [3] In any case, not all export subsidies show up in the form of lower prices for export than for domestic sales. Concessionary credit terms, for example, may influence a producer's sales strategy without leading to a price differential. Those GATT signatories who accepted paragraph 4 of Article XVI also accepted the Working Party's list, but as illustrative rather than as exhaustive. The definition of an export subsidy thus remains open.

Finally, there is no agreed definition of primary as opposed to non-primary products in this context. But there is a significant difference in the way in which subsidization of the two classes of goods is to be tolerated. It is not surprising, given this fuzziness or absence of crucial definitions, that there are serious weaknesses in GATT procedures for dealing with the contentious issues of subsidy and countervail.

First, the tolerance with which export subsidies on primary products are treated in Article XVI.3 militates against the interests of efficient primary producers. This paragraph provides no criteria for judging what would be a country's 'equitable share of world trade' in a given product in the absence of subsidization and, hence, no way of judging whether a subsidy contravenes the General Agreement. Primary producers who suffer from their competitors' export subsidies feel that they are not being offered any significant protection in the agricultural field and are therefore, not encouraged to respect the stricter provisions concerning subsidization of non-primary products (Article XVI.4) when these are not in their interest.

Second, non-signatories of the Declaration implementing Article XVI.4 are under no legal subsidization restraint regarding non-primary goods other than the general commitment to notify and consult other Contracting Parties when they employ measures having an impact on international trade. But very few countries have taken the initiative of providing meaningful details of their own subsidy programs and their likely trade effects. Since importing countries can impose CVDs whenever injured, this lack of restraint on subsidization might seem unimportant. But the right to countervail offers little redress against import replacement subsidies and none at all when one exporting country loses sales to a competitor's subsidized exports in a third country's market. [4] An example of this latter situation would be the loss of European markets for Canadian aluminum products as a result of British subsidization of smelting and fabricating facilities in the United Kingdom.

Third, the provisions of the two relevant GATT articles appear to have become inconsistent since Section B was added to Article XVI in 1955. While this section prohibits, as we have seen, certain types of subsidy, the difference between tolerated and prohibited subsidies is ignored by Article VI, which requires proof of injury before any countervailing action can be taken, regardless of the legality of the original subsidy.[5]

A fourth and not insignificant weakness of the whole GATT procedure at stake here is its unilateral character. Determination of injury is to be made by the injured country itself, and there is no provision for notification or consultation before such a country imposes CVDs.[6]

Finally, the exemption from need to prove injury before taking countervailing action, claimed by the United States, continues to envenom the whole issue. Other countries' representatives feel that the time for 'provisional' accession to the GATT by the United States has passed and that by now that country could be expected to have brought its legislation in line with that of other Contracting Parties, instead of which, the US Administration must still impose CVDs on subsidized exports whether or not there is any evidence of injury to US industry.[7] This situation represents a continual threat to the United States' trading partners, particularly Canada, which has already suffered under it, and thereby lessens the likelihood of achieving a practical consensus on the basis of the existing GATT provisions.

THE RATIONALE FOR SUBSIDIES

At the same time concern about subsidization grows, more and more sophisticated forms of government assistance to producers[8] are coming to light, so that it becomes increasingly difficult to circumscribe the notion of 'subsidy.' Yet a definition is necessary, not only for negotiating purposes and conflict resolution, but also for establishing common ground (particularly concerning the question of economic efficiency) for multilateral discussion.

Harald Malmgren has recently proposed one of the most complete definitions of a subsidy. He describes it as 'any government action which causes a firm's, or a particular industry's, total net private costs of production to be below the level of costs that would have been incurred in the course of producing the same level of output in the absence of the government action.'[9] This definition draws attention to the specificity or discretionary nature of a subsidy which benefits a particular firm, industry, region, or activity by placing it in a favored position as compared with the regular, run-of-the mill situation. The main channels of subsidization include fiscal, manpower, research and development, transportation, credit, and marketing programs.

It may be noted that Malmgren's definition makes no reference to international trade. As we shall see later, there is no clear dividing line between subsidies that have and those that do not have a foreign trade impact. That is why it is necessary to understand the rationale for subsidies in general before returning to their significance for the trade negotiations.

Governments often resort to subsidies for a variety of social and political reasons that are difficult to justify in economic terms but which cannot be ignored by the negotiators in Geneva. Thus, in addition to subsidization aimed at temporarily modifying market signals, one may find examples of subsidies directed at intergroup or interregional compensation or redistribution, or of perceived national interest. In a world in which nations attach different weights to different national goals, it is obviously difficult to develop meaningful and acceptable concepts and criteria for international negotiation of domestic subsidization. An economic examination may, nevertheless, be relevant to the MTN in revealing the respective efficiency of alternative subsidy measures in attaining desired goals.

The economic justification for subsidizing is to eliminate distortions in the allocation of resources that are not self-correcting within the market system.[10] Such distortions are usually attributed to one of three causes—externalities, 'infant-industry' situations, and foreign government interference.[11]

So-called 'externalities' exist when there is a difference between the private and the social benefits (or costs) of a productive enterprise. Investment leading to the creation of a technologically advanced manufacturing industry using new labor skills is an example of an undertaking in which the long term social benefits are believed to be greater than the returns accruing to the individual investor. He may make a heavy investment (in training labor, for example) which cannot be protected by patent. Similarly, initial investment contributing to the establishment of self-sustaining industrial activity in a backward region yielding substantial social benefits may bring in private returns which compare unfavorably with opportunities elsewhere.

'Infant-industry' and, by extension, 'infant-exporter' situations can be treated as particular types of externality. A country may be a potentially efficient producer and exporter of a given product but be unable to realize its potential because of startup costs that appear prohibitive, difficulties of breaking into established markets, lack of information, and so on. This argument is, of course, often invoked by the late arrivals on the market to justify their use of special tariff protection and subsidization to allow infant industries to develop their latent comparative advantage. Since it is extremely difficult to gauge both the degree of distortion which existed before corrective action was taken and the effects on overall resource allocation that can be legitimately attributed to this action, the infant-industry argument has usually come under attack from economists while being widely invoked by policy makers.[12] If it can be shown however that resources are, in fact, being mis-allocated on account of externalities, subsidies are generally believed to be a more efficient corrective measure than are either tariffs or quotas. The relevant theoretical literature also strongly suggested that subsidizing domestic production is preferable on grounds of efficiency to subsidizing export activity (Ref. Malmgren).

Discussion of the relative efficiency of export versus production subsidies brings us back to the problem of distinguishing one from the other, a problem that the contracting parties to the GATT have so far left unsolved. Attempts have been made to differentiate export from domestic production subsidies according to various criteria such as (a) the intentions contained in the enabling legislation, (b) the policy tools used (concessionary export financing or multiple currency rates would identify an export subsidy, for example), or (c) the consequences experienced by the subsidizing country's trade partners.

Yet when examined closely, any distortion-correcting measure will have some trade impact, however minor. Therefore, from a trade, as opposed to an efficiency, standpoint the difference between the effects of export subsidies and of other production subsidies may only be one of degree. The major trading countries' representatives in Geneva are divided, as we shall see, as to whether it is (a) feasible and (b) necessary to differentiate between the two different classes. All appear to agree, however, that subsidization will continue and become increasingly sophisticated.

THE US POSITION

Since the United States is the main protagonist of countervailing duties and, officially at least, one of the staunchest opponents of export subsidies, its negotiating strategy in the Subsidies and Countervail Subgroup is of major importance to the other delegations in Geneva. This is an area within the MTN which has been given high priority by both Congress and the US Administration and in which the US delegation is under close scrutiny from domestic agricultural and industrial lobbies.

From the legal standpoint, the United States is in a strong position. Since mandatory legislation was in effect when the GATT came into being in 1947, the United States was exempted from Article VI.6, which requires proof of injury before CVDs can be levied.[13] Therefore, until the Trade Act was passed in 1975, not only was there no need to find evidence of injury in order to impose CVDs, but the Treasury was obliged to levy them once a complaint of subsidization had been substantiated.

The US power to automatically countervail foreign subsidies can be justified on logical, as well as on strictly legal, grounds, if one gives any weight to Article XVI.4, which prohibits certain types of export subsidy.

Since these have been outlawed by seventeen of the main trading nations, it seems reasonable for one member of this group to take automatic countervailing action when another member uses one of the prohibited measures. Developing this line of argument, US negotiators believe that all governments (not only their own) should have the right to offset certain of the potentially most damaging export subsidies without having to prove that a domestic industry is in jeopardy.

Despite its apparent force, the United States' traditional position is vulnerable, on several counts. First, the GATT prohibition of export subsidies is, as we have seen, limited, poorly defined, and subscribed to only by a minority. Second, in using its 'grandfather' privilege to countervail foreign subsidies unconditionally, particularly those clearly not falling under Article XVI.4, the US Treasury is likely to provoke widespread resentment and hostility regardless of the legality of its position.

Third and most important, experience has shown that despite the 'grandfather' exemption, the status quo does not satisfy American interests. Although countervail actions have multiplied and been processed more rapidly, US business and agricultural leaders feel that their interests are still being undermined by ubiquitous foreign assistance programs that spring up as soon as tariff reductions are implemented, effectively sabotaging trade liberalization. Meanwhile, the anarchy reigning in this area of international trade relations is revealed by the fact that the US Administration has recently found itself levying countervailing duties on imports benefiting from measures similar or identical to those that it itself uses to promote US exports.[14]

In this context, notwithstanding its rights under the Protocol of Provisional Accession, the United States is anxious to negotiate a new agreement regarding subsidies and countervail. Evidence for this is provided by the temporary negotiating concessions contained in the 1974 Trade Act and by the more flexible manner in which the Treasury Department has recently been interpreting its countervail mandate. However, not all of the US Administration's recent reactions to foreign subsidies have been lenient. It is, moreover, clear that the United States intends to act to offset the effects of foreign subsidies which injure its exports in third countries even if there is at present no internationally agreed procedure for so doing.

The US delegation in Geneva has proposed that a comprehensive code covering both subsidies and countervailing action be drawn up and negotiated as part of the MTN. The main principles US representatives appear to want to see enshrined in a subsidy/countervail code include (1) that subsidization cannot be allowed to continue to nullify negotiated trade liberalization measures; (2) that the problems created by subsidies must be considered at the same time as the question of regulating countervailing action; (3) that subsidies to producers of non-primary goods, notably agricultural goods, should not be automatically excluded from the Subgroup's negotiations; and (4) that governments must have some means of offsetting the damaging effects of subsidization of competing exports in third countries' markets.

In order to get discussions going on countervail and subsidy issues conjointly, the United States has proposed a three-part classification of subsidies together with the countervail procedures to which each would give rise. Subsidies, according to this proposal, would be classified as (a) prohibited export subsidies that could automatically trigger the imposition of CVDs by the importing country; (b) subsidies which can have a substantial trade impact and would be subject to CVDs if it was found that they had caused or were threatening to cause material injury to an importing country's industry; or (c) domestic subsidies with minor, indirect trade effects that would not be subject to countervail.

Such a classification of subsidies supposes that agreement can be reached on a definition or on an exhaustive list of prohibited measures. These would be automatically countervailable at the discretion of the importing country, so that the present inconsistency between Articles VI and XVI of the GATT would be eliminated. Rules for the finding of injury in the second class of subsidy would be determined according to a GATT code, which would also draw up procedures for dealing with injury from subsidization in third markets. From the US standpoint, this partial acceptance of the need for an injury test is a major concession. But as we will see below, other countries are hesitant to bring all forms of subsidy under a GATT code and are very reluctant to accept the principle that any subsidies could trigger automatic unilateral countervailing action by the importing country.

NEGOTIATING PROSPECTS: ALTERNATIVE APPROACHES

The other major delegations to the MTN tend to see the subsidy/countervail issue from a perspective different from that of the United States. The main problem in their eyes is to bring the United States' countervailing powers within the purview of an operational international agreement. Some negotiators refer to a 'return to legality' and suggest suspension or abolition of the Protocol of Provisional Accession under which US countervail legislation is exempt from GATT rules. Once the United States has accepted the need for an injury test and renounced its unconditional right to countervail subsidies, it will be relatively simple, the European and Japanese representatives seem to believe, to negotiate satisfactory amendments to Articles VI and XVI.

The European Community (EEC) delegation supports the idea of a countervail code similar to the Anti-Dumping Code, which would lay down objective criteria and procedures for determining whether a litigious subsidy was causing material injury to a foreign industry. The subsidy's effects would be evaluated in two distinct stages —first, with regard to changes in the subsidized product's penetration of the notifying country's market and, second, and only if the first test showed positive results, with regard to changes in the situation of the affected industry, (its turnover, prices, employment levels, etc.). Subsidization would have to be the 'principal' (and not just 'a major') cause of injury to justify the imposition of countervailing duties in the EEC's view.

European Community negotiators are opposed to the idea of automatic triggering of unilateral countervailing action under any circumstances. Even if injury were conclusively proved, bilateral consultations with the subsidizing government should be undertaken first, followed, if unsuccessful, by multilateral consultation and, only in the last resort, by the levying of CVDs. European opposition to the right to automatic countervail stems partly from scepticism about the possibility of international agreement on a set of prohibited export subsidies.

Their negotiators have suggested continuing to build on the existing GATT provisions to develop an empirical jurisprudence concerning the different kinds of subsidy. The EEC representatives seem to believe that the two-price criterion is still useful and want to retain the different treatment of assistance measures for primary and for non-primary producers. This would continue the status quo on the subsidy side and maintain the anomaly of ostensibly prohibiting some types of measures but making any consequent offsetting action conditional on an injury finding.

The Japanese position appears to be quite close to that of the EEC. Although the Japanese are prepared to assist in drawing up a list of prohibited export subsidies, they stress the importance of objective determination of injury before any offsetting action can be taken. They see no need to attempt a general classification of subsidies within a countervailing code and would be opposed to an official listing of permitted, 'green' assistance measures on the lines of the US proposal.

The developing countries, for their part, support the adoption of strict injury tests before CVDs can be levied. But, in addition, they want recognition of their right to use export subsidies without any fear of countervailing action because of their special status as unequal partners in world trade. Some of the industrialized countries are reluctant to recognize this claim, since many developing countries are already benefiting from special tariff rates for their exports under the General System of Preferences. Moreover, the developing countries best equipped to take advantage of export subsidies are those considered by many to have already graduated from 'developing' status.

In preliminary negotiations, many industrialized countries' reaction to this claim for exemption has been that once a meaningful test of material injury is accepted as a condition for countervailing action, most of the developing countries' problems will be solved. In any case, few negotiators are prepared to offer a special developing country solution to the subsidy-countervail issue before they know what general solution will be agreed upon.

THE CANADIAN POSITION

As we saw earlier, Canadians have a lot to gain from an end to the United States' unconditional countervailing powers. Adoption of an injury test would remove much of the unpredictability at present surrounding the US Treasury's use of CVDs. Canadian policy makers would then be better able to weigh up the options open to them in their pursuit of industrial goals by means of discretionary assistance.

Yet at the same time the Canadian representatives at the MTN support the United States' position that subsidies as well as CVDs should be dealt with in a countervail code. They believe that a more operational definition of export subsidies than that at present provided by the GATT could be drawn up. Rather than relying on the existence of dual pricing, a Canadian proposal would classify a subsidy according to whether or not it was intended to stimulate increased exports or to maintain current exports at levels higher than they would otherwise reach. Export subsidies, so defined, should be prohibited in the Canadian view. But like the Europeans, Canadian representatives are reluctant to accept the automatic countervailing procedure contained in the US proposal.

In particular, Canadians stress that the distinction between an export subsidy and a domestic production subsidy may be particularly difficult to establish in the case of a country with a small market which provides assistance to a high-volume producer. Inevitably, a larger proportion of subsidized shipments will be exported than would be the case if the same amount of assistance were given to a similar sized plant operating in a much larger market. First-hand experience of this situation reinforces Canadian insistence on the need for proof of injury and for agreed international procedures regulating the use of countervailing duties.

THE NEGOTIATIONS

The Subsidies and Countervail Subgroup has met five times since the Tokyo Round negotiations got underway in 1975. Progress has been slow primarily on account of the basic difference in approach explained above. There are also two more general explanations for slow progress.

First, the fundamental disagreement between the United States and the European Community on the procedure for negotiating agricultural issues has acted as a break on the Subgroup's negotiations. The EEC's desire to deal with agricultural issues separately from the rest of the MTN obviously impinges on attempts to revise the GATT's different treatment of subsidies on primary and on non-primary production. The first meeting of the Agriculture Group in December 1976, at which a compromise was reached allowing the Group to consider issues which are also under discussion in the other MTN groups (and subgroups), may mean that the US–European procedural disagreement is now less of an obstacle to progress in the Subsidy/Countervail area. The second general explanation for the negotiators' difficulty in concluding agreements is the need to take account of the developing countries' position. The Tokyo Declaration, in recognizing their right to special treatment whenever possible, has strengthened this group's claims to prior exemption from whatever rules may be accepted as binding on the industrial countries.

No conclusive results had been expected in this field (nor in other areas of the MTN) until a new US Administration took office in 1977. The US delegation came under fire at home in the first half of 1976 for presenting a proposal in Geneva that would make recourse to countervailing action contingent upon injury in certain circumstances. So it is clear that it will take a firm commitment on the part of the Administration to reach a multilateral agreement to the problem for the US negotiators to go through with their proposal. In the early rounds of the talks, the Europeans and Japanese were reluctant to make any *quid pro quo*. Their official position was that they should not have to pay, by means of trade concessions, for the Americans to conform with existing GATT provisions. But, as the negotiations are revitalized with President Carter's backing, their position may be modified.

The subgroup's acceptance of the Canadian delegation's offer to draft a countervail code was a sign that the deadlock may be ending. There was no commitment on the part of the delegations to subscribe to the draft and the document which was submitted to the Subgroup on 28 February 1977 inevitably raised a lot of questions. Yet its drafting is itself a hopeful sign. In the preceding stage, the Secretariat had been asked to compile the delegations' often conflicting positions on the various ramifications of the subsidy/countervail issue. Since Canada is seen to share many of the concerns of both the United States and the European Community, there is hope that its delegation's draft will be received with understanding when (or if) political considerations permit a compromise. Agreement on this joint issue is certainly vital to the success of the MTN, as, without it, gains won elsewhere will appear ephemeral and hence the concessions made in exchange, unjustified.

The Subsidy/Countervail issue is, furthermore, not only crucial to the success of the MTN, but is also, as we saw above, symptomatic of fundamental problems within the General Agreement itself. It has become clear that many of the GATT articles need overhauling and that its regulatory mechanisms must be strengthened if it is to play an effective role in preventing a relapse into protectionism. However, a new understanding of government activity in the international market place and a renewed consensus regarding contracting parties' shared powers and responsibilities seem to be prerequisites to the implementation of these much needed reforms.

Notes and References

1. The US Treasury processed 65 CVD cases from 1897 to 1974 compared with 38 in 1975 alone.
2. The most important of these attempts was that of the 1960 GATT Working Party which drew up an illustrative list of prohibited export subsidies (see footnote 3).
3. The following measures were listed: (i) currency retention schemes; (ii) direct subsidies to exporters; (iii) export-related remission of direct taxes or social welfare charges; (iv) excessive border tax remission; (v) provisions of inputs to exporters by governments at prices lower than those charged to non-exporters; (vi) government export credit guarantees at premiums lower than necessary to cover costs; (vii) export credits available at rates lower than cost; (viii) governmental bearing of costs incurred by exporters in obtaining credit.
4. Article VI.6 (b) authorizes a country importing subsidized goods to impose a CVD to offset a subsidy that, while it may not be injuring the importer's industry, is injuring the exports of another country in the importer's market. But this provision has not been used, since it is not in the importing country's interest.
5. US representatives refer to this inconsistency in arguing for automatic countervailing of prohibited subsidies.
6. Article VI.1 may be used as an argument against this conclusion, but as already mentioned, it has proved quite ineffectual. Historically, the United States has frequently consulted its trading partners prior to imposing CVDs but at present is under no clear obligation to do so.
7. The Trade Act has modified the mandatory nature of US countervail procedures by introducing an injury test for non-dutiable imports and by granting waiver rights to the Secretary of the Treasury, but the waiver rights are only temporary and can be overruled by either House of Congress.
8. Subsidies to consumers are not dealt with in this paper, as they are much less likely to have a trade impact than are producer subsidies.
9. See Harald Malmgren, 'Subsidies and Trade Policy,' a paper presented to a meeting of the Trade Policy Research Centre, Bellagio, June 11–13, 1976, p.18.
10. This statement begs the question of which is the particular welfare area whose resources are to be allocated efficiently. As Denton and O'Cleireacain have pointed out, the policy decisions will be different as one attempts to

maximize resource use on a regional, a national, a trading bloc, or a world basis. See G. Denton and Seamus O'Cleireacain, *Subsidy Issues in International Commerce* (London: Trade Policy Research Centre, 1972).

11. A fourth cause of distortions is an inflexible disequilibrium exchange rate. Although some countries, particularly in the Third World, may find themselves with such an exchange rate (for example, if devaluation is liable to reduce total receipts from commodity exports), the current flexibility of exchange rates weakens the argument in favor of correcting distortions due to exchange rate disequilibrium through domestic subsidy programs.

12. See Malmgren, *op cit.*, p. 25, and Denton and O'Cleireacain, *op. cit.*, p. 13, for a discussion of the conditions under which assistance to an infant industry is economically justified.

13. See Kenneth W. Dam, *The GATT Law and International Economic Organisation* (Chicago: University of Chicago Press, 1970), Chap. 19, for an explanation of the provisional nature of the contracting parties' endorsement of GATT articles. Briefly, a generally accepted interpretation is that mandatory (but not permissive) legislation predating a country's accession to the GATT is allowed to stand even if it runs contrary to GATT articles. The US practice of disregarding injury considerations is thus inconsistent with, but not in violation of, the GATT. (The United States' trading partners might, however, argue that the amendments introduced in the Trade Act of 1974, passed in January, 1975, constitute new countervail legislation not protected by the Protocol of Provisional Accession.)

14. See transcript of the press briefing by David R. Macdonald, Assistant Secretary of the Treasury, on Final Determination in Thirteen Countervailing Cases, Washington, 5 January, 1976. Secretary Macdonald said, 'So I don't think there is anything inconsistent about our subsidizing our exporters and our countervailing subsidization of imports. We have it both ways.' (p. 18).

5 US Policies and Practices on Subsidies in International Trade

RICHARD N. COOPER

Modern governments intervene in their economies in countless ways. This is true even of such countries as the United States, with its strong commitment to an economic system of 'free enterprise.' The concept is relative, for enterprise today is anything but free, if by that is meant free from government regulation or influence. A few of the US government's actions, such as import tariffs, the cabotage rules on coastal shipping or the oil import quotas (now in abeyance), are aimed specifically at foreign trade in goods or services. Most actions are not, but they have an influence on international trade—via the competitiveness of the firms subject to regulation or influence, and through them indirectly to all firms —that varies from negligible to substantial.

It is useful at the outset to list the various ways in which government actions influence foreign trade. We are concerned here mainly with 'subsidies', that is, with actions that make the affected firms more competitive in foreign markets than they would be in the absence of the government action. But what is a 'subsidy' in this sense turns out to be a tricky question when one goes beyond the reasonably direct and obvious—and sometimes even in those cases. As we shall see, many government actions, even those that raise costs, can have the same effect as a subsidy to some other industry when traced through the whole economic system, especially now that we have floating exchange rates. Also, given the high degree of government intervention of a cost-*increasing* character, some 'subsidies' may still leave a firm in a worse competitive position than if there were no governmental regulation, although better off than in the absence of the subsidy alone.

Section 1 of this paper lists a wide variety of US government actions which improve the competitiveness of some industries, running from the more direct in the early part of the list to the indirect and even the unexpected in the later part of the list. This list is intended to be suggestive rather than exhaustive, but it includes the relatively small number of direct government subsidies to US exports.

Section II of the paper considers US policy and practice toward the subsidies of other countries, that is, it considers US measures to countervail foreign subsidies and to deal with other 'unfair' trade practices. Section III briefly outlines the proposals that the US government has put forward in the current round of Multilateral Trade Negotiations (MTN) to rationalize international agreement on subsidies and on countervailing action, especially in the General Agreement on Tariffs and Trade (GATT).

A final section offers a different perspective from the one that has been adopted in international discussion of these matters in the MTN, and suggests an alternative, somewhat more relaxed approach to dealing with government influences on international competitiveness.

It may be useful at the outset to review briefly the GATT rules on the question of export subsidies and methods for coping with them. Article XVI of the GATT states in Section A that every contracting party to the GATT must notify other contracting parties of any subsidy that directly or indirectly increases exports and that 'In any case in which it is determined that serious prejudice to the interests of any other contracting party is caused or threatened by any such subsidization, the contracting party granting the subsidy shall, upon request, discuss with the other contracting party or parties concerned, or with the contracting parties, the possibility of limiting the subsidization.' Section B of Art. XVI, added in 1955, goes further and provides that 'contracting parties shall cease to grant either directly or indirectly any form of subsidy on the export of any product other than a primary product.' Developing countries have not subscribed to this last provision, but are covered by Article XVI, Section A.

Under Article VI of the GATT importing countries may impose countervailing duties to an amount not exceeding the subsidy on an import, subject to the condition that the subsidy 'is such as to cause or threaten material injury to an established domestic industry, or . . . to retard materially the establishment of a domestic industry'.

US GOVERNMENT SUBSIDIES AND OTHER POLICIES THAT INFLUENCE EXPORTS

The US government engages in a host of actions that influence the competitiveness of American exports. They range from direct actions to encourage exports through activities to stimulate production and general support for business activity to actions which by discouraging certain industries lead indirectly to encouragement of others. The following list proceeds from the most direct form of export encouragement to less direct forms. [1]

1) Economic and military assistance to less developed countries, tied to the procurement of American goods. In this case the US government in effect buys the American goods and gives them away, or lends them on very easy terms. Foreign aid represents an extreme form of export subsidization, but it is accepted as contributing to economic development or national security, and the importing countries in this case would not hold the United States accountable under Article XVI of the GATT, or impose countervailing duties under Article VI. But third countries may lose export orders because of foreign aid shipments tied to US procurement. The subsidization of American exports would cease if foreign aid grants and loans were freely usable for the purchase of goods and services anywhere, as is the case with loans from the World Bank. US foreign assistance amounted to about $4 billion in 1976, or less than 4 per cent of total exports of goods and services.

2) Under US tax law, corporations that derive at least 95 per cent of their gross receipts from exports can qualify as domestic international sales corporations (DISC) and can defer payment of corporate profits tax until dividends are remitted to the parent corporation. This provision, which cost in excess of $1000 million in revenue foregone in 1976, amounts to an interest-free loan from the government for expenditures involved in the promotion of exports. (The subsidy element—about $60 million—is much less than the foregone revenues, since the taxes must eventually be paid.)

3) The US government subsidizes both the construction and the operation of merchant vessels under US registry. Construction subsidies do not increase exports since such subsidies are available only to purchases by US flag companies, but of course operating subsidies to shipping make it easier for US vessels to 'export' shipping services. Both programs are of long standing and the operating subsidy, which is not subject to GATT, in 1976 amounted to around $200 million. Ship construction, and indeed shipping services generally, involve heavy government involvement throughout the world.

4) The Export-Import Bank provides medium-term credit for American exports. For a number of years the interest rates were below market rates, so a direct subsidy was involved. Recently the Bank's interest rates have been raised to $8\frac{1}{2}$–$9\frac{1}{2}$ per cent, depending on maturity, and it is the Bank's intention to keep its lending rates above its borrowing rates by enough to cover its operating costs, except when necessary to meet foreign competition. The subsidy to American exports is thus now the more subtle (and smaller) one which arises from the use of US government credit in borrowing in the capital market plus the absence of a requirement to pay dividends on the Bank's capital. In early 1976 an agreement among the major industrial countries limited competition among government supported export credit agencies by requiring interest rates not to fall below $7\frac{1}{2}$ per cent.[2]

5) Until 1973 the Commodity Credit Corporation gave substantial subsidies to US exports of many agricultural products, the counterpart of a system of high domestic price supports combined with the view that in the absence of agricultural policy the United States would be a substantial exporter of agricultural products, especially grains, cotton, tobacco, etc. The high price supports stimulated output, so the program also involved limitations on acreage. It is difficult to say whether agricultural exports were larger or smaller than they would have been in the absence of the government support program, since the support prices and the acreage controls could be expected to have opposite effects on production. (In addition, the United States shipped abroad substantial amounts of agricultural products as foreign aid, but that was covered under item (1) above.)

At present there are no export subsidies for agricultural products. Support prices continue, but for most products they are well below world market prices, and acreage controls have been removed on all but a few products—rice, peanuts, and tobacco. Recently domestic production of peanuts has been given a subsidy, but in view of acreage controls it is difficult to discover whether exports will be augmented by the subsidy, compared with the absence of both subsidy and limitation on acreage.

6) Investment in plant and equipment in the United States enjoys a 10 per cent investment tax credit. The credit in effect lowers the cost of domestic investment by ten per cent, and thus stimulates the productive capacity of the economy. The credit operates for all investment, however, and since national income equals national output, it is not obvious whether on balance exports or imports are stimulated more by the tax credit. The first round effects of increased production and income could go either way. The major long-run effect of the investment tax credit is to make American industry somewhat more capital intensive than it would be without the credit.

Depletion allowances for oil and other minerals have the effect of stimulating domestic production of such products and thus serve to reduce imports or to increase exports. Until 1975 this tax privilege was available to American mineral investment anywhere in the world, but now it is limited to production in the United States.

7) There are many areas of direct government expenditure for activities that support business enterprise. Examples are Federal spending, net of user charges, for airports and air traffic control, for dredging rivers and harbors, and for providing postal service. These activities clearly represent government support for commercial and economic activity, and it is quite likely that exports are larger than they would be without such spending, although imports are undoubtedly also encouraged by such measures.

8) Price controls on domestically produced crude oil and natural gas

cheapen energy for all American users as compared with the world market price, and hence provide 'subsidies' (but not revenue reducing ones) for American exports as well as for domestic sales of products that require energy to be used in their production.

9) Government expenditures on research and development help to cover the initial costs of new economic activities, which often later lead to exports. The classic example is agricultural research, which has been financed by government for over a century and has led to vast improvements in the productivity of American agriculture and to improvements in the quality of agricultural products. Sometimes too, large export sales are a distant by-product of military research and development expenditures, as was the case with the jet engine. Currently the government is spending substantial sums on research and development in the energy sector, both on nuclear power and on such possibilities as liquification of coal. To the extent that the last proves to be economically feasible, for instance, it may augment future exports of American coal.

10) Extensive government purchases sometimes lead to the development of products which are highly competitive in world markets, by helping private firms to spread their own research and development costs as well as other overhead expenditures over a larger number of sales. The list of products here in principle is a long one, but the point is quantitatively important in relatively few industries, such as military equipment or ground tracking stations for satellites.

11) The most pervasive influences, and quantitatively probably the most important stimulus to exports of particular goods, but also the least obvious, is the host of government regulations on US production which have been introduced to improve the working environment or the natural environment. Such items as effluent controls, safety regulations, minimum wage legislation and restrictions on child labor can have a profound effect on the competitiveness of particular industries, and hence on the relative competitiveness of other industries less directly affected. Since most observers would not mention such government actions in a list of export 'subsidies'—and indeed they do not normally give rise to a loss of government revenue, except where the government occasionally incurs some of the costs, for example, of anti-pollution actions—it is worthwhile to trace through the influence on exports of one of these regulations, the minimum wage. The key assumptions in this analysis are that over time balance is maintained in international payments, for example, by movements in the exchange rate of the dollar, and that the government takes whatever steps are necessary to assure full employment of the labor force. So we are looking here for *sectoral* effects, the relative stimulation or retardation of production in particular sectors of the economy which arise from the regulation in question.

The minimum wage, if it is set high enough to exceed the wages that would otherwise be paid in some industry, reduces the international competitiveness of that industry by raising costs. The industry will find it more difficult to compete with products from abroad. Imports will rise, and to restore equilibrium in the balance of payments will require some depreciation of the dollar (relative to what it would otherwise be). The depreciation, in turn, will *increase* the competitiveness of all sectors where wages are not influenced by the minimum wage. Put more concretely, it is likely in the United States that the minimum wage discourages the production of textiles (which are displaced to some extent by imports) and encourages the production (and export) of machinery. Thus in an indirect fashion, via adjustment of the exchange rate, the export of machinery is 'subsidized' (but again not in a fashion that reduces revenue to the government). A similar argument holds, *mutatis mutandi*, for other government regulations. For example, meeting required safety standards will raise costs more in some industries than in others, and via adjustments in the exchange rate will increase the competitiveness of industries or firms whose costs for safety have been increased least.

So the influence of government actions on international competitiveness may be pervasive, but it may also be so indirect as to be difficult to trace in detail with any confidence. But it may nonetheless be substantial, even when it flows from actions aimed at objectives quite different from a desire to stimulate exports.

I will close this section with reference to a special feature which the United States shares with a few other countries, such as Canada, Australia, and West Germany, namely the federal structure of its government. The Federal government accounts for only about 35 per cent of total government expenditures in the United States, and for 19 per cent of civilian government employment. For the most part, the influence of state and local governments on the structure of production and costs falls into the categories (7) and (11) in the foregoing list: expenditures which support business enterprise in a general way, and regulation on the conditions of production or marketing. In addition, local governments sometimes support business activity in the form of cheap land or low utility rates or cheap credit. During the 1960s a number of localities used their privilege of floating securities, whose interest was exempt from Federal taxation, to provide cheap credit to new firms through the issue of so-called industrial development bonds. Congress moved to block this rapidly growing activity in 1967 and it has been negligible since then.

The business-promoting activities of state and local governments are not of course aimed at encouraging exports from the United States, but from the particular state or locality to the rest of the United States, and only incidentally to other countries.

US POLICY TOWARD EXPORT SUBSIDIES OF OTHER COUNTRIES

The United States has had a countervailing duty law since 1897, requiring the Secretary of the Treasury to impose countervailing duties whenever he finds that a dutiable import into the United States has been subsidized by a foreign government or by a private organization. The countervailing duty provisions were revised in the Trade Act of 1974, mainly to put a six month time limit on the period the Treasury can take, following a petition, to discover whether a subsidy exists or not, and a further six months to negotiate the removal of the subsidy or to impose the countervailing duty. Until December 1978 the Secretary of the Treasury may however waive the imposition of a countervailing duty if he finds that adequate steps have been taken to remove the subsidy or that there is a reasonable prospect for an agreement to remove the subsidy or that imposition of the duty would jeopardize such negotiations.

In addition, the 1974 law allows for judicial appeal on any negative findings of export subsidy (previously only positive findings could be appealed), extends the provision for countervailing duties to items on the duty free list (but only with a showing that domestic industry has been injured), and allows the Congress on simple majority vote of either house to override the Secretary of the Treasury's decision not to impose a countervailing duty. The law does not however alter the criteria which had earlier been established for determining the presence of an export subsidy (to be described below). The new opportunity for countervailing duties on duty-free goods derives its importance from the extension of duty-free treatment to many manufactured goods from less developed countries introduced in the same trade act.

GATT Article VI allows countervailing duties, but only on a showing of injury to the domestic industry in competition with the subsidized import. US law does not require a showing of injury (except on duty-free goods), and avoids violation of the GATT under a grandfather clause, since the US practice antedates the GATT. This discrepancy between US law and the GATT provision has become an irritant in trade relations between the United States and a number of other countries. It should be noted, however, that *any* additional competition 'injures' established firms, in that their sales would be larger and their profits higher than in the absence of the subsidy. So it is not clear that a showing of injury here should be the same as the injury test required for imposition of restraints on imports, for example, under escape clause action. The correct course depends on the ultimate objective. If, as Article XVI of GATT suggests, export subsidies are prohibited among industrial countries (except on primary products), then the deterrent effect of automatic countervailing without a showing of injury may be desirable.

In practice, the imposition of countervailing duties has been only sparing until recently. From 1897 to 1959 countervailing duties were imposed on only 41 occasions, and between 1959 and 1967 none were imposed. Between 1967 and 1974, in contrast, countervailing duties were imposed 17 times. The large increase reflects in part the overvaluation of the dollar starting in the late sixties, the successful conclusion of the Kennedy Round of trade negotiations (negotiations in process usually inhibit any restrictive action), and perhaps also increasing reliance by other countries on various export-promoting devices.

Several generalizations can be made from the nature of the counter-vailing action that the United States has undertaken.[3] Countervailing duties have been imposed on direct subsidies, on indemnification for loss in exporting, on multiple exchange rate practices with the effect of an export subsidy, on rebates of direct taxes, on over-rebates of indirect taxes, on rebates of indirect taxes on overheads or other indirect costs of production, on preferential transportation prices or credit terms' for exports, and on price support or regional development subsidies when a firm's production is predominantly exported to the United States. Examples of the last were the Michelin Tire case (1973) where a plant in Nova Scotia benefitting from Canadian regional development subsidies exported about 80 per cent of its output to the United States, and the Greek tomato case (1972) where direct payments to tomato producers were countervailed on the grounds that 90 per cent of the production was exported.[4]

Many petitions to Treasury before 1974 were dismissed on grounds that the subsidy was *de minimus*—an implicit form of injury test. Others were simply postponed, prompting the stipulation in the 1974 law that Treasury had to make a preliminary finding within six months and, if appropriate, impose a duty within a year of the petition. During 1975 Treasury began investigations on 38 cases under the countervailing duty law, including 30 pending from prior years. This was a record number.

Of the 37 cases concluded within 1975 and the first three months of 1976, 15 were terminated by the petitioners, 11 resulted in a finding of no subsidy, and 11 resulted in a finding that the exporting country was subsidizing. Of the last eleven, five (float glass from Italy, footwear from Taiwan, leather handbags from Brazil, non-rubber footwear from Korea, and castor oil products from Brazil) resulted in the imposition of countervailing duties by the United States, while in the remaining six cases (mostly agricultural products from Europe) imposition of duty was waived on the grounds of not jeopardizing ongoing trade nego-tiations relevant to the foreign practices.[5] It is clear from the sharp increase in activity that the Treasury Department is under greater pressure with respect to foreign subsidies, but its basic method of approach remains relatively unchanged except with respect to the speed with which it must reach a conclusion.

Two further provisions of US trade law permit government action against foreign subsidies. Under Section 337 of the Tariff Act of 1930 the President can exclude articles from being imported into the United States if they involve 'unfair methods of competition', a term that is undefined, and if the effect of such importation is 'to destroy or substantially injure an industry, efficiently and economically operated, in the United States, or to prevent the establishment of such an industry, . . . ' In the Trade Act of 1974 this provision was amended to permit the International Trade Commission to issue the exclusion order on a finding of unfair competition, and as an alternative to issue a cease and desist order. In practice this provision has been applied mostly to cases of infringement of a US patent, and that history continued in the seventeen cases which were under consideration during 1975, although some of those cases involved tie-in or exclusive dealing arrangements rather than patent infringement. But it is conceivable that some forms of government subsidy could be judged as a form of unfair competition.

The Trade Act of 1974 introduced a new provision that bears on the handling of export subsidies. Under Section 301, if the President determines that a country 'provides subsidies (or other incentives having the effect of subsidies) on its exports of one or more products to the United States or to other foreign markets which have the effect of substantially reducing sales of the competitive United States product or products in the United States or in those other foreign markets', he is enjoined to take steps to stop the practice and he is empowered to withdraw trade concessions that have been granted to the offending country and to impose whatever duties or other import restrictions on the products of the country that he deems appropriate. This provision applies to services as well as to goods. It can be invoked, however, only if the normal countervailing duty procedures are inadequate to the task of deterring the subsidies. It is obviously designed to deal with cases in which the damage is to some American export industry in third markets, where the normal countervailing duty procedures are not applicable. Of the five complaints brought under this provision in 1975, one (Guatemalan discrimination against non-Guatemalan shipping companies) was found to be an unjustifiable trade practice, but the complaint was withdrawn before an appropriate remedy was determined. In late 1976 several American steel companies brought action under this provision against the informal agreement between Japanese and European steel firms, which restricted Japanese steel exports to Europe and allegedly resulted in a diversion of Japanese steel to the United States.

It is worth noting, to sum up this section, that in all likelihood a number of American practices would be countervailable under US law, or would otherwise lead to restrictions or retaliation. The DISC, the

Commodity Credit Corporation export subsidies before 1973, and Export-Import Bank low-interest loans before recent changes could all be considered export subsidies that are subject, under US law, to automatic countervailing duties. The same might be true of the investment tax credit, if the bulk of the output of a foreign firm was sold in the American market. Moreover, operating subsidies to American flag shipping would almost certainly be considered an 'unjustifiable and unreasonable' trade practice if some other country had the same policy and it reduced the sales of US shipping services.

In addition, as noted above, US law differs from GATT in not requiring injury before countervailing duties may be imposed, and in not distinguishing between primary products and manufactured goods.

US PROPOSALS IN THE MULTILATERAL TRADE NEGOTIATIONS

In the current multilateral trade negotiations the United States has pointed out the inconsistency between GATT Article XVI, which prohibits export subsidies on goods other than primary products, and GATT Article VI, which makes the reaction of other countries to violations (for example, through imposition of countervailing duties) conditional on a showing of injury. If a practice is prohibited, the US argues, sanctions against it should be conditional only on showing that the prohibition is violated. The GATT provisions for sanctions are deficient in addition by failing to provide against subsidies by one country that damage another country's exports to third markets. Moreover, the range of subsidy-like actions which governments have adopted in recent years has greatly increased; and some less developed countries want blanket exemption for any actions they take to promote exports. Thus, the entire area of export subsidies in international agreement needs to be rationalized and brought up to date. To that end, the US Government has proposed a three-fold classification of government actions which may have the effect of stimulating exports: (1) a list of prohibited actions, which would call for automatic countervailing, but from which less developed countries might be exempt from countervailing action if there were no injury; (2) an intermediate range of actions, which would call for countervailing only on a showing of injury to domestic industry; and (3) a permissible range of actions which could not be countervailed.

The list of prohibited actions would cover all subsidies to exports. The second list would cover subsidies which affect exports and domestic sales equally (for example, regional subsidies or general investment subsidies). The third list would cover actions which can be expected to have a minimal effect on international trade, and in addition it might include certain approved actions. In addition, the United States would like to revise the GATT so as to allow sanctions against a country that is damaging another country's sales in third markets.

There is still considerable disagreement among countries on how subsidies affecting international trade should be treated, and support for the US proposals is at present not strong.

AN ALTERNATIVE PERSPECTIVE ON GOVERNMENT SUBSIDIES

We should attempt occasionally to stand back and observe how' the world trading system operates as a whole, to provide perspective on the particular pieces we are focusing on at the moment. To gain such perspective, we must take into account the role of government in modern society, and especially the balance of payments adjustment mechanism, governmental responses to under-utilization of resources, and governmental behavior with respect to internationally agreed rules of behavior.

Today; in contrast to the 19th century, government intervention in the economy is pervasive. Few areas of modern economies remain un-touched by government action, and all such government actions will affect international trade, although many of the effects will be small and others will cut in opposite directions, possibly leaving a small net effect. This pervasive influence arises because government action affects relative costs and prices, and hence the relative competitiveness of the nation's goods and services with respect to foreign markets. Some of the actions will just offset others (as when a government 'subsidizes' the purchase of anti-pollution equipment to comply with a government requirement to reduce pollution); others will have substantial net effects on trade.

A rigorous extension of concern with the pervasive subsidization of various economic activities in modern economies would require a complex set of countervailing duties, on a country-by-country basis. Alternatively, governments would be required to 'harmonize' all aids and restraints to domestic economic activity so that the same incentives and restraints would apply to all producers throughout the world. The first approach would be an administrative nightmare, since as noted in Section I some 'subsidies' are extremely subtle and indirect in their effects. The second approach, which is that desired by the Commission of the European Community within Europe, would not be politically feasible and, I would argue, undesirable as applied to the world as a whole. It is undesirable because different national communities under-standably have different preferences regarding the nature and extent of the role of government in their economies, differences which arise from differences in history, in circumstance, and in ideology. In a pluralistic world these differences should be accommodated as much as is possible without intruding strongly on the preferences of other countries.

Even if one were to opt for a complex system of countervailing duties, a key ambiguity concerns the 'baseline' from which such duties are calculated. Should it be for a hypothetical economy with *no* government interference? And since each national economy is part of a larger world economy, and responsive to what happens abroad, should the baseline also suppose no government interference elsewhere as well, including in the country imposing the countervailing duty? Or should the baseline presuppose just such government interference as is required to offset certain market imperfections, such as pollution and the inadequacy of private incentives to support as much education as is socially desirable in the absence of compulsory education? Here the baseline would become an idealized market system with corrections for externalities. Or should the corrections include anti-monopoly actions as well, so that the baseline becomes an idealized competitive system? And what assumptions should be made about the 'legitimate' methods for raising government revenues? For example, the petition of the US steel industry against the border tax adjustments in Europe for the value added tax implicitly denies the right of those countries to levy indirect taxes on the destination principle, that is, to tax consumption rather than production. And how, when all these questions are settled, does one in practice calculate the countervailing duties so as to compensate for the subsidies thus defined?

An alternative approach is to view each country's 'comparative advantage' in producing different goods as reflecting not only its natural endowments, its capital stock, and the skills and working habits of its labor force, but also the conditions of work and of environment that are socially acceptable. These acceptable conditions will be reflected in political decisions (or their absence) with respect to air and water pollutants, hours of work, minimum wage and safety standards, equal wages for women, restrictions on child labor, and so on—all of which governmental decisions affect comparative costs and hence the structure of imports and exports.

This view could be taken a step further, and treat in the same way national desires (as reflected through the political process) to reduce the uncertainties of international trade, to improve national security, to develop new technology, and even just to build modern monuments in the form of high cost production facilities. Such a pluralistic view of the world economy would allow nations to use their resources as inefficiently as they like, or as efficiently in the pursuit of diverse non-economic objectives.

It will be objected that the residents of other nations have a legitimate interest in how each country uses its resources insofar as it bears directly on them. That is surely correct, provided the interest is not pressed too far. Should Saudi Arabia be obliged to increase its oil output as rapidly as possible to provide cheap energy to the rest of the world? Or Canada to develop its northern water resources to satisfy the thirst of American industry? Or the United States to sell nuclear fuel reprocessing plants to other countries to extend their limited supplies of natural uranium? In each of these cases the future interests of the potential exporting country may suggest that the answer is no. The best way to accommodate the interests of the international community in the actions of any one country is not always through specific prohibitions or requirements, although such rules are often useful. Rather, in the case of government subsidies, and other actions that influence international trade, the interests of residents of other countries reside in the proposition that they should not have to bear the costs, which are often transitional or adjustment costs, arising from the actions of other countries.

Any costs associated with a government's actions should insofar as possible be borne by residents of the country making the change in policy. Achievement of that objective is made easier if countries take steps to maintain full employment (steps that are within their capacity to take) and if we have a relatively smooth balance of payments adjustment mechanism, something that has been improved with the shift since 1973 to flexible exchange rates. The pressures that have led to export subsidies have often reflected inadequate national policies for employment, giving rise to a desire to 'export' the unemployment through subsidization of exports. Balance of payments considerations, associated with undue rigidity of exchange rates, have also played an important role in motivating policies of subsidization. In an environment of full employment and active labor market policies, the social cost of changes in industrial structure—some industries expand, while others contract—will be low. The overall rate of economic growth is also an important variable, since a relative decline in an industry need not imply an absolute decline; rather, new entrants to the labor force are drawn into other activities. Thus rapid European growth in the 1960s facilitated the adaptation of European industry to the removal of tariffs following formation of the European Economic Community, with surprisingly little economic disruption. Rapid growth, combined with a ten year transition period, together greatly reduced the costs of adjusting to a major change in economic policy.

Under conditions of full employment and greater flexibility of exchange rates, to take a concrete example, the costs of the Common Agricultural Policy of the European Community will fall overwhelmingly on the residents of the European Community—both the consumers of food and the producers of manufactured goods. Subsidies for exports of grain or dairy products, by leading to more appreciated currencies than would otherwise obtain, reduce the competitivenes of

European automobiles and other manufactures. The producers of Volkswagens and Fiats are paying for the subsidies to French and German farmers. This is as it should be: domestic political decisions regarding structure of output should encompass the costs as well as the benefits.

This perspective on the problem suggests that perhaps we should not worry so much about government subsidies to economic activity—or rather government intervention of all types—as far as their effects on foreign trade are concerned, provided the interventions are introduced sufficiently gradually so that they do not impose acute adjustment costs on economic activities outside the country in question.

A regime that focuses on the distribution of costs would call for advance notification and gradual introduction of any change in policy that is likely to influence strongly the structure of imports and exports. Procedures would be necessary for discussing new policies and for considering proposals that would achieve the same objective but would reduce the external impact. They would cover any major change in policy with external repercussions on particular industries, and would have the objective of modifying the proposed action so as to reduce the imposition of costs on other countries. A gradual introduction of the new measures, like the multi-year staging of tariff reductions, is one way to reduce the costs of adjustment. The principles involved here cover subsidization of domestic production that competes with imports as well as subsidization of exports.

A natural place for such consultations to take place would be under the auspices of the General Agreement on Tariffs and Trade, although in certain respects that would take the GATT into new territory. The OECD Trade Committee would represent another possible forum, on matters of predominant interest to the industrialized countries.

On this general view of the matter, if a country wants a particular industry so badly that it is willing to subsidize foreign and domestic consumption of the product, that would be all right so long as others have ample time to adjust to the new situation, which might take a decade or two—an appropriate period when one is concerned with the structure of production. If other countries also want the same industry, of course, a conflict of objectives will result if the total desired output exceeds the world market for the product, even with subsidies.

Under these circumstances, one can imagine letting different countries 'bid' for the activity through the granting of ever higher subsidies, just as firms bid for a job through price reduction, until the fiscal burden becomes so great that enough countries drop out of the competition to bring world supply of the activity into line with world demand. While such a system might work well in the abstract, however, it is not likely to be an efficient one in practice, either in economic terms or in terms of international relations. A process of discussion and negotiation may well be a superior way to reach some principle of allocation. Such allocation often rests on historical shares, which is satisfactory (in terms of minimizing adjustment costs) as a starting point so long as some provision is made for gradual reallocation of those shares, and in the latter process least cost considerations should play an important role.

The appropriate nature and format for the negotiations to assure that objectives are consistent and to work out a mutually satisfactory solution to the allocation of production depend on the particular issue. Questions of international civil aviation, for instance, have an intrinsic bilateral character, although the underlying principles can have greater generality. International trade in textiles, in contrast, poses an issue of global allocation and change of pace.

Even under this relatively laissez-faire regime—laissez-faire in the sense that national governments are left relatively free to pursue their diverse economic objectives—nations may find it expedient to prohibit certain forms of governmental action by international agreement, for self-protection against domestic pleas for particular actions that are not in the broader interests of the individual countries themselves. International agreements often provide a welcome restraint on behalf of national governments with respect to their own special-interest constituents. Direct subsidies to exports may fall into this category, since it is difficult to find national objectives that are better served by export subsidies than by other actions.

Also, business firms and publics at large are sensitive to the 'unfair' competition which government subsidization may be perceived as being. Thus governments may want to avoid direct subsidies to exports for this reason as well—although, if a country is willing to subsidize the residents of other countries at no cost to the latter group, should they object? Thus, the issue returns to the question of who bears the costs.

On this more pluralistic perspective, no explicitly special treatment is required for less-developed countries. They would be free to adopt policies they feel are suitable, provided the adjustment costs elsewhere are not large. In the early stages of development, a country's exports are likely to be small and adjustment costs in importing countries are likely to be minimal. In later stages of development, special aids to exports should not be necessary. If manufacturing activity in general is to be encouraged, any special aids should be to total production, not merely to exports.

Notes and References
1. A discussion of many of these subsidies can be found in Robert E. Baldwin, *Nontariff Distortions of International Trade*, (Washington: The Brookings Institution, 1970) Chapter 5.
2. See International Monetary Fund *News Survey*, 15 March, 1976.

3. See Peter B. Feller, 'Mutiny Against the Bounty: An Examination of Subsidies, Border Tax Adjustments and the Resurgence of the Countervailing Duty Law', *Law and Policy in International Business*, vol. 1, (Winter 1969), pp. 17–76; E. B. Butler, 'Countervailing Duties and Export Subsidization: A Re-emerging Issue in International Trade', *Virginia Journal of International Law*, vol. 9, (December 1968), pp. 82–152; Robert V. Guido and Michael F. Morrone, 'The Michelin Decision: A Possible New Direction for US Countervailing Duty Law', *Law and Policy in International Business*, vol. 6, (1974) and B. Balassa and M. Sharpston, *Export Subsidies by Developing Countries: Issues for Policy*, (World Bank Staff Working Paper No. 238, July 1976) (mimeo.).

4. The problem of regional subsidies is an especially delicate one, since to countervail them automatically seems to deny any country the right through its fiscal system to give preference to one region of the country over another. One principle, which the US Treasury is moving toward, would permit fiscal preferences to economic activities in a region which is designed to offset the economic disadvantages of the region, but not beyond that. Such a principle raises a host of practical difficulties, however, of identifying and quantifying the economic disadvantages of a region. But at least it provides a rough standard against which a given subsidy might be compared.

5. 'Annual Report on International Unfair Trade Practices', (US Treasury, March 1976) (processed).

6 Japanese Subsidy Policies

NOBUYOSHI NAMIKI

The considerable misunderstanding about the different stages through which government intervention in the private sector has evolved as well as the changing nature of industrial policy, has prevented a balanced estimate of the current determinants of the international competitiveness of Japanese firms. It has also precluded an accurate assessment of the role subsidies play and the problems Japanese industry faces in adjusting to more complex patterns of competition.

Starting in 1960, Japan began to liberalize international current transactions and a little later capital transactions. These became multilateral obligations with her accession to the Organization for Economic Cooperation and Development (OECD) in 1963 which included adherence to the OECD Code of Liberalization of Capital Transactions. Although the formal implementation of these policies was achieved before the oil crisis, and legally Japan is now prevented from recourse to restrictions on foreign direct investment, in rare cases, controls have still played a protective role. Thus the Japanese government requested an American firm to suspend its direct investment in the caustic soda industry. However, this was an exceptional instance, since this sector is undergoing restructuring as an antipollution measure. In this context, American investment might be fatal to several Japanese firms which are suffering from heavy financial burdens necessitated by the introduction of costly antipollution technology.

Similarly, trade barriers have been liberalized. As a result of the internationalization of her economy and in accord with her policy of removing obstacles to commerce, Japan has reduced tariffs and quotas through her participation in successive rounds of GATT negotiations. The lowering of such barriers has not only removed the possibility of resort to traditional protectionist measures, but it has also contributed to the reduction in the effectiveness of subsidies as well as their importance and magnitude. At the present moment, subsidies do not play as large a role in Japanese industrial policy as they did in the past or as they do now in the cases of other advanced industrial nations. Moreover, these various changes have shaken and altered the relationship between government agencies and the private sector. Throughout this period of liberalization, the potential strains on firms have been relatively small due to the increased global competitiveness of Japanese industries.

Although industry now faces numerous transitional problems in which government may play a role, these fundamental changes in business/government relations and the international competitiveness of Japanese products based on more efficient production methods apparently remain obscured to observers in other countries.

Only after a review of the policies that were necessary in the 1950s and 1960s to re-establish Japanese competitive equality with the major industrial powers, will it be possible to consider the pressures from the Third World and the advanced nations with which Japanese industry must contend. While this must include a consideration of current attitudes toward GATT articles on subsidies and countervailing duties, foreign concern about state aids in Japan must be modified to take into account the transformation of the Japanese economy. Thus two of the major problems facing industry in the future are restructuring in the face of changing patterns of comparative advantage and sectoral negotiations in areas where Japanese industry has a superior competitive advantage.

THE MYTH OF 'JAPAN INC'

In spite of Japan's acceptance of GATT and IMF rules, there are many people who believe that an article on contemporary efforts to deal with national subsidies and countervailing duties should include an analysis of Japanese industrial policy. Since Japanese exports continue to be a major source of concern in other countries, the belief persists that they enjoy an unfair advantage as a result of a unique and close relationship between government and business. In addition, her imports are alleged to be institutionally controlled to a very great extent, even though from a bilateral point of view, Japan's restrictions have been no worse than those of her partners. After all there have been very considerable discriminatory restrictions imposed against Japan in the form of 'voluntary' export restraints. And Japan does not exercise any discriminatory restrictions as a member of a trading block.

These views demonstrate that there is a widely held misunderstanding concerning the nature and reasons for postwar policy toward industry, particularly as it involved the evolution of the relationship between government and the private sector in recent years. It seems to me that undue emphasis has been given both here and abroad to Japan's 'peculiarities', particularly in regard to the belief that subsidy policies are somehow qualitatively different from those pursued in other OECD states. On the one hand, there has been a failure to take into account that these policies have not been determined because of some exceptional and unchanging structural feature of the Japanese system. People in a similar geopolitical and geoeconomic situation who aspired to be a modern country would probably have reacted in a similar fashion. Moreover, there is a lag in perceiving both the reduced role of subsidies in Japanese policy as well as the new context within and pressures under which industry must operate.

What was in the eyes of history only a passing phenomenon has continued to be mistaken for a permanent structural feature. The so-called vertical society theory and the 'Japan Inc' syndrome are examples of such mistakes. They are illusions which may have been socially meaningful in the programmatic sense, but could produce adverse effects if people blindly believed in them. However, since they had led and continue to lead to conclusions about the causes of Japanese international competitiveness in the late 1970s which are no longer entirely accurate, what is needed is a fresh and realistic look at current developments in the Japanese economy.

In this regard, the image should change within a few years. The relaxation of the controls which have existed, or do now exist, have fundamentally altered Japan's relationship to the world economy. Japan's adaptation to the international rules of behavior on trade and capital have opened her economy to an array of pressures from the Third World, the United States and the European Community. The inevitable concomitant of the process of reducing protective walls against foreign competition has been the necessity for adapting industries to the demands of the international economy. This new context with its diverse pressures has had important implications for the evolution of Japanese industries, their relationship to government, and in particular, official Japanese reaction to various aspects of the subsidy issue.

In the following pages I will explain the goals of Japanese industrial policy after World War II and also the nature of 'Japan Inc' which has been considered the mechanism of this policy. In this context it will be necessary to clarify the subsidy issue by being more specific about the contemporary sources of comparative advantage for Japanese firms as well as place this issue in the broader framework of the evolution of key industrial sectors.

FOUR PERIODS IN JAPANESE INDUSTRIAL POLICY

The postwar history of the Japanese economy may be divided into four periods. The first lasted from 1945 to 1952. This transitional period came to an end in 1952 when government controls on prices and distribution were lifted with the abolition of the Special Law Concerning the Adjustment of Supply and Demand for Goods and Commodities. The second lasted for the remainder of the 1950s. It was one in which qualitative improvements were made. Industrial policy during those years aimed primarily at the rationalization of major industries and the development of new ones, while in the first period, the emphasis had been on the reconstruction and expansion of basic industries such as coal, steel, electric power and shipping.

In the third period, covering the 1960s, internationalization of the Japanese economy was promoted. The first significant step was taken in June 1960 with the formulation of a program of trade and foreign exchange liberalization. For the sake of convenience, this period could be extended to 1973 when the oil crisis occurred. Essentially, however, the third stage ended in the 1960s, since the features of the Japanese economy were somewhat different in the early 1970s. The fourth period is that following the oil crisis.

Generally speaking, Japan Inc. played an active role in the two decades from 1952 to 1970, and it was during this period that the functions of Japan Inc. were most clear. It was a period in which the Japanese economy, having gone through the immediate postwar transition, made a tremendous effort to catch up with the developed nations of the West. Partnerships between government and business were promoted to increase the efficiency of these 'catching-up' efforts.

HISTORICAL NATURE OF JAPAN INC.

Three major factors contributed to the development of Japan Inc. One comprises historical factors, another involves Japan's economic structure, and the third relates to the managerial organization of Japanese corporations.

Historically, the Japanese nation consists basically of a single ethnic group speaking a single language. This fact is largely responsible for the ease with which consensus has been obtained and maintained in Japanese society. It has also been true that in pursuit of national goals the Japanese people have tended to display an ingenious mix of Japanese and foreign attributes. That is to say, the Japanese people have vigorously tried to absorb 'things Western' while at the same time retaining their 'Japanese spirit'.

As for economic structure, it has generally been believed that the lifelong employment system based on seniority has made it easier to carry out innovations, and that the heavy dependence of Japanese corporations on external capital has made it possible to concentrate funds in key sectors. These aspects, however, have posed certain problems since the oil crisis. Concerning factors related to managerial organization, it must be pointed out that Japanese business managers tend to base their decisions on the prevailing opinions of middle management. In a corporation headed by a dictatorial leader it is impossible to promote genuine cooperation between government and enterprise. But the 'bandwagon' approach based on consensus, or something close to it, can create a climate which is conducive to government–business cooperation.

All these factors, it has been argued, are concomitants to the establishment and development of Japan Inc. This argument, however, is not valid now, although it is true that these factors did affect the actual shape of Japan Inc. in the past.

Japan Inc. in principle has represented a system of measures designed to expedite the process through which a semi-developed country can catch up with developed nations. Therefore, the potential for such a system exists at least in theory in every semi-developed nation. Setting apart the question of socialist countries with their centrally planned economies, semi-developed nations which maintain the capitalist system and the market economy formula have opportunities to establish something similar to Japan Inc. However, given the fact that domestic and international conditions are subject to rapid change, such possibilities are not always realized. What happened in Germany following the Franco-Prussian War in the latter part of the nineteenth century may be cited as a historical example of the national catching-up process.

What has Japan Inc. accomplished? It was able to promote the development of both basic and new industries.

In the steel industry, for example, positive rationalization and modernization efforts were made under the first (1951–55) and second rationalization programs (1956–60). In 1958 the open-marketing system was introduced, and starting in 1959 investment coordination was promoted. In the 1960s, production cutbacks based on official recommendations were carried out from July 1962 to October 1963 and from July 1965 to August 1968. In the machine industry a law concerning special measures to promote this sector was passed in June 1956. Similarly laws were passed to promote the electronics industry in June 1957, the aircraft industry in May 1958, the petrochemical industry in June 1955, the synthetic rubber sector in June 1957 and a five year program to develop the synthetic fiber industry was passed in March 1953. As for the automotive sector, in October 1952, the government adopted a policy of giving priority to the assembly of Japanese-made cars, and in 1955 the government invited private companies to formulate a plan to put a standard national small scale motor vehicle (the Japanese Volkswagen) into production. In 1959 the first large scale plant for mass auto production was constructed.

These industrial promotion measures had several major features in common. First, medium and long-term demand estimates were made, then capital investment plans were formulated and rationalization goals set. Corporate investment plans properly reflecting the goals of these broad development plans were accorded preferential treatment in the areas of financing and taxation. Such promotional measures were taken mostly in the second period of Japan's economic growth, that is the period in which qualitative improvements were made.

It was during these years that government banking institutions such as the Japan Development Bank played an important role. At that time, we had a so-called coordinative credit system, under which the Japan Development Bank covered only a small portion of the demand for long-term credit by private business. Loans were based upon recommendations given by government ministries in charge of industries. These small amounts, however, were very important for private companies, because they made it easier for the rest of the credit requirement to be covered by coordinated loans from the private banking system.

With money scarce in those days, the private banking system was socially responsible by complying with the coordinative credit system. It was a good business too. Those in the private banking system who were involved with coordinative lending could claim that they were exempted from financial risk because of the cooperation with the Japan Development Bank. However, the conditions of credit were not different from ordinary commercial loans and assured a normal rate of profit.

After this second period the role of the government financial institutions in the field of long-term credit receded into the background, and the era of the private banking system began. The second period, however, was probably the most productive one for Japanese bureaucrats in charge of industrial policy. In fact, Japan's policymakers during this period may be likened to impeccable orchestra conductors. In the third period, their batons and instruments were synchronized. However, an astute observer would have found that the conductors had all but lost their command. And in the fourth and current period, the tempo of their batons has tended to lag behind that of the instruments. In fact, it is becoming increasingly apparent that the conductors are losing their credibility.

TRANSFORMATION OF GOVERNMENT/BUSINESS RELATIONS

Why did all of this happen? There is a combination of reasons. First, Japan Inc. with its primary goal of catching up with the developed nations was bound to lose its raison d'être once its mission had been accomplished. As a matter of fact, Japan Inc. in this traditional role is on the brink of collapse. Its employees are so deeply caught in a web of fixed ideas that they cannot effectively respond to new developments. Second, as a result of the evolution of the Japanese private sector, changes also occurred in business/government relations. Two events in the third period of Japan's economic development—the period of internationalization—demonstrated the growing disunity in the conductor's performance. One involved the unexpected failure to enact a law on special measures to promote selected industries (1962–64). The other was the Sumikin case (1965–66). This incident occurred after steel makers had reached a stalemate in negotiating production cutbacks and MITI stepped in with administrative guidance. Sumitomo Kinzoku Kogyo Ltd. (Sumikin) alone refused to comply and continued producing as it wished, marking a break in Japanese intercompany cooperation.

It is worth going into greater detail about these developments since they entail a relative shift of power from government to banks. This discussion will provide a new point of analysis for the reasons for Japanese international competitiveness.

In the third period, each big private Japanese bank tried to foster so-called 'one-set' industries around itself as a basis for a new form of competition among lending institutions. Each bank wanted to have in its group of clients one big petrochemical, textile, electrical machinery and trading corporation etc. This goal has several times had results contradictory to the intentions of the government. For instance, parallel with its liberalization policies, the Japanese government wanted to have firms concentrate in order to increase the competitive power of the economy in the face of foreign competition. This was quite similar to the European goal of creating 'national champions'.

But it was always the will of the private banks which prevailed. The failure to enact the law on special measures to promote selected industries in the face of this is sufficient evidence that power had shifted from the government to banks and private business. Because we have a dozen big banks we could not have national champions. Instead of champions we have had a strong competition among several oligopolistic firms sponsored by different banks.

Ironically, the secret of the improvement in the competitiveness of the Japanese economy should be sought in this wild vitality of private business circles and not in government policies such as subsidies, etc. There is a widespread misunderstanding in this regard even among experts in foreign countries. Moreover, in recent years, there are several companies which have become too large to be members of a single bank's group. These include Hitachi, Toyota, Matsushita and Shinnittetsu. However, even after the government has withdrawn from the front stage and large companies have emerged with a degree of independence, banks still remain at the height of their control over private business.

THE NATURE OF 'PLANNING' UNDER JAPAN INC

Now let me touch briefly on the question of whether Japan Inc had any real long-term plan. Planning has not only been considered one of its most salient aspects, but it has been viewed as distinctly different from the practices of other OECD countries, particularly in regard to its comprehensiveness, accuracy and ease with which it could be implemented.

In the period up to the oil crisis, the government formulated seven medium and long-term plans. Insofar as the number of plans goes, Japan ranks first among the developed nations. But what were the nature of these plans?

Plans were formulated and carried out only in certain industries where the overriding need was to catch up with the developed nations. Japanese society as a whole had no plans at all. For example, the lack of planning is evident in such areas as housing, land use, urban development, and national land development—all areas in which planning is of vital importance. Thus, one former prime minister managed an enterprise which made its profits through land speculation. Such a thing would not have happened had it not been for the lack of meaningful planning.

Next, Japan had to formulate so many plans because each had to be revised within a few years in order to bring it into line with reality. The growth rate estimated under each plan was easily surpassed by the actual growth rate, because the constraints built into each estimate turned out not to be bottlenecks. Nonetheless, planning was a game which gave everyone some assurance about future prospects, and the plans also became incentives. In addition, there were a number of development plans for individual industries.

In Japan, as in other countries, the decisions of entrepreneurs are influenced by long, medium and short-range forecasts. Such forecasts are often made by government and large enterprises in a modern industrial country. They can then be coordinated implicitly, as in the case of the United States and the Federal Republic of Germany or explicitly and institutionally as in the case of Japan and France. The coordination formula adopted in the French case is *l'économie concertée*.

The Japanese and French systems of coordination, implemented according to this formula, resemble each other to a fairly large extent in the way public and private forecasts are coordinated and in the content of deliberations based on these forecasts. The fundamental difference is that the chairmanship of the French council for such deliberations is assumed by a government representative and its rapporteurs are also government officials. A similar Japanese council is chaired by a representative of the private sector and its rapporteurs are also from private circles. In a sense the Japanese private sector charts its own economic course based upon the suggested guidelines prepared by government officials.

NEW DIRECTIONS FOR INDUSTRIAL POLICY AFTER JAPAN INC

What will happen now that Japan Inc has collapsed in the wake of the oil crisis? Not only have the prospects for government guidance become more limited, but it has become more difficult to achieve a consensus on industrial goals and policies. It has become necessary to search for new instruments and ends.

There has been discussion about changing the structure of the economy. Takao Sofue has presented a new interpretation of the 'vertical society' theory, which he believes can change and is changing. This theory has been given so much attention that it has come to perform a function which differs from the original concept. It has served to vindicate, in the name of collective rationalism, the egotism of those who stand to gain from it. This approach should be destroyed. What is needed is a horizontal society in which strong, independent-minded individuals would play an active role.

In order to develop such a society, it is essential that corporations assume greater independence. The need for this cannot be overestimated in an economy which operates on market principles. These principles have been advocated ever since the Meiji era, 1868–1912, but economic conditions did not support them. If our economy is to remain healthy, industries will have to become more independent from banks. This is admittedly difficult, since Japanese corporations have developed a habit of relying heavily on banks for investment funds during the period of high economic growth.

Next, a new vision of industrial society is necessary. Government must keep in mind that considerable work is indispensable to determine a new direction. In regard to future industrial structure, current analysis has focused on reducing those sectors which require huge amounts of energy and raw materials and expanding those which have been termed 'knowledge-intensive'. These include electronic computers, aircraft, industrial robots, atomic power related industries, fine chemicals, new ceramics and sophisticated assembly industries.

To a large degree the realization of new ideas and industrial goals will be deeply influenced by the changed international environment. The world in which Japan pursued her liberalization policies and policies of adaptation was one of neo-classical economics within which subsidies and other protective measures were to be abolished. However, in today's international economic system things are not as simple as described by neo-classical premises. This is a world of dynamic, complex growth, and no general theory exists to analyze this process of development, particularly in regard to north/south relations. At the present moment, we can apply only case by case analysis to actual situations. We have to revive and renew the ideas of Friedrich List and combine them with a neo-classical framework in order to analyze the problem of industrial subsidies. Only from this broader point of view can we approach the problem of industrial subsidies and determine the premises upon which Japanese industry and government must rely.

JAPANESE INDUSTRY IN THE LATE TWENTIETH CENTURY

The problems faced by Japanese industry are considerably more complex than twenty years ago. Not only is there competition among the industrialized states, but the developed states have become serious competitors too. Japan is faced with responding to the range of policies, including subsidies, used by both Third World and OECD states to influence their industries.

INFANT INDUSTRY PROTECTION

Japan is surrounded by rapidly industrializing developing countries such as Korea and Taiwan. Hong Kong is also a threat to Japanese light industries. These are among the most successful Third World developing economies. Within a quarter of a century, mainland China with her huge population will also become a very important competitor for several Japanese heavy industries, such as chemicals, general and precision machinery, consumer durables, to say nothing of light industries.

Nowadays, the developing countries are using various methods to establish manufacturing industries. Sometimes conditions of factor endowment determine comparative advantage and labor intensive industries can grow without government subsidies. For example, in South Korea and Taiwan, at the end of 1975, the productive capacity of their textile industries almost reached half of the productive capacity of the Japanese textile industry. Each country has about a quarter of Japanese capacity. Within two to three years, when the Japanese economic situation will have improved and stabilized, demand for textiles will resume and lead to a huge increase in imports as was the case in 1973. In this event, Japan will probably be obliged to introduce import restrictions. We have already asked Korea and China to introduce voluntary export restrictions on raw silk and silk fabric. This has been necessitated in order to protect sericultural farmers, and thus it is agricultural, not industrial protection. But Japan will also face the problem of industrial protection.

For example, as a result of the introduction of British technology and technical support from Japanese shipbuilding, South Korea now has a shipyard which can build 500,000 ton tankers. This company is owned by a Korean family which owns other industries among which is a contract construction firm. When this contractor succeeded in obtaining a contract to construct a harbor at Jubail on the east coast of Saudi Arabia, the Korean government lent support by granting exemption from military service to young workers who volunteered to go there, and also promised to give priority to them to rent public owned houses after returning home. In this latter case, the Korean government is providing quite effective support to a Korean company without undertaking any additional government expenditures.

Generally speaking in Japan's neighboring countries there are no material government supports for infant industries. However, this is not true in other parts of the world. For example, in Bahrain the aluminum smelter industry enjoys an exceptionally cheap price for natural gas. This is a delicate matter, because there is no established international price in Saudi Arabia and Bahrain at the present moment. Thus it is not possible to judge whether the present price of natural gas is appropriate and it will only be some time in the future when an international price is set, whether the competitive power of the Bahrain aluminum smelter can be maintained. However, in the meantime, the behavior of these 'non-economic' smelters is disturbing the world market for aluminum ingots and is harmful to the less competitive Japanese smelters.

Apart from the rather exceptional case of the Korean contractor in Saudi Arabia and the delicate case of the Bahrain aluminum smelter, there are many cases of overt protection of infant industries in developing countries. Sometimes even for labor intensive industries such as textiles, but frequently for capital and technology intensive ones such as automobile assembly and shipbuilding, developing countries have protective measures such as import restrictions, high tariff rates and subsidies.

In Brazil a Japanese shipbuilding company has a subsidiary with a capacity for building 500,000 ton tankers. But it lacks competitive power due to excessive protective measures. In those countries, there is a vicious circle between heavy protection and lack of competitive power. Because of deficient competitiveness, governments feel obliged to apply protective measures, and then due to the existence of protective measures, the industry cannot become competitive.

From a theoretical point of view, it is possible to argue that it is unfair for developing countries to enjoy a comparative advantage for light industry and at the same time apply protective measures for heavy industry. However, it is difficult to criticize them because of the precarious position of the non-oil producing states among them.

KEY TECHNOLOGY INTENSIVE INDUSTRIES

The next problem is a north/north issue, the strengthening of the competitive power of key industries in advanced countries. As is well known, governments are not the least hesitant in providing subsidies for reasons of national prestige for the research and development of new airplanes. It is possible to argue that this constitutes an infringement of GATT rules, but no one is prepared to criticize government support, because everyone engages in these practices. For instance, Lockheed, because of its close relationship with the American government for the support of military aircraft, is not in a position to criticize the Concorde with its huge subsidies from the French and British governments. An additional reason has been Concorde's failure to be profitable.

The Japanese government intends to grant a subsidy to a Japanese firm which is engaged in a joint project with Boeing and an Italian company. The amount is estimated as $194 million and will be disbursed between 1977 and 1981. Total Japanese expenses for this project are expected to be $345 million, a tiny amount compared with other countries' efforts.

In the case of nuclear power usage, many governments provide fiscal and financial support. In Japan, the annual government allocations for nuclear development were $210 million in 1973, $218 million in 1974 and $288 million in 1975. This represents a steady, but not an adequate, increase.

In regard to electronic computers, governments are eager to make their industries as competitive as possible by providing fiscal and financial support. In Japan, the government has decided to give subsidies of about $100 million within the four year period ending 1979 for the development of the super-LSI to catch up with the FS, the equivalent IBM model. To facilitate the financing of rentals, Japanese producers jointly founded a company, Japan Electronic Computer Co (JECC) in 1961 with paid-in capital of about $4 million. This rose to $200 million at the end of 1976. The shareholders consist of six private firms producing computers.

JECC borrows money from the Japan Development Bank and also from private banks to be able to finance the rental business. Thus if a producer finds a customer for its product on a rental basis, it can sell the computer to JECC. In turn, JECC rents the machine to the customer. At the end of 1975, money borrowed from private banks amounted to ¥118.7 billion ($396 million) with an interest of 9.2 per cent and money borrowed from the Japan Development Bank amounted to

¥ 119.6 billion ($399 million) with an interest rate of 7.5 per cent. JECC bought about 40 per cent of total computers produced in 1970 and it was responsible for about the same share in 1975. In 1975 about 30 per cent of total production was sold directly to the customer (not rented), and about 20 per cent was rented directly by producers with their own funds, chiefly the Hitachi Co. But in 10 per cent of the cases the machines were too small to be covered by the JECC system. In recent years, Hitachi, which is the largest producer of electrical machinery and has considerable financial resources has not been utilizing JECC. For Hitachi, freedom from JECC means the expansion of its capability for negotiating with a customer, because the effective rate of interest for Hitachi is almost the same as that of JECC. In the beginning, JECC activities constituted a major support for the Japanese computer industry, but lately, as the case of Hitachi amply illustrates, the importance of the JECC role is diminishing. In the future, if the existence of JECC were deemed a hindrance for the export of Japanese computers, it could be liquidated quite easily.

Governments also grant subsidies for the development of sea bed and aerospace technology. For those technology intensive industries already cited above, the US is the leader through the development of the mechanism of the so-called military-industrial complex. Industries in other countries have been handicapped by the relative scarcity of fiscal aid by the government. One can easily imagine that the spillover effect is quite immense for American industry. But no one can accuse the American government for its huge defense expenditure. It has provided the effective countervailing power to Soviet military power. The necessity for defense is the last word.

REGIONAL DEVELOPMENT

Increasingly, populations tend to concentrate in metropolitan areas. In order to achieve effective geographical dispersion of industry and population, it is necessary to establish a regional development plan, a task which seems almost beyond reach.

Kukuei Tanaka tried to remodel Japan, but was too rash to succeed. Since the task is so difficult, I do not think subsidies to promote regional development can be considered as having the effect of an export subsidy. A subsidy for regional development is a compensation for the handicap of installing new industry in underdeveloped regions of a country. There are usually domestic competitors in developed regions of the same country. If no subsidy is given to competitors in the developed regions, there would be no trade deviation, and we would have no basis for worrying about it.

INTERNATIONAL ECONOMIC POLICY ISSUES

Problems caused by subsidies are only part of a wide range of international economic policy issues. In order to place these problems in a proper setting, it is necessary to explore a variety of measures available for dealing with international conflicts as well as to determine in which areas subsidies are the cause of frictions.

SECTORAL PROBLEMS

As was mentioned, the dramatic improvement in Japanese competitiveness has allowed us to liberalize import and capital transactions and reduce protective measures such as subsidies. But it has also made it necessary for us to revalue the Yen. Future relative changes in competitiveness will require new exchange rate adjustments. However, problems in many sectors such as ships, iron and steel and color TVs would occur, even if we had kept our basic account in equilibrium. For example, the US/Japanese textile issue has no direct relation to the two countries' trade balances. Sectoral problems, in this case, are partly structural ones. There are four factors which cause them: wage levels, technology, prices of raw materials including energy and efficiency of management.

Recently Japan was able to resolve the passenger car conflict with the United Kingdom by introducing voluntary export restraints, that is, an export cartel. But Japan still has problems with the European Community with shipbuilding, ball bearings and iron and steel and with the United States with iron and steel and color TVs. It has been assumed that world economic recovery fostered by demand management, would solve these problems. For iron and steel and ball bearings, I admit, economic recovery would be helpful in reducing the gap between supply and demand. But for other goods such as ships, cars and color TVs, the problems are mainly structural. Under a rate of exchange which can maintain equilibrium in the basic account, relative competitiveness of such goods produced in Japan is superior to those of several competing nations. Even for iron and steel, Japan is more competitive.

Given the good labor relations which assure the quality of products and intense domestic competition among oligopolistic large firms which stimulate technological improvement, relative competitiveness in these goods will not be weakened, even if we would continue to revalue the Yen at a steady pace. Under these circumstances, there is no theoretically practical solution. Industrial adjustment under GATT rules is not easy because it is usually quite difficult to determine alternative employment opportunities. The only practical and pragmatic solution is through negotiation and compromise.

Over a year ago in an analysis of future demand for ships, we found that recovery of this sector could be expected at the earliest by 1980. For color TVs, economic recovery will not contribute much to the domestic absorption of output. It will take quite some time for other countries to improve the competitiveness of their products through technological innovation and modernization of production equipment. Thus some kind of negotiation and compromise are inevitable. This is not a desirable solution. It is second, or rather third best. The better way would be to determine in advance the possibility for such problems to occur by comparing and checking the evolution of production in major countries. To this end about three years ago in the Industrial Committee of the OECD, we proposed the establishment of medium-term estimates of industrial sectors of member countries, and explained the Japanese versions of making such estimates based on the analysis of demand.

The work is going on in the industrial committee. However, many countries do not have adequate statistics to establish a coherent analysis of their industries. Consequently, there is little reason to be optimistic about the results. It is also doubtful how useful estimates would be for solving the problem of industrial transformation. Even in the face of the necessity of compromise, national sovereignty will assert itself. At any rate, such estimates are an improvement over the status quo.

INDUSTRIAL CONVERSION

Industrial conversion is one aspect of international industrial adjustment. It involves the efforts of developed countries, and the voluntary restriction of exports from developing countries. The international rule which should harmonize these conflicting interests is the safeguard mechanism contained in GATT Article XIX. There is a long history of the efforts to revise this article, including the Rey Report.

For the fiscal authorities of developed countries, it is not an easy task to provide sufficient resources to convert, rationalize or revitalize declining domestic industries. Instead of industrial conversion, developed country governments are more apt to have recourse to import restrictions—as in the case of the international textile agreement. To cope with this difficulty, it might be desirable that the United Nations Conference on Trade and Development (UNCTAD) adopt a resolution calling for each developed country to establish an Industrial Conversion Fund to accelerate the transformation of declining industries or the rationalization of decaying ones. UNCTAD could decide on the amount of an annual contribution to this fund, at least .01 per cent of GNP.

Theoretically, it would also be advisable to fix the permissible safeguard period for each category of industry, for example 1.5 years for the spinning industry, 2.5 years for chemical and synthetic fibers and so on. Within this period, a developed country could apply safeguard measures and could convert or rationalize the industry in question. During the safeguard period, the exporting country would be given the opportunity to increase its access to the market of the importing country. In any case after the expiry of the safeguard period, the government would have to abolish safeguard measures, and in principle, the renewal of such measures would not be allowed.

These are examples of revisions to be added to the ideas in the Rey Report. But it is one thing to think of the revision of GATT articles, and quite another to realize them. Anyhow it is not necessary to blame the lack of efforts by governments in this field, since there is little risk of excessive revitalization of declining industries by government subsidies.

SUBSIDIES AND COUNTERVAILING DUTIES IN GATT NEGOTIATIONS

In the current multilateral trade negotiations (MTN) the central problem which must be negotiated first is whether it is necessary to establish an exhaustive list of prohibited subsidy practices based upon a newly proposed list or to be content with the existing more restrictive one. The original list, the so-called 'A' Declaration adopted by the GATT General Assembly on 19 November 1960 contained eight.[1] More recently, a list was proposed by working group 1 of the committee on trade in industrial products which contains 21 items.[2] The second important problem is the establishment of an international countervailing duty code. The following brief remarks are on these issues.

WHICH PRACTICES SHOULD BE PROHIBITED

The expanded list of prohibited practices is rather detailed and creates the impression that it intends to be exhaustive. For almost all of the items, there might be no grounds for opposition. However, there are several items which need comment or clarification.

GOVERNMENT LOANS TO EXPORTERS

The matter has been dealt with for a long time in the OECD, with the goal of trying to harmonize the terms on which loans are made available. I think there is no other way to treat this problem.

GRANTS BY GOVERNMENTS OF EXPORT CREDIT INSURANCE ETC.

In almost every country, the export credit insurance business operates on the principle of equilibrium between revenue and expenditure. However, in several countries there is insurance against inflation. This insurance is running in the red. It is quite difficult to operate insurance on a sound accounting basis, and in this way, insurance tends to be export stimulating.

MEASURES OFFSETTING EXCHANGE RATE ADJUSTMENTS

It is hard to consider this measure as export stimulating, especially for short-term transactions. For long-term loans accompanying the export of plants and equipment, there is insurance against exchange rate fluctuations in many countries, with the exception of the United States and the United Kingdom. In Japan our system proved ineffective due to quite restrictive operations with very high premiums. The IMF suggested that this problem is caused by the exchange rate system and might fall under its competence. At any rate this problem belongs to the so-called grey zone, in the effort to determine whether particular subsidies should be allowed or prohibited.

REMISSION OR DEFERRAL OF DIRECT TAXES

There are several kinds of infringements to this prohibited practice. The DISC of the United States is one example. In Japan there are two funds: the reserve fund for overseas market development and the reserve fund for specific and exceptionally large scale overseas contracts. The first is available for small and medium scale firms whose paid-in capital is less than about $3.3 million. Trading companies with paid-in capital between $.33 million and $3.3 million can retain 1 per cent of their export earnings for five years during which they are temporarily tax exempt. However, if the company does not use these retained earnings for expenditures on overseas market research, each year 20 per cent of the reserve becomes taxable. For trading companies with paid-in capital of less than $.33 million, the rate of reserve is 1.7 per cent. For manufacturing companies with paid-in capital between $.33 million and $3.3 million, the rate is 1.5 per cent, and for companies with paid-in capital of less than $.33 million, the rate is 2.3 per cent. It is only for small and medium sized firms. The subsidy element is only the interest on the deferred part which can be treated as a case of *de minimis*. Although it is not necessary to continue this measure in the future however, several politicians may feel it is.

The second reserve fund is a good measure for promoting economic cooperation with the developing countries. By 'specific' is meant that the partner of the contract should be a foreign government or public corporation. The total amount of the contract must be over $1.3 billion. This contract must be related to a development assistance project which is based upon an official exchange of letters for economic cooperation between the Japanese government and government of developing regions, that is, other than the states of Eastern Europe. Private firms undertaking these projects can retain annually 7 per cent of the amount of construction work performed each year as a reserve fund for five years. After five years 20 per cent of the reserve will be transferred annually from the fund to be added to current profit, and will be taxed. These conditions show that the objective of this measure is solely to promote economic cooperation with the developing countries and not to stimulate exports.

There are several other export promotion measures which are not covered by the list of twenty-one items. Preferential lending of long term loans to companies whose chief business is exports is an example. It is supposed to exist in France, but detailed information is not obtainable. And it is not realistic to think that we can enumerate every prohibited practice and can make a thorough list. So it might be wiser to make a short list of prohibited practices which are mandatory and to leave many others in the grey zone. Grey zone examples should be treated on a case by case basis, and sometimes will become the subject of countervailing duty actions. With the accumulation of experience, it will be possible to specify which grey zone measures should be permitted or forbidden.

COUNTERVAILING DUTIES

Within the past five or six years, only the American government has invoked countervailing duties. At the end of March 1975 there were 22 items from eleven countries on which they were levied. The eleven countries are Australia, Canada, Cuba, Denmark, France, the United Kingdom, Ireland, Italy, Greece, Brazil and Spain. There were no Japanese exports which became subject to American countervailing duties until April 1977.

The problem involved in the American resort to countervailing duties is that a determination of material injury is not required. Duties have been imposed on products imported without any injury to American industry, if there was proof that a subsidy had been granted on the imported products by the government of the exporting country.

In the case of anti-dumping duties, the determination of material injury is required before a duty can be imposed. During the Kennedy Round, an international code on anti-dumping was established, and it is now planned to establish a similar code on countervailing duties. Since there are several common elements between the two, it should not be difficult to accomplish this. There are at least several items which should be dealt with in such a code: (a) the scope of subsidies which are liable to be the object of a countervailing duty, (b) cooperation between governments of both parties during prior consultation, (c) proof of injury, (d) temporary remedial measures, (e) discretionary actions, (f) the dispute settlement committee, (g) third country countervailing duty problems.

One point still to be discussed is the treatment of developing countries. There are proposals from Brazil and India. Both request special treatment for export subsidies and for export commodities from Third World states. The Brazilian proposal asks for the establishment of a 'positive' list for export subsidies by developing country governments. In light of the present situation of non-oil producing developing states, we must admit preferential measures. However, it is not necessary to clearly define this in an international code. Provisions of a general nature are appropriate here.

CONCLUSIONS

From the Japanese view point, the role and significance of industrial subsidies and countervailing duties should recede into the background of international economic policy. These are problems chiefly among the developed countries. And developed countries are well aware of the necessity for abolishing these artificial export promoting measures.

Instead of these problems, we are confronting two quite difficult problems. The first is that of international industrial adjustment. For developed countries this involves industrial conversion. Under lower growth rates as a result of the energy crisis, it has become difficult for Japan to find a way out through industrial conversion. For Japan, the textile issue with the United States has been the most important international trade problem since the end of World War II. This time it is Japan which will impose restrictive measures against textile producers from developing countries. The United States and the West European nations are not innocent in this respect. Moreover developed countries will be obliged to have recourse to import restrictions for other products in the coming five years.

Even more of a source for concern is the limitation of energy supplies. Oil economists predict a shortage within three years. The only possibility left for us is American influence on Saudi Arabia to increase production in excess of her need to cover expenditures required for the realization of her national development plan. In the face of these difficulties, developed countries are in the same boat.

Notes
1. See Appendix B.
2. See Appendix C.

7 The European Community and National Subsidy Policies

STEVEN J. WARNECKE

The American position in the current round of trade negotiations for revising GATT Articles VI and XVI includes a proposal for a tripartite differentiation of national subsidies.[1] This so-called 'traffic light' or 'red, green, amber' system is in many respects quite close to existing European Community (EEC) practices. Since the EEC represents the most far-reaching attempt to liberalize trade among industrialized states, its experience with subsidies, albeit a highly specialized issue, may not only provide useful insights for understanding the American proposal, but also be relevant to efforts to reform the pertinent GATT articles. These include such questions as the extent to which and under what conditions general rules and obligations can be defined which are economically relevant, politically acceptable and enforceable multi-laterally among a group of industrialized states; the frame of reference a multilateral organization can develop for evaluating national subsidies; the pressures it can bring to bear on its members; and the limits imposed on policy formulation. In the EEC's case one limit is a result of the fact that the Community constitutes a suboptimal area from the perspective of the international economy.

The EEC is a particularly valuable subject for a case study, since the Commission has rather broad powers under the Rome Treaty to regulate competition, and in exercising these powers has tried to deal with the *causes* as well as the *effects* of subsidies. Moreover, the EEC is of considerable interest because of the Community's structure. All too frequently, the discussion of subsidies ignores or is insufficiently related to the problems presented by government organization for translating economic analysis into effective policy. In regard to subsidies the domestic dimensions are the responsibility of departments with a national constituency, whereas the international aspects are in the domain of departments with global responsibilities. Coordination between the two groups is often absent or inadequate. In the

Community's case, this problem of departments with different foci exists on both the EEC level as well as that of the individual member states.

The decision making structure of the EEC not only raises questions about how intra-Community subsidy policy is formulated and implemented, but how the EEC fits into the international system. For states such as Japan and the United States, there is no intermediary between the national government and the GATT. In the case of the EEC there is not only an intermediary, but the nine member states have been obligated to pursue trade liberalization on two levels simultaneously, regionally and internationally. Thus the Commission is responsible for defining an intra-Community subsidy policy as well as responding to pressures to reform Articles VI and XVI of the GATT.

Many observers have questioned the usefulness of the Community's experience with subsidies for the GATT. As with so many other EEC functional policies, its value for other circumstances seems to have been diminished, because the European federalists have linked competition policy to the establishment of a supranational Community. In spite of this programmatic connection, subsidy policy can be treated separately from any impact it might have on the transfer of sovereignty to Brussels, since regulation would be necessary in any event irrespective of whether the Community were a customs union or a new political entity.

ROME TREATY ARTICLES ON SUBSIDIES

Although it has been difficult to reach agreement about when a subsidy has an adverse effect on trade as well as to develop methods and criteria for measuring these effects, the EEC as a result of the goals of the Rome Treaty has had to deal with this issue in depth. From the strictly practical viewpoint the establishment of a free trade area requires a central policy concerning competition. This follows logically not only from the economic ends of the customs union, but is also a political necessity as well. Economically, the new geoeconomic area was established to permit a better allocation of resources. Thus it has been essential to reduce or eliminate government measures which place firms on an unequal footing with each other and distort market forces. Politically, competition policy has been essential for reconciling conflicts among the member states which might ultimately contribute to undermining the consensus on which the Common Market is based.

Rules governing state aids are contained in Articles 92–4 of the Rome Treaty following those on competition (Articles 85–91).[2] Article 92 states that 'any aid granted by a member state or through state resources, in any form whatsoever, which distorts or threatens to distort competition by favoring certain enterprises or the production of certain goods shall, to the extent to which it affects trade between member states, be deemed to be incompatible with the Common Market. Sections 2 and 3, in contrast, contain rather broad lists of aids that can be considered compatible with the Common Market. Section 2 includes: aids granted for social purposes; aids for damage caused by natural disasters; and aids to those areas of the Federal Republic of Germany affected by the division of the country. Section 3 deals with exemptions which must be specifically authorized. They are: regions having underemployment or low standards of living; to promote an important project of common European interest or to remedy a serious disturbance in the economy of a member state; to facilitate the development of certain activities or of certain economic regions provided that such aid does not change trading conditions to such an extent as would be contrary to the common interest; [3] aids to shipbuilding; [4] categories to be specified by the Council of Ministers.

Although the Rome Treaty has clearly made the Commission responsible for implementing these provisions, Article 92 left a number of key problems unresolved. Among them were: the definition of which aids are to be included; the specific economic and political criteria for deciding when aids are incompatible; what exactly the 'Community' interest was and how it was to be enforced; what the role and powers of the Commission should be; and the extent to which Articles 92–4 were applicable to direct and indirect state involvement in the economy. In contrast to Articles 85–91 involving private sector competition, the relatively small number of decisions published in the *Official Journal* in which the Commission has ruled upon, much less forbidden state aids as incompatible with the Common Market, raises the impression that there has been little activity in this area. This is not at all correct. Since the establishment of the EEC, the competition policy directorate has been one of the strongest and most effective departments of the Commission. The department has had a consistent influence behind the scenes and has consistently tried to take a tough line against useless subsidies. The charged nature of the issue explains why much activity has been secret as well as why the role of this particular directorate has evolved slowly.

Before turning to the substantive questions raised by Article 92, what *formal* powers does the Commision have to deal with subsidies and how have these been asserted? Its specific procedural powers are enumerated in Articles 93–4, and provide it with the capacity to review aids in advance of their application. Article 93:1 states that the Commission in cooperation with the member states is responsible for keeping all aid systems under surveillance. This includes the introduction of new or the revision of existing legislation. When necessary, the Commission can propose to the states any appropriate measures required by the progressive development or functioning of the Common Market. The states, for their part, are obliged under Article 93:3 to inform the

Commission of the introduction of new or the revision of existing aid systems. Article 92:2 states that the Commission must give notice to the parties concerned (which includes states and enterprises) to submit comments. If it finds an aid incompatible on the basis of Article 92 or being misused, it must decide whether the subsidy should be abolished or altered, as well as the time limit within which this must be done. In practice the Commission has left the choice of the time limit up to the states.

If the member state does not comply, the Commission or any other interested state can apply to the Court of Justice. However, a member state can apply to the Council of Ministers, which acting unanimously can vote a derogation from Article 92 under the clause providing for relief as a result of exceptional circumstances. Hardly any use has been made of this provision, because difficult problems are resolved through negotiation. However, application to the Council of Ministers suspends action under Article 93:2, if any is under way. Article 93:3 states that the Commission shall be informed in sufficient time by the states in order to be able to submit its comments on any plans to grant or alter aid. Member states shall not implement proposed measures until the Commission has ruled. Finally, Article 148:2 empowers the Council of Ministers to implement Articles 92–4 through regulations proposed by the Commission. This is done by qualified majority.

As with other sections of the Rome Treaty, the elaboration of these articles has been inextricably bound to the establishment and legitimation of the Community's central institutions and the development and maintenance of consensus and support for EEC policies. These boundaries have fluctuated as the member states have resisted strengthening central institutions out of principle or necessity, and in turn this has affected the speed and extent to which the competition policy directorate has been able to define its powers under Articles 92–4. In spite of the uncertain foundation for Commission policies, the competition policy directorate has had a unique position among the various departments in Brussels. It has the firm backing of the Rome Treaty provisions establishing a customs union, the precedent of the European Coal and Steel Community, the resurgence of interest in competition after 1945, and the determined influence in the early years of Walter Hallstein, first president of the Commission, and Hans von der Groeben, first Commissioner responsible for competition policy.[5]

The elaboration and implementation of Articles 92–4 can be divided roughly into two overlapping periods dealing with two distinct sets of issues: early discussion to interpret the Treaty and decisions necessitated by the progressive removal of quotas and tariffs, 1959–67; and efforts to develop systematic approaches to aids for industrial, regional and general economic growth policies. From the outset the competition policy directorate has developed its authority in close cooperation with national officials. Shortly after the establishment of the Community, the directorate set up working groups including national officials to define legal concepts such as 'aids granted by states or through state resources', compile inventories of aids, determine criteria for evaluating them, rule on existing programs, and develop notification procedures and mechanisms for examining aid systems.[6]

In the course of the 1960s the directorate was able to enforce its right to examine existing legislation and new bills, and established its authority within the Commission in regard to such directorates as regional, social and industrial policy. The accepted interpretation of the phrase 'aids granted by states or through state resources' has delimited the scope of its jurisdiction. This phrase includes the member states themselves, the Laender of the Federal Republic of Germany, administrative districts of states such as provinces, regions, departments, associations of municipalities and municipalities which receive their funding either through transfers or subsidies from the national budget or through levying taxes on their own authority. It also covers public entities, associations or other public law bodies as well as compensatory and support funds which have been established by government regulation.[7]

Finally, although all specific cases which arise from actual government grants of subsidies are investigated solely by the competition policy directorate, complaints can be initiated by the directorate on its own behalf, by member states or by firms. Thus the directorate initiated cases against the Belgian government in 1964 as a result of a subsidy to Ford to locate a tractor plant in Belgium, in 1973 it opened another case against the Belgian government as a result of its efforts to expand refinery capacity in Antwerp, and in 1975 it initiated an informal inquiry as a result of the British government's decision to provide a subsidy to Norton Villers. Most frequently, firms initiate complaints, particularly in the textile industry, or as in recent years German enterprises have brought complaints against Italian competitors who receive subsidies from state holding companies such as ENI and IRI. Most often these cases are settled through private negotiations, and solutions are not always made public.

REPRESENTATIVE CASES DURING THE 1960s

Procedural powers are only one side of the coin. The keys, of course, to the operation of Articles 92–4 are the definition of subsidies, the criteria which are applied, and the extent to which states are prepared to accept Commission rulings. Although the Treaty does not indicate what forms subsidies can take, the Commission provided a representative list in 1963 in response to a question from the European Parliament. Thus, the wording of Article 92 is considered to include every type of allowance, regardless of form, given directly or indirectly by the state to individual enterprises or sectors of the economy. This covers non-repayable money payments as well as exemption from taxes and fiscal charges, exemption from charges similar to fiscal charges, interest reduction or reimbursement, loan guarantees under particularly favorable circumstances, transfer of buildings or land either free of charge or under particularly favorable conditions, covering of operating losses or any other measure having an equivalent effect, regardless of whether the enterprise which benefits is public or private. Credit guarantees may be considered as subsidies only if they are made under other than normal market conditions. Where aids are granted in the form of reduced transport rates, the corresponding Treaty provisions Articles 80 and 95 will prevail only if specific provisions are made. Otherwise, Article 92 applies especially in the numerous cases in which aid is given in the form of tax benefits.[8]

This is only a catalogue, and the gradual evolution of criteria can be gleaned from decisions taken by the competition policy directorate between 1959–70.[9] They include: ensuring conformity with the basic principles of the customs union; development of standards for prior review of national subsidy legislation to remove potential economic and political conflicts in advance and to further elaborate a legal basis for Commission action; development of economic criteria through which national calculations of effects of domestic policy goals can be related to and examined against a Community framework; and application through specific cases.

Commission decisions in regard to ensuring conformity to basic Common Market principles have ranged from the general to the specific. For instance, during the first years of the Community, the Commission had to deal with how far existing aids should be assimilated to customs protection and as such made subject to the same reductions as the customs duties applied between the member states. Or in 1961 the Commission ordered the abolition of indirect aid to the Italian motor car industry as being discriminatory, because it involved credit facilities available for the purchase of Italian manufactured agricultural machines. In the last year, the Commission has initiated an action against the British government for subsidizing the construction of deep sea oil rigs in British shipyards.

In regard to prior notification and review of aid schemes, as required, the member states have submitted all new bills for comment and approval. Among them have been a 1963 Italian draft law for aid to the Mezzogiorno, the 1964 revision of the Belgian law for economic expansion of 1959, the 1964 French system outlining new arrangements for granting relief to promote the expansion of business and facilitate structural adjustments. In 1966 the Commission met with national experts to examine Dutch measures for industrial restructuring in the province of Limbourg. In each case the competition policy directorate was concerned about the specificity of goals, aid levels, procedure for application, and opportunities for Commission review and supervision. Such meetings are a general practice and take place for every major aid scheme. They provide member states with the opportunity to express possible concern with a proposed scheme before it is accepted by the Commission.

Cases involving specific sectors reflect an effort to develop economic criteria. In 1961 the competition policy directorate reviewed the Tambroni bill to amend existing aid systems to Italian shipbuilding. Although it was approved because the Commission felt it could come under Article 92, section 3c, approval was conditional. The restructuring program outlined had to be carried out without prejudice to the competitive positions of other Community shipyards and, in order to ensure this, the Italian government was required to make half yearly reports to the Commission. In 1964 the Belgian government was ordered to withdraw aids granted to Ford Tractor Ltd in Antwerp under the 17 July 1959 law for the promotion of economic expansion and the establishment of new industries. The aid was in the form of interest rebates which were adjudged invalid not only for legal reasons but because there was a communitywide overcapacity in the production of farm tractors, gear boxes and differentials. In 1970 the Commission ruled that an Italian law for aid to restructure the textile sector could not include a ten year exemption from any direct tax on income from investments. In addition, the Commission required that the criteria for granting aid be amended to prevent any increase in productive capacity in this sector. Finally, in 1965 in a draft directive submitted to the Commission, the competition policy directorate made a first try at developing a sectoral policy for one industry, shipbuilding. In a Commission memorandum of 13 Jan 1966, *A Community Approach to Shipbuilding*, rationalization in relation to main non-member competitors and difficulties in converting inefficient EEC shipyards was discussed.

THE DEVELOPMENT OF A MORE SYSTEMATIC FRAMEWORK

If the 1960s were a period in which the competition policy directorate tested its powers and explored the parameters for a Community subsidy policy, it was only with the appearance of the *First Report on Competition Policy* in 1971[10] that the directorate presented an outline for a systematic approach. This required tackling the central problem of exactly how a Community perspective differed from a national one. For the Commission, at a minimum, this meant ensuring that member states' aid programs take the interests of their partners into account. Governments acting individually would be better informed of nationally anticipated gains from their own subsidy policies, rather than about the negative implications at the Community level. Economically, such unilateral initiatives in a multistate customs union might lead to the reciprocal neutralization of national policies, waste of domestic and Community resources, shifting economic difficulties from one state to another, or the creation of new difficulties, such as competitive outbidding. Seen in this context, governments might underestimate the reaction of their partners.

To avoid these conflicts the report noted that more than discussion was necessary, and it proposed increased coordination among national structural policies and a greater role for the Commission. However, the prospects for both of these developments depended on several prerequisites. The member states would have to share the Commission's view of the solidarity and interdependence of national interests, thus permitting the discussion of national policies to be raised to a Community level. Even if they were prepared to evaluate the relative seriousness of their regional and structural problems not only within a domestic frame of reference but also in relation to the Community as a whole, would states be prepared to accept the necessary 'coordination'. Coordination meant decisions on expansion and contraction, and even the development of new sectors. To what extent would states be prepared to allow a regional secretariat to influence these distributive decisions?

While such a 'Community' solution might be extremely desirable from a liberal perspective, Article 92, the basis for the Commission's role, unfortunately contained conflicting standards. Section 1 is a classical liberal statement concerning the *economic* criteria for dealing with subsidies which are compatible with a customs union. Aids are incompatible if they distort or threaten to distort competition and thus the operation of markets to produce an optimum resource allocation; they are also incompatible if they adversely affect trade between the member states. On this basis, individual national policies would be evaluated in reference to the Common Market. The Commission's role would be rather mechanical and passive, restricted to the guardianship of trade liberalization by neutralizing government measures that undermine tariff and quota concessions. Logically, this would expand the leeway available to the private sector.

Sections 2 and 3, however, place *political* limits on the application of these strictly economic criteria. Although the Rome Treaty has established a legally defined market common to all member states, it is still one in which the states are the basic datum. The catalogue of exceptions, particularly those contained in section 3 is a recognition that interests as defined by the states may conflict with a 'Community' evaluation and solution. The competition policy directorate is keenly aware of this power structure and the political constraints it places on implementing an EEC subsidy policy, although it has been accused of trying to define unrealistic principles of competition or induce perfect economic rationality in the state aid area.

Pierre Mathijsen, the former director of that section of the competition policy directorate that deals with state aids, public discrimination, public enterprises and state monopolies, has tried to reconcile these apparently conflicting goals. '. . . Competition constitutes an essential instrument of economic development and implies in principle that the undertakings enter upon the market entirely on their own, with their own resources, at their own risk.' State aid can lead to inequality. On the other hand: 'If state aids proper affect competition and interstate trade, they also constitute an instrument of structural development policy when certain legitimate objectives of economic growth cannot be attained by the sole interplay of market forces (or not within an acceptable time limit) or would cause unacceptable social frictions.'[11]

The heart of the conflict is the modern state's ambivalent reaction to market forces. If, on the one hand, the establishment of the Common Market was a recognition by small states that there were political and economic limits imposed on them by their size, on the other hand, states which were not prepared to accept the full play of market forces at home were equally unprepared to accept similar forces as a result of membership in a customs union. The progressive lowering of tariff barriers and quotas, both in the EEC and internationally, have had as their concomitant, increased resort to national industrial, regional and similar policies.

Why have the nine EEC member states attempted to impose limits on how their firms respond to the Common Market? As described in chapter 2 by Guy de Carmoy, the Nine, particularly those members who aspire to have 'complete economies' such as France, Britain, Italy and Germany, are concerned about the types of industries they have. This phenomenon is clearly evident in lead sectors such as computers, aircraft, nuclear reactors, telecommunications and chemicals. It includes the size and structure of firms, their geographical location and the locus of both their legal and actual control. But state intervention also extends to industries which are under strong competitive pressures due to changing patterns of comparative advantage. In these sectors, one problem may be that adjustment is neither as simple nor as rapid as required by liberal theory, or as in the case of automobiles, the industry looms so large politically and economically in the national context that a sectoral policy is not a simple matter.

Ideally clashes among the Nine would not exist in their present form if 'Community' firms had developed. Thus the division of labor and degree of competition would be judged in the context of a common market and not in terms of the distribution of firms among the individual states. In the ideal case, competition policy would be limited to regulating relations among firms in a single continentalwide market such as in the United States. But since the states remain the primary datum and try to limit or influence the impact of market forces on their industrial structures, they are reluctant to allow the Commission or other member states acting in cooperation with the Commission to become either a major factor in or arbiter of structural change and industrial distribution.[12]

In fact, behind the facade of the Community is a struggle among the member states to influence the international distribution of industry among themselves, a struggle that often seems to have mercantilist overtones. States frequently disregard whether their economic bases are sufficiently large to warrant the development of certain kinds of industries, a policy which leads to the necessity for export markets, both in the EEC member states and abroad. And since the Nine have similar structures of production and similar industrial goals, they try to expand in the same areas and inevitably come into conflict with each other. Furthermore, liberal theory which examines firms and sectors from the strict view of efficiency economics disregards the role such industries often play in maintaining a precarious national stability. One need only cite the parentella/clientalla relations between the ENI and IRI groups on the one hand and the coalitions of regions and classes on the other hand. It can be argued that strong multilateral obligations are useful because they may permit national policy makers to upset such economically inefficient patterns and force resources out of weak into strong sectors. But it is a rather large step from the general validity of this observation to its translation into a specific policy.

These circumstances might suggest that the Commission's role has been limited to either implementing the general principles necessary to maintain a customs union or of being an honest broker trying to strike a balance among competing national political and economic interests. To a certain extent this is accurate. But the competition policy directorate as a result of its unique role, the intent of the Rome Treaty, and the effects of regional trade liberalization and competitive national policies has had to try to move beyond a passive liberal role for itself. If it limited itself to ensuring the removal of government barriers to the operation of EEC wide markets, those states such as Germany which were highly developed industrially would expand both their lead and power and shift the burden of adjustment to the less competitive members. This would be politically and economically undesirable.

Even though the Nine individually are concerned about losing control over their structural policies, the international nature of sectoral problems and the obligations of the Rome Treaty have often driven them to Brussels. They have half-heartedly turned to the Commission for assistance in dealing with overcapacity and adjustment in such areas as shipbuilding and textiles. The Commission has some power and leverage as a result of its responsibilities for the common external tariff and the negotiation of international trade agreements for all of the member states. Thus the Commission has had to face both the effects and causes of national subsidy policies.

DELINEATION OF AN EEC APPROACH

Commission efforts to implement Articles 92–4 must be evaluated against this background. Obviously without some framework supported by the Nine, the Commission would be deprived of means for assessing the legality of national aims, the methods of member states' interventions and the economic consequences both for the states and the Community. But in achieving these goals the Commission has had to confront the facts that aids are not always easy to identify nor are the means through which they are granted always visible. In addition, it is frequently difficult to unravel the sectoral and regional consequences of some systems of an excessively general nature. Thus the first step has been to bring some order into the plethora of subsidies and goals. One of the main elements supporting the Commission's role has been its right to review in advance and pass on the compatibility of aids with Article 92. This has compelled the member states to submit their aid systems to a multilateral examination and raised discussion to a Community level with the Commission representing a 'Community' interest. This is a continuous and close process, which by its nature has reinforced the awareness of reciprocal obligations.

The Commission has tried to distinguish aids into three groups: regional, sectoral and general, and to evaluate them in terms of the specificity of their application, calculability of their aid levels and the degree of discretionary power left in the hands of government agencies. The following sections of this chapter will look systematically at the Commission's application of Article 92. For purposes of analysis it is useful to work with a twofold distinction: general aids not applicable in advance to specific industries and specific aids for specific sectors. All conclusions about the implications and effectiveness of the EEC subsidy policy will be contained in the final section.

GENERAL SUBSIDY PROGRAMS NOT TIED IN ADVANCE TO SPECIFIC SECTORS

REGIONAL POLICIES

Aid for regional development has posed one of the most serious problems for the European Community. The member states are often in direct competition with each other for investments, and this has led to a proliferation of types of aid, the number of zones to which they are applicable, and an escalation in available aid levels. These policies have had a variety of negative consequences: national initiatives to attract investments have become more costly, the advantages offered frequently exceed the material inconvenience imposed on firms which have decided to locate in these regions, and the aid levels may no longer correspond to the relative seriousness of problems in the various regions whether assessed at national or Community level.[13]

Moreover, since national regional aid systems are often general, it is difficult for the Commission to fulfill its responsibility of prior review, because it cannot determine in advance the incidence and therefore compatibility of the aid with Article 92. Furthermore, since all industrial sectors can potentially benefit from such schemes, under cover of worthwhile regional objectives sectoral development can be encouraged which may produce harmful effects from the perspective of a Community interest. This is not a theoretical problem, since regional subsidies are not always used for strictly regional goals.

Although the Commission has had to accept the inevitability of regional subsidies, this has not been allowed to entirely outweigh the case for their control and harmonization. In the first place even though trade distortions caused by such subsidies may be minimal, the fears they engender may lead to other countries' producers pressing their governments to take countervailing measures. The result will be the creation of other nontariff distortions. In order to avoid such escalation of trade barriers it is necessary for governments to operate *transparent* policies which clarify the situation and leave no excuse for retaliatory measures. In addition, transparent policies offer governments an opportunity to evaluate costs in a context larger than the national economy, an opportunity all the more essential in a customs union. But achieving control of regional aids hinges on the long standing problem of determining the criteria governing the definition of regions in need of assistance, and the development of a set of criteria to determine when regional aids distort trade. It is no easy task to clarify the impact of regional aid on trade flows and to devise criteria for a code of conduct to define what is an acceptable regional aid program, as well as to prevent distortions from arising.

In 1968 after several years of having dealt with the regional policies of the then six EEC member states without systematic criteria, the Commission proposed an inductive method for attaining such a coordinated approach. The states should agree to prior notification of significant cases of application of regional aid systems, and these would serve as a basis for gradually arriving at a coordinated method. Several states objected to the development of systematic criteria based on individual cases, and preferred that agreement on a comprehensive policy be derived from the aid systems themselves.

On 23 June 1971 the Commission sent a memo to the Council of Ministers outlining such an approach. On 20 October 1971 the governments of the member states meeting within the framework of the Council of Ministers expressed their agreement with the Commission's views and adopted the First Resolution on General Regional Aid Systems.[14] It contained a list of principles to be applied to general systems of regional aid already in force or due to enter into force. (These principles would also eventually be applied to other kinds of aid systems.) They included:

1. *Regional Specificity*. Aids must not be applicable to an entire national territory with the exception of Luxembourg. They must clearly define either geographically or by means of quantitative criteria, the regions or zones with such regions which are to receive benefits.

2. *Transparency*. The openness of regional aid systems would be improved by prior knowledge of the geographical and sectoral locations of the main investments benefiting from such aid. It would also be necessary to determine the relative percentage of all aid granted to an investment in relation to the total amount of the investment, by applying a common method of evaluation worked out with the assistance of experts from the member states. This would require a clear indication of the gradation and types of aid involved. Since all sectors are potential beneficiaries of regional aids, it would also be necessary to work out a method to evaluate the sectoral incidence of such subsidies.

3. *Single Intensity Ceiling*. The Commission must relate the level of aid to the nature and seriousness of the problem it is supposed to solve. Thus aid levels must be adapted to the nature, seriousness and urgency of the problem, and the gradation and variation of aid rates according to area and region must be clearly indicated.

4. *Supervision of Coordination*. Outbidding might be considerably reduced if member states had to submit regional aid policies to Brussels for approval. This might permit the emergence of a 'Community attitude' in regard to the main problems: ascertaining the most urgent regional and sectoral problems and fitting them into a

common framework. Aids must not be of an *ad hoc* operational nature, but must structurally improve existing industries and not keep declining businesses alive. The Commission would exercise its authority on the basis of *a posteriori* communications submitted by the member state concerning most significant cases.

All criteria were to be applied to what were defined as the central and peripheral zones, but the most essential, the single intensity ceiling was only applicable to the central regions. The central regions are generally fairly industrialized, even if sometimes rather out of date, and as a result face reconversion problems. Since they all have well developed infrastructures and are geographically close to one another, the effects of outbidding are most visible. They include all of the EEC with the exception of Berlin, the Zonenrandgebiete, the Mezzogiorno and the south and southwestern parts of France. The peripheral zones correspond mostly to large areas far from consumers and industrial centers. Agriculture is still important, living standards low and unemployment acute. For the Commission, coordination in the central regions would constitute a first step toward eliminating outbidding. As of 1 January 1972 all cumulative regional aids for central regions, regardless of form, were fixed at 20 per cent of the investment in net grant equivalence calculated on the basis of a common method for aid evaluation. Peripheral areas could receive government aid whose value is equivalent to more than 20 per cent of net investment in buildings and plants without interference from Brussels, although all projects in peripheral regions would have to obtain Commission clearance.

In keeping with this approach the Commission struck down investment grants in the German coal sector, asked for revisions of the Belgian draft law on economic expansion, and ruled on a French regional bonus scheme and Italian assistance to industries in the region of Friuli-Venezia-Giulia.[15]

With the expansion of the Common Market to include Great Britain, Ireland and Denmark, the stability of this approach was threatened. As of 1 July 1973 all of Ireland was designated a peripheral region and Denmark with the exception of Greenland and several islands was defined as a central region. The United Kingdom, however, wanted a redefinition of central regions in regard to itself, because under existing EEC standards the declining industrial areas of Great Britain could not have been included. The competition policy directorate disapproved of the existing UK definition of regions, because this might not only affect existing, but new aid programs. In addition, the directorate disapproved of British regional employment premiums, because they were seen as a form of ongoing subsidy. It wanted time limits set to this aid. Furthermore, it wanted any extension of employment premiums limited to fresh investment projects, rather than allow them to be used across the board as a disguised form of regional devaluation.[16]

For its part, the UK wanted all of its hardcore special development areas, its development areas and its intermediate areas to be counted as EEC peripheral regions. If this were allowed, under EEC rules agreed to in October 1971, some 65 per cent of British land area and 55 per cent of the population could qualify for unlimited state aids subject only to Commission approval. If too much were conceded to Great Britain, there was a danger that several of the original six Community members, mainly Italy and France, might seek to extend the size of their own peripheral areas. Overbidding for footloose foreign investments by granting aids in undeserving regions might then start up again.[17]

With George Thomson as Commissioner for Regional Policy, new criteria were introduced for defining regions. They included rates of unemployment, regional income per head, and local emigration. All three raised the prospect of national governments gerrymandering boundaries inside which these statistics were calculated. Thomson also suggested that these criteria must be related to changes in the indicators in reference to the levels at which they were originally calculated as well as in reference to the over and undervaluation of currencies.[18]

The British government increased its pressure on the Commission when, in June 1973, Prime Minister Heath met with Albert Borschette, the Commissioner then responsible for competition policy. He indicated his government could fall if Britain did not get its way over the areas in which it was allowed by Brussels to give regional aids to industry unchecked. The Commission finally gave way by simply defining Britain's so-called central regions as all those that do not at present receive aid plus the intermediate areas where aids are generally too low to worry Brussels. All the rest of Britain would not be designated peripheral as was usual with other EEC states. This outcome meant that Britain would not only be exempted from the 20 per cent limit on net investment in plant and equipment that the Commission insisted on in EEC central regions, but that it would also not be subjected to the tests of transparency and specificity normally applied outside the central regions.[19] This concession had important ramifications for Community coordination of regional aid policies, since it led to the necessity of a reclassification of all central and peripheral regions. It also had implications for efforts to establish a Community regional policy fund, since the operation of such a fund was also dependent on the definition of regions. The Dutch, Danes and Germans had been arguing for as restricted a definition as possible, both for economic and political reasons.

GENERAL SUBSIDY SYSTEMS

Efforts to subject regional aid policy to controls concerning specificity of application and calculability of subsidy levels can be undermined through comprehensive national laws for fostering general economic growth, modernization of the national economy and restructuring of firms in difficulty. Such systems are likely to be applied to all enterprises regardless of sector or region, involve large sums of money and confer wide-ranging discretionary powers on national authorities.[20]

Many of the problems the Commission has faced with this kind of legislation have been similar to those it has had with regional aid systems. Legally, since these are general laws, they have no specific relationship to particular industries or regions. Consequently, they cannot qualify for derogations from the aid incompatibility rule provided for in Article 92, section 3 for aids designed to help the development of 'certain activities' or 'certain regions'. Next, the Commission has no way of determining on the basis of an examination of the rules governing such schemes what areas or sectors would benefit from aids, or when such systems might be applied. Thus it had no means of assessing their impact on competition and trade. Lastly, whereas a member state wishing to establish an aid scheme with a specific industrial or regional objective is subject to procedures outlined in Article 93, another state using a general aid system could pursue the same goal under cover of this law while escaping treaty provisions.

Since such general legislation involves fundamental prerogatives of the state, which needs such laws with wide discretionary powers without being bound in advance, the Commission is faced with a dilemma. How can it fulfill its legal responsibilities in an area that brings it into direct conflict with national sovereignty. In the face of this difficulty, the Commission has had to give ground. It has proposed two alternatives to the states: the competition policy directorate would allow such schemes to continue provided the states apply them in the future under programs having an individual industry or regional nature in line with treaty requirements on the specific character of subsidies. These programs would be defined gradually as needs emerged and submitted in advance to the Commission; or should states feel that they could not break down general aids into regional and sectoral ones, they might submit significant concrete cases in advance to the Commission.

The Commission has achieved acceptance of both of these points in principle. The Belgian draft law on economic expansion submitted to the competition policy directorate at the end of 1969 was challenged by the Commission as to the compatibility of the aid scheme with Article 92. The Belgian government agreed to revisions. In regard to such national institutions as the French Economic and Social Development Fund, the Dutch Nationale Investeringsbank, the French Institut de developpement industrielle and the Belgian Société Nationale d'investissement, the Commission has gained acceptance of the principle that governments will submit significant cases of application to the competition policy directorate for review and approval.

These principles do not preclude that in certain exceptional circumstances, the Commission will accept general aids for very short periods as outlined in Article 93, section 3b, when the aim is to remedy serious disturbances occuring in a member state's economy. An example of this was the Commission's approval in July 1971 of Italian government measures to deal with serious disequilibria. With the increased economic difficulties of the EEC member states, resort to this provision has become all the more attractive and, consequently, disruptive of the competition policy directorate's role and cooperation among the Nine.

APPLICATION OF ARTICLES 92–4 TO DIRECT AND INDIRECT STATE
INVOLVEMENT IN THE PRIVATE SECTOR

State involvement in economic activities by means of intermediary enterprises, practically or wholly controlled by public authorities, is an important component of modern European national economic systems. These include nationalized industries, state holding companies such as ENI and IRI, the French Economic and Social Development Fund, the British National Enterprise Board and the Dutch Nationale Investeringsbank. Although Article 222 of the Rome Treaty in no way prejudices state involvement in the private sector, how state controlled enterprises fit into the EEC customs union had become an increasing source of concern even before the economic downswing of the late 1960s. During the recession concern has intensified as the Nine have stepped up measures neither necessarily exclusively in the form of regional or sectoral aids, but also including the injection of additional funds into individual firms, notably in the form of loans or the acquisition of holdings.

The Commission is now working on a directive, based on Article 90,[21] to achieve these goals: (1) to make clear that the same rules of competition apply to state controlled enterprises as to independent companies; (2) to put the Commission in a better position to check on compliance with the treaty by member states operating through public undertakings; (3) and to make financial links more transparent, if not for the purpose of curbing subsidies at least to make the subsidy element more visible.[22]

Before he was forced to give up his post as a result of illness, Borschette had been thinking about provoking a test case possibly involving the Italian state holding companies ENI and IRI and the UK National Enterprise Board.[23] There had already been several Commission rulings in this area which are worth noting. In a 1972 decision on an Italian law to provide assistance to small and medium sized firms in financial difficulties, the Commission had an opportunity to define its position on the temporary acquisition of capital by financial agencies established by governments. Under the Italian law, the Instituto Mobilare Italiano could grant preferential credits or temporarily purchase holdings in firms adversely affected by difficulties in the Italian economy. In addition, the Gestione e Participazioni Industriale, which was set up by various semi-public groups (IRI, ENI, IMI and EFIM) under instructions from the Interministerial Committee for Economic Planning, could also acquire temporary holdings and grant credit with or without reduced interest rates. [24]

The Commission, in its decision, distinguished between temporary holdings and preferential credits. The latter were general aids, and, therefore, incompatible with Article 92. Nevertheless, in this case, the problems of the Italian economy warranted such aids 'to remedy a serious disturbance in the economy. of a member state.' However, in regard to temporary holdings, only *ex post facto* information could help the Commission determine whether the acquisition had had the effect of an aid. Thus the Commission required continuous monitoring of these subsidies. The Italian government would have to submit regular reports showing the firms which had benefited, their location, their economic and financial situation at the time of purchase, the terms of purchase, the manner in which the acquisitions were eventually liquidated, and how the firm's financial situation evolved during this period. If at the end of this process, it was determined that competition had been distorted, it is questionable whether the Commission would be able to take any corrective action. [25]

In addition, the Commission initiated action against the French Economic and Social Development Fund which grants loans on favorable terms. The goal was to subject it to one or the other control procedure outlined in the prior section: notification of programs for specific industries or failing this, notification of significant cases. The French government accepted the Commission request. In regard to the Netherlands, the Commission made a similar request concerning state guarantees through the Bijzondere Financierung which guarantees operations carried out by the Nationale Investeringsbank. The Dutch too acceded to the Commission's request.

SUBSIDIES GRANTED TO SPECIFIC SECTORS

Prior review of the provisions of general and regional aid systems is one thing, specific industries another. Such subsidies not only confront the Commission with the legal problem of determining an aid's compatibility with Article 92, but with either supporting or deterring a national economic policy. The problem is all the more acute with sectoral policies in which the industries which are to receive subsidies are known in advance. In addition to determining whether a subsidy will distort competition, the Commission is also faced with making an entrepreneurial judgement concerning the viability of a firm or a sector. But this not only requires an analysis of a firm's efficiency in the national context, but also in reference to the Common Market, and when necessary to the global economy.[26]

While a government will probably emphasize the difficulty of its domestic industry and seek a strictly domestic solution, from the Brussels perspective, one or more member states may have similar industries with the same problems. As with regional aids, competitive sectoral aids can neutralize one another, lead to unfair competition, or, if one country is more successful than another, shift the burden of adjustment to the weaker country's industry.[27] The number of sectors with one difficulty or another range from 'declining' to lead industries, and include shipbuilding, textiles, synthetic fibers, pulp and paper, steel, cars, computers, nuclear generators, uranium enrichment facilities, aircraft and telecommunications. The reasons for these problems vary from sector to sector, but difficulties frequently arise because modern states have similar structures of production. Productivity increases often exceed increase in demand in such sectors as textiles, shipbuilding and synthetic fibers, or in the case of lead industries, too many small states with inadequate domestic markets try to force the growth of large scale firms that can only survive through access to foreign markets.

Under these circumstances, the Commission cannot base its decisions on *ad hoc* criteria. Some general criteria are desirable, but this means broaching the problem of the *causes* of interstate sectoral conflicts as well as trying to mitigate the most immediate *effects*. Thus, the Commission has proposed several criteria for judging sectoral aids. They should be of a selective nature, and only granted to enterprises where there is a presumption that they will be competitive in the long run if allowed to reorganize. Sectoral subsidies should be sufficiently temporary and even digressive in order to speed up the re-entry of firms into the competitive market place. Aid simply to maintain a more competitive firm or sector and aid for plant operation must be excluded. In addition, these aids must be as transparent as possible, in order to permit an evaluation of their true incidence and their effectiveness with regard to the aims to be attained. Finally, they should be in a form which meets the objectives of national policy, while having the least possible negative effect on intra-Community cooperation and trade.

But such guidelines require the Nine member states to agree upon the parameters of a Community sectoral policy and the powers of the Commission. Commission rulings on national sectoral policies would mean the power to influence the contraction, expansion and distribution of industries as well as the capacity to block or foster mergers. In regard to mergers which lead to the establishment of large scale internationally competitive 'Community' firms, the competition policy directorate has had to rely on a combination of removing national obstacles to cross frontier concentration and market forces. To the extent that this has not produced restructuring and concentration on a Communitywide basis, those who have favored a dirigiste policy have had to attach their hopes to the powerless and ineffective industrial policy directorate set up in 1967. But this leaves the question open of whether the Commission's competition policy directorate can be the instrument through which to pursue a variety of structural policies. It would be useful to look at the role it has played in such sectors as textiles, shipbuilding, aircraft, computers and cars.

TEXTILES

Textiles, the prototypical declining sector in advanced industrial states has been the object of national policies for some time. In the 1960s the Community tried to limit subsidies which expand capacity and encourage those that reduce marginal production units.[28] On 30 July 1971, the Commission issued a memorandum for the coordination of member state aids for the textile sector. The memorandum excluded aids which directly affect price formation or support current operating expenses. Aid for investment would only be permissible for modernization and reconversion which did not increase overall capacity, or distort competition among Community firms. In those cases such as the various British plans for retrenchment in the wool and cotton textile sectors, the Commission has simply to respond favorably to initiatives taken by member states. If member states take no initiatives or firms have access to private sources of capital, the Commission is powerless to act. Moreover, efforts to reduce capacity in the declining part of the textile sector, namely natural fibers, have been undermined by growth in the expanding part, synthetic fibers. The growth of synthetic fibers has led to a rejuvenation of the European textile industry and, in turn, structural problems have developed in the chemical sector. Finally, efforts to control or mitigate the impact of international competition on EEC firms led to the Commission signing the Long Term Arrangement on Cotton Textiles during the 1960s and becoming a signatory to its successor the Multifiber Agreement which also includes wool and synthetic textiles. Thus, internally, the Commission has pressed for restructuring and rationalization and externally it has participated in 'stabilizing' international competition through membership in the Multifiber Arrangement and the negotiation of 'voluntary' export limitation agreements with advanced states such as Japan, and developing states such as India.

SHIPBUILDING

During the 1960s the Commission had concluded that distorted conditions of competition in world markets had been and continue to be one of the decisive reasons for the decline of the EEC shipbuilding sector. Since shipyards must build for a world market, resort to traditional protectionist instruments was not possible, both because of GATT obligations and the possibility of retaliation. In 1966 the Commission proposed a dual policy of negotiating an international agreement and rationalizing productive capacity in the EEC. Since shipyards are often located in declining areas, a sectoral policy would also involve a regional development dimension.

The Commission submitted a draft regulation to the Council of Ministers in 1965. This was only adopted in July 1969, and fixed the ceiling of national aid granted shipbuilding at 10 per cent of the selling price, a percentage which was felt to correspond to the prejudice suffered by Community shipyards in relation to non-EEC competitors. Simultaneously the EEC began participating in OECD negotiations to tackle directly the problem of world overcapacity. A second directive issued in 1971 lowered the subsidy to 4 per cent of the selling price but the Nine could not reach agreement on a third directive in 1973. In its draft the Commission asked for greater powers to deal with structural problems. This included the elimination of direct aids and their gradual replacement by subsidies to investments, which moreover would have to be notified in advance to the Commission if above a certain threshold. The Commission also wanted its authority expanded to include a greater variety of subsidies such as cost increase guarantees. Neither the French nor British governments were pleased with this draft. The second directive was extended, and the third directive which finally came into force on 10 July 1975 did little more than prevent the introduction of new forms of direct aid, but nothing to eliminate existing subsidies. The Commission had attempted to tie the third directive to an EEC 'industrial policy' for reducing capacity and rationalizing the remaining shipyards.[29]

LEAD SECTORS

Initially, the competition policy directorate took a fairly orthodox approach to national subsidies to encourage the development of lead sectors. Subsidies *per se* were incompatible with the Common Market, particularly if they distorted intra-Community competition. However, with the increasing recognition that large scale internationally competitive 'Community' firms were not evolving either through voluntary cross frontier mergers between private firms or through national efforts to create 'national champions', the competition policy directorate reversed itself. This reversal was partly a response to the establishment of the industrial policy directorate which attempted to develop sectoral plans for such industries as aircraft and computers. In both of these sectors, the industrial policy directorate searched for strategies which would either induce private firms to merge or influence member states to give up the pursuit of uneconomical national undertakings and cooperate with other member states. Since the industrial policy directorate had no instruments of note, it had to rely on rulings from competition policy officials. Thus, the competition directorate ruled that national aids to production and export of aircraft were legal as a result of Article 92, section 3b which permitted aid to promote the execution of an important project of common European interest. Aids could be either for suppliers or purchasers, be long-term credits with or without interest rebates, insurance against commercial risk, or guarantees against exchange rate fluctuations. However, the Commission attached a very important condition to this decision. Governments could only grant such aids if they facilitated joint cooperation among aircraft firms, particularly in regard to planning to improve the international position of this sector. A similar condition imposed on national aids to the computer industry influenced the formation of UNIDATA by Siemens, Philips and Companie Internationale Informatique.[30]

These exceptions to traditional competition policy did not have the desired effect. UNIDATA collapsed, and the French firm CII turned to Honeywell. In the aircraft sector the major British, French and Italian firms preferred American to European partners. These developments revealed another limitation on national and Community structural policies. Community policy was based upon the assumption that the EEC constituted the most desirable geopolitical and geoeconomic unit, a view not necessarily shared either by firms or governments.[31]

AUTOMOBILES

In the midst of the recession, several major EEC automobile firms simultaneously experienced difficulties. Demand had dropped precipitously causing major cyclical problems, but, in addition, many deep-seated structural difficulties became more visible. Among them were the interrelated issues of overproduction and lack of competitiveness. The French, British and German governments responded to pleas for aid which came from Citroen, Leyland, and Volkswagen.[32] The French government granted a loan of 1 billion French francs through the ECSF at a rate of 9.75 per cent for a duration of fifteen years. It was to be used to bring about a link with Peugeot. The British aid package was more complicated, since it involved a total amount of £900 million to be granted between 1975 and 1978. It included a maximum of £200 million in the form of a financial guarantee together with a majority equity stake of a further £200 million, and a long-term loan of £500 million at the normal market rate. The German government resorted to regional policy measures to assist the areas affected by increased unemployment as a result of redundancies in the Volkswagen group. The budgetary resources to be made available over a period of three years amounted to 210 million German marks. The Commission would have preferred a major contraction in the size of this sector including national policies of voluntary adjustment of employment levels. It was also concerned about the extent to which these subsidies would distort trade within the Common Market. The competition policy directorate was hampered in judging these measures, since they were vague, as a Commission spokesman indicated, in regard to the details for restructuring and reorganization. However, given the significance of this sector as well as the fact that the UK referendum on continued EEC membership was to take place on 5 June, the Commission had no choice but to reluctantly approve these aids in a decision taken on 29 May 1975. At the end of the year, Albert Borschette did raise extremely strong objections against the British government's bailout scheme for Chrysler. But the other Commissioners outvoted him, fearful of a showdown and worried that the British might ignore a veto.

CONCLUSIONS

THE EFFECTIVENESS OF AN EEC SUBSIDY POLICY

In discussing the development of an EEC subsidy policy considerable emphasis has been placed upon the delineation of the Commission's formal jurisdiction, the establishment of evaluative criteria and specific cases. However, since the Community is a complex multistate organization, an analysis of the effectiveness and long range viability of a subsidy policy administered by a regional secretariat requires more than the definition of legal norms and a study of particular instances where they have been applied. The relationship of these norms to the dynamic political and economic relationships among the member states and between the states and the Commission must be examined. Only then will it be possible to determine those broad conditions that either contribute to or detract from a consensus about the Commission's role as the interpreter of the Treaty's subsidy provisions, as well as the extent to which general rules can be applied equally to all of the nine member states.

In the first place, the extent to which the Nine will agree to abide by general rules on subsidies which are equally applicable to all of the states not only depends upon the specific industry involved or the conflict between supranationalism and intergovernmentalism. An even more basic consideration is the overall economic relationships of the Nine to each other, as well as how they perceive their individual relationships to the global economy. This, of course, is the central factor which determines the stability of the EEC and the degree of cooperation among the member states. If there are major divergences among the member states in growth rates and the evolution of patterns of production, there will be increased resistance to the Commission exercising the power it has, much less expanding its authority into new areas. The role of the Commission has been weakened as the Community has split into a two tier system of states which are economically strong such as Germany and those which have become chronically weak such as Italy and the United Kingdom. The weak states have increased their pressure on the Commission to make exceptions in the application of Treaty commitments not only because of the impact of the recession but because of the long range macro- and micreconomic problems faced by these states. Thus, the degree to which general rules, such as those on subsidies, can be applied evenly to all of the member states, depends on several factors. The Nine must either be roughly equal in terms of their level of economic development; or perceive their relative inequalities as not affecting their interests and ability to support general rules; or see their long run economic development as being positive and acceptable in terms of continued membership in a customs union.

Article 92 attempts to take into account the possibility that exceptions to EEC subsidy policy may be necessary from time to time. In fact, regional policy, by its nature, is a recognition that certain designated areas of the Community, are subject to specific and exceptional provisions concerning national subsidy policies. While Article 92 can provide a basis for temporary and occasional digressions from treaty provisions, it does not deal with those cases where member states may feel compelled to opt out of their reciprocal commitments, or ask for special exemptions for all or major parts of their economy.

Such national difficulties can be projected directly into the Commission and the competition policy directorate. As a result of Borschette who had a reputation as a crusading economic liberal being replaced in 1976 first by Thomson and then by the Luxembourger Raymond Vouel, there was a change in some of the directions pursued by the directorate. For instance, Thomson rejected three separate recommendations from the directorate's staff that the Commission should attack parts of the British government's plan to aid industry. The first recommended that the Commission veto the UK's National Enterprise Board plan to provide money to machine tool makers, the second that it ask the British government to amend proposals to aid the textile machinery industry, and the third that it should get Britain to think again about aiding manufacturers of paper and printing machinery. Thus, Thomson fought the battle for the British government against the competition department's free market officials. He was also among the Commissioners who rejected the department's advice that the UK bailout of Chrysler be banned.

Thomson's role was accidental as a result of Borschette's illness, and he was replaced by Vouel. But both Thomson and Vouel are Socialists in contrast to Borschette, and this has raised some concern that as a result of their political preferences they are suspicious of a policy which has been so overtly dedicated to promoting free competition. There were some indications that Vouel seems less bothered about stopping the state aids to industry which have multiplied throughout the Nine during the recession. But his reluctance may be explained partly by the fact that a new Commission was to take office on 1 January 1977, and he was interested in retaining his position. However, the political leaning of the EEC Commissioner responsible for competition policy toward state subsidies is not a secondary matter.

A further consideration affecting EEC subsidy policy is the effect that enlargement to include Greece, and potentially Spain and Portugal, may have on existing Community policies on regional, sectoral and general aid schemes. The admission of Greece as a full member will greatly increase the range of economic disparities with which the Commission must deal. In fact, the different levels of development between Greece and the other Common Market states is already recognized in certain exceptions contained in the present association agreement. And if Greece were to become a full member of the Community, all of the country with the possible exception of the Athens/Pireus area would be designated a peripheral region under existing EEC practice.

The rules developed by the competition policy directorate, whether for regional or sectoral subsidies, are principally efforts to coordinate the means used by states to influence investment patterns and to exercise some control over the goals to which they are used, when possible: for example, influencing the reduction of capacity in the textile sector. But regional and industrial policies are in part pursued by governments because reliance on markets alone does not necessarily lead to the distribution of investments, industries and ultimately growth, in patterns which are geographically and politically acceptable. But the question of the fair or acceptable distribution of investments, industry and growth is the Achilles heel of a customs union, or any liberal economic system for that matter. In regard to the competition policy directorate, subsidy policy is mainly a passive instrument through which to influence distribution. Although the EEC Regional Development Fund and the guidance section of the agricultural fund are supposed to be available for active policies to influence structure, adequate compensatory EEC policies involving sufficiently large resource transfers as an augmentation to improving markets and influencing industrial structure in a general way are nonexistent. Thus the resort to subsidies by the Nine must be understood both as a response to strictly domestic pressures as well as a reaction to the relative competitive positions of one state to another. Increased disparities among the member states of the EEC will make it all the more difficult to rely on formal rules to improve competition or influence the use of subsidies, if the economic and political results are unacceptable.

Next, it is necessary to recognize how the reasons for subsidy policies have changed or how they differ among states at varying levels of economic development. The subsidy issue has generally been discussed as a simple form of unwarranted protectionism, as part of the infant industry problem, or in regard to that stage of industrialization when growth in the manufacturing and service sectors requires transfer of workers out of agriculture. However, for most of the EEC member states, which now have very small agricultural populations, there are two new factors. We are dealing with advanced, highly industrialized states in which the problem is not one of industrialization, but of moving to a new generation of industries upon which continued growth can be based. This is a major political problem, because it also includes the relative strength of a state *vis a vis* other states. And if, as Ohlin has noted, population growth has slowed and additional workers are not to be gained from further reductions in the agricultural sector, all structural change must be accomplished by more contraction in weak sectors, if manpower is to be steered to the expanding sectors. Expanding sectors, in turn, must be able to force other industries or services to relinquish some of their factors of production. But what happens when a group of states faces the same constellation of problems simultaneously, with private sectors of varying strengths, economies with different growth rates, and governments more or less prepared to intervene in influencing markets. National policies must be seen in part as depending on what other governments and national industries are doing in response to similar problems.

A related dimension influencing the development of national subsidy policies is the effect a customs union has on comparative advantage and industrial structure. According to theory some degree of complementary intra-regional specialization should have occurred. On the contrary, like other OECD states the Nine have tended to imitate each others' patterns of production, and instead of comparative advantage being based on complementary specialization, it has been based on product differentiation. During the 1960s, a period of rapid economic expansion, in several important sectors productivity often outstripped demand. With the onset of a severe recession, the underlying structural problem of overcapacity, both within the EEC and on a global basis in many of the sectors which have been discussed in this paper, became highly visible. Obviously, it is impossible for all states to expand simultaneously, and contraction also presents difficulties. In this context, the competition policy directorate is in a very exposed position, if it must play a significant role in limiting expansion or influencing contraction. It is one thing to free some factors of production through contraction, it is another to ensure that they flow into new, more productive areas. Liberal theory has dealt extensively with the first problem, and very little with the second. But the second has become increasingly important not only because attention is shifting from focusing entirely on negative trade effects of subsidy policies to dealing with sectoral changes, but because many of the advanced states will attempt to improve their growth rates by shoring up the same existing industries and encouraging the development of similar new industries.

From a strictly welfare economics viewpoint, it is possible to see regional and industrial policies as a means to maintain and improve income and employment levels. It is also correct to note that a policy which is essentially conservative is not likely to foster growth and change, and it is also essential to ask whether the particular form of intervention chosen achieves an economic goal at the least cost. But while it would be ideal if policy could be formulated in terms of strict economic considerations, such policies may either be limited by or collide with other factors that weigh upon policymakers. Freeing factors of production to move from inefficient sectors to more productive ones may have political implications which governments are not prepared to deal with. The migration of workers from the Mezzogiorno to the north of Italy has had a major impact on the alignment of political parties. The British Labor Government's bailout for Chrysler involved saving a subsidiary located in Scotland, a move which can be explained by Labor's fear of losing voters to increased nationalism in Scotland. The efforts to shake up ENI and IRI which are major contributors to the inefficiency of the Italian economy will unsettle those parentella/clientella relationships that provide some modicum of stability in Italy. While such a change is desirable, destabilizing what exists without being clear about what a new political balance will look like or whether it is possible, is counterproductive. And in the case of France, the reluctance to allow the Commission to reduce government control over shipbuilding, computers or aircraft is part and parcel of a national policy to ensure, if not French pre-eminence, at least eminence in these sectors.

The competition policy directorate's right to review new legislation in advance of passage and modification of existing aid schemes has led to the continuous examination of major national legislation on a multilateral basis. This has required the elaboration of legal and economic criteria for evaluating the compatibility of national programs with

Rome Treaty obligations. The positive benefits of this process are evident in the effective pressure which can be exerted on the member states to reduce the vagueness of their aid schemes. This includes being precise about the conditions under which subsidies will be granted, the degree to which aid levels are made visible and calculable, and the extent to which governments' discretionary powers to implement subsidy schemes are subject to some limitation and control. In addition, EEC level discussions of regional and sectoral subsidies force intra-Community comparisons, and compel states to consider their goals in reference to similar ends pursued by other EEC members.

The order and comparability introduced into national legislation can be supplemented by those instances in which the competition policy directorate is empowered to make decisions on individual cases. The general pressure the directorate can exert on states to consider the economic rationale of subsidy legislation, becomes more specific in particular cases. In these instances, the competition policy directorate as a result of its power to approve or disapprove subsidies can influence the expansion, contraction and reorganization of various sectors. It is essential to note, however, as the examples cited in this paper illustrate, that the Commission is not always politically in a position to act in those areas in which it has the legal right.

Finally, the Commission can represent the Nine in international negotiations that deal with the problems of particular sectors such as ships and textiles. As in the case of trade negotiations, by acting collectively, the Nine may be in a better bargaining position. Moreover, as the Kennedy Round demonstrated, the Nine collectively are probably more prepared to negotiate liberalizing agreements, although in the case of national industrial policies and state subsidies, this may not be the case.

THE EEC AND EFTA MODELS AND THE GATT

Many observers feel that the EFTA model is much more directly relevant to the substantive and institutional problems involved in reforming GATT Articles VI and XVI. There are several important differences between the Community and the GATT which are cited to support this view. Unlike the GATT which is a flexible, multistate organization with the limited goal of ensuring continued trade liberalization through the reduction of tariffs and quotas, the EEC is an effort to move beyond regional trade liberalization to form a supranational entity with common political institutions and economic policies. Consequently, the two organizations are fundamentally different in structure and purpose, since the GATT's goal is to achieve economic benefits for its members with the least pooling of sovereignty necessary.

Moreover, even if it were desirable for the GATT to have a strong role in dealing with subsidies, the EEC Commission has considerably stronger economic and political powers because of the obligations imposed upon the nine member states by the Rome Treaty. Both the treaty and the geographic contiguity of the member states has created a framework which provides considerable support for central institutions to develop and enforce policies on the Nine. In regard to subsidies, the treaty provisions for competition policy are quite important, and in particular, Article 95 empowers the Commission to review national legislation in advance of passage as well as to approve or disapprove the granting of subsidies in individual cases.

In contrast, the goals and structure of EFTA seem much closer to those of the GATT. The Stockholm Treaty established a free trade area in industrial products, but did not include agriculture or require the signatories to agree to a common external tariff. EFTA has been described as being flexible and pragmatic, particularly because it has assumed economic benefits could be gained without loss of national sovereignty.

However, there has been a high degree of convergence in EFTA toward the Rome Treaty view on competition policy and subsidies. As Middleton has observed:[33]

> There has been increasing acceptance by the EFTA member states, first of the fact that effective cooperation in the free trade area requires a greater sacrifice of sovereignty than they had envisaged at the outset and, second, that the acceptance of further-reaching obligations in the area of non-tariff distortions of trade, brings with it the need for effective supervision of compliance by the EFTA organs (and, not least, that the Secretariat must be adequately equipped to assist this supervisory activity).

In other words, dealing with tariffs and quotas alone is insufficient. A free trade area is in danger of moving backward unless these other issues are addressed. Nowhere has a shift in view been more marked than the British position before and after joining the European Community.

Although Articles 13–14 of the EFTA Convention deal with subsidies, the usefulness of the association's experience for the GATT is open to question. There was only one major case involving state aids, British subsidies to the aluminum industry, and after nearly a decade of discussion the results were inconclusive. Moreover, the few conflicts in this area may have been a result of the structure of EFTA. Of the original seven members only one has aspired to have a 'complete economy', the United Kingdom, while the others were highly specialized and thus by and large complementary to the UK economy. Finally, the subjects of industrial restructuring and distribution were not broached.

For want of more elaborate practices and criteria, EFTA members have relied on the frustration clause[34] of the Stockholm Agreement. While useful in the early years of the association when great flexibility was desirable, in the long run its general wording has left too much open to interpretation. And in any event, now that the United Kingdom has joined the Common Market, it is no longer joined by treaty to complementary, but to competitive economies.

EEC experience with Article 92–4 is indicative of the kinds of problems involved in revising Articles VI and XVI of the GATT to encompass the causes as well as effects of national subsidy policies. Whether an international organization has the requisite authority and legitimacy to imitate the practices of a regional one is unclear, particularly since the Community has had to cut into an area traditionally protected by national sovereignty. Even if there are limits to regional or international regulation of subsidies, EEC policies on classifying, clarifying and examining them are directly relevant to the reform of the GATT articles. Commission procedures have had the salutary effect of placing the policies of the nine EEC member states under multilateral scrutiny and pressure. Without attempts to do this, there will be no counterweight against the continued proliferation of subsidies, and efforts to find solutions will gravitate to other fora. As in the case of shipbuilding, states will try to force settlements on the basis of some notion of 'fair shares'.

Notes and References

1. See pp. 100–101 and 116–117 for discussions of this proposal.
2. For the full text see Appendix D. Articles 90 and 222 are also relevant and are discussed on pp. 156–60.
3. This provision has been the basis for most of the measures taken under such legislation as the French Fourth Plan or the economic development policies of the German Laender.
4. The complete section reads as follows: 'Any aid to shipbuilding existing on 1 January 1957 shall, to the extent that such aid merely offsets the absence of customs protection, be gradually reduced under the same conditions as apply to the abolition of customs and duties, subject to the provisions of this Treaty relating to the common commercial policy in regard to third countries.'
5. For an early authoritative statement see Hans von der Groeben, 'Policy on Competition in the European Community', in *Bulletin of the European Community* (Brussels: Nos. 7–8, 1961).
6. A record of the directorate's activities for the period 1959–70 will be found under the heading 'Competition' in the *Bulletin of the European Community* for those years.
7. Hans von der Groeben, *Handbuch für Europäische Wirtschaft* (Baden-Baden: Lutzeyer, 1975, 132 Lieferung), p. 220.

8. Written question no. 48, 27 June, 1963. *Official Journal of the European Community* (No. 125, 17 August, 1963), p. 2235.

9. For a thorough discussion of the various interpretations and applications of Articles 92–4 see von der Groeber, *Handbuch, op. cit.*

10. Commission of the European Community, *First Report on Competition Policy* (Brussels: April, 1972), pp. 112–6.

11. See P. S. R. F. Mathijsen, *A Guide to European Community Law* (London: Street and Maxwell, 1975), p. 130.

12. Steven J. Warnecke, 'Industrial Policy and the European Community' in Steven J. Warnecke and Ezra N. Suleiman, *Industrial Policies in Western Europe* (New York: Praeger, 1975).

13. *First Report on Competition Policy, op. cit.*, p. 116 ff.

14. *Official Journal of the European Community*, C111, 3 November 1971, p. 1 ff.

15. Regional aid cases are summarized in the reports on competition policy which first started appearing in 1971.

16. Commission of the European Community, *Third Report on Competition policy* (Brussels: May, 1974), pp. 76–8.

17. *The Economist*, 12 May, 1973, p. 56; 21 April, 1973, pp. 55–60; and 26 May 1973, p. 61.

18. *The Economist*, 17 March 1973, p. 56.

19. *The Economist*, 30 June 1973, p. 54.

20. Commission policies on general subsidy schemes are discussed under that heading in the various reports on competition policy starting with the first one in 1971.

21. Article 90 states: Member States shall in respect to public enterprises and enterprises to which they grant special or exclusive rights, neither enact nor maintain in force any measure contrary to the rules contained in this Treaty, in particular, to those rules provided for in Article 7 and in Articles 85–94 inclusive.

22. *The Economist*, 10 July 1976, p. 67.

23. *The Economist*, 15 May 1976, p. 75.

24. Commission of the European Community, *Third Report on Competition Policy* (Brussels: May, 1974), pp. 96–7.

25. Commission of the European Community, *Second Report on Competition Policy* (Brussels: April, 1975), pp. 106–9.

26. Commission policies on subsidies to specific sectors are discussed under that heading in the various reports on competition policy.

27. It should be noted that French industrial policy of the late 1950s and 1960s was motivated partly by a desire to have large French controlled firms in key sectors as a balance against German industry, a basis for national independence, and an instrument for ensuring continued economic growth.

28. Camille Blum, 'The Textile Policy of the European Community' in Warnecke and Suleiman, *op. cit.*

29. European Report, no. 193, 11 Dec 1974, no. 244, 2 July 1975, and no. 247, 12 July 1975. See also Commission of the European Community, *Fifth Report on Competition Policy* (Brussels: April 1976), pp. 76–7.

30. See *Second Report on Competition Policy, op. cit.*, pp. 89–95.

31. John Zysman, 'French Electronics Policy: The Costs of Technological

Independence' in Warnecke and Suleiman, *op. cit.*

32. *European Report*, no. 226, 26 Apr 1975 and no. 235, 31 May 1975.

33. Robert Middleton, *Negotiating on Non-Tariff Distortions of the Trade: The EFTA Precedents* (London: Macmillan, 1975), p. 160.

34. Article 31, section 1 reads: 'If any Member State considers that any benefit conferred upon it by this Convention or any objective of the Association is being or may be frustrated and if no satisfactory settlement is reached between the Member States concerned, any of those Member States may refer the matter to the Council.'

8 Subsidies and other International Economic Issues

WILLIAM DIEBOLD, JR.

How broadly to define subsidies and how narrowly to limit the range of practices one tries to deal with by international agreement are major questions that run through the other chapters in this volume. The difficulty of believing that there will soon be widespread agreement on concrete rules covering many different kinds of subsidies could lead to the conclusion that one should concentrate on establishing principles even if practice develops more slowly. This entails the question of whether such principles should apply to all international arrangements touching subsidies, even if they deal mainly with such broader matters as international investment, economic development or the problems of certain troublesome industries.

Most of the contributions to this book concern subsidies in national industrial policies and their relationship to international trade negotiations. But efforts to work out global agreements on a wide range of other subjects must, at least part of the time, deal with government aids to industry. Since subsidies, in one form or another, are ubiquitous, serious efforts to deal with them through international action are almost certain to be quite selective, particularly in regard to the kinds and aspects of them which might be regulated multilaterally as well as the forums in which they are handled.

This chapter is concerned with how these issues intersect. The central question it examines might be put so: how do efforts to reach international agreements on such subjects as coordination of macroeconomic policies, investment and multinational enterprises, industrial policy and north/south relations affect what is done about subsidies in such places as the GATT, and vice versa? If not only explores, in rather general terms, several areas of negotiation in which subsidy issues will arise, but also covers key problems caused by the principles of selection that are applied. These include which kinds and aspects of subsidies might be dealt with by arrangements which have quite a different major purpose from that of the GATT; whether separate and parallel efforts are desirable; and whether these will lead to conflicting standards or can be made to complement and reinforce one another? In addition, it also considers the implications that the choice and availability of institutional settings may have for concluding agreements, particularly as it permits flexibility in negotiating on this complex issue. Thus a problem which was intractable as an isolated subsidy issue, leading for example, to a persistent use of countervailing duties, might be more amenable if approached in a different framework such as a sectoral negotiation. In somewhat similar vein, one can imagine that countries which are not prepared to commit themselves to a set of propositions about all kinds of subsidies, whether in the GATT or elsewhere, would look differently on commitments about specific kinds of subsidies made as part of an agreement that involves related practices as well.

An equally serious problem which affects the legitimacy and effectiveness of multilateral agreements is who the participants are. Much of the time, different sets of countries are involved in negotiating about different issues. The second part of this chapter briefly examines some of the implications of this fact. For example, what difference does it make if some changes are made in GATT rules that apply to all signatories while the OECD countries work out arrangements on additional points among themselves? Suppose several sets of north/south arrangements about multinational corporations and, say, the location of processing industries in effect regulate the use of subsidies in still other ways. Is it better to be pragmatic about reaching some agreements among a limited number of countries or to insist on broader arrangements? Are there subjects that can be adequately dealt with if only a few countries commit themselves to certain arrangements? Are such practices likely to damage outsiders?

Thus the emphasis on intersections in the following pages is a reminder that if governments fail to agree on rules about subsidies or abandon the effort as too difficult, they will nevertheless find themselves having to deal with the same subsidy issues in the course of coping with a host of other problems.

FIELDS OF NEGOTIATIONS

There is no need here to elaborate on the many things said in other chapters on the relation of subsidies to other aspects of trade negotiations.[1] Questions about the monetary system as a whole and possible directions of further reform lie farther afield than we need go. However, the matter of flexible exchange rates (or the lack of them) will turn up from time to time as it does elsewhere in this book. That leaves four fields to which this section is addressed: the coordination of macroeconomic policies; international investment and the multinational corporation; some possibilities of international negotiation about industrial policy that go beyond what others have considered and finally, the whole complex of north-south relations.

COORDINATION OF MACROECONOMIC POLICIES

The record of the industrial countries in trying to coordinate their macroeconomic policies is a mixed one. Inability to keep their economies in line or to accept parallel trade-offs of inflation and unemployment has been a major factor frustrating efforts at monetary unification in the European Community. Working Party Three of the OECD has for years provided unprecedented opportunities for key officials to exchange information on policies, plans and expectations. This work seems to have had a serious influence in some periods as have the frequent discussions among bankers at Basle and elsewhere. At other times, and perhaps more often than not, domestic pressures have outweighed these efforts and separate national responses to the inflationary forces of the early 70s swamped coordination. However, the rather frightening impact of the oil crisis of 1973 with its threat of almost universal balance of payments deficits and the accompanying problem of recycling petrodollars made all governments aware of the importance of acting together at least to avoid the worst results of conflicting policies. Subsequently high level meetings in Rambouillet in 1975 and Puerto Rico in 1976 stressed the need to work along similar lines to overcome recession. Soon after the change of administration in the United States at the beginning of 1977, the signals from Washington stressed the key parts the United States, Germany and Japan could play in sustaining the recovery that had started, even if other countries could not move as fast. For the long-run future there is no doubt that continued economic cooperation among the interdependent industrial countries will put an even higher premium than in the past on the coordination of macroeconomic policies.

On the face of it, subsidies might be thought to have no part in these activities. They are, essentially, microeconomic devices focusing on structure and not on the business cycle. Still, governments when they feel themselves in trouble about unemployment, prices or the level of economic activity, are very likely to see in subsidies means of dealing with a number of urgent matters such as holding down key prices, underwriting employment, keeping some industries in operation, promoting exports or checking imports. Individual firms, even individual plants, will sometimes be the targets. Distinctions will fade between macro and micro devices, between structural and cyclical aims.

Inevitably, such practices will sometimes frustrate one another. What one country seeks to achieve another will try to avoid. The risk of retaliation arises. This was recognized at the outset of the oil crisis in May 1974 when the OECD countries made a pledge not to deal with their balance of payments problems by measures that would push the burden of adjustment on others. The resulting effort which was quite successful was thought of largely in terms of avoiding import restrictions and competitive devaluations. But in principle it applied just as much to any measures that would have produced the same results, such as export subsidies. This insurance against untoward results is something less than positive coordination of macroeconomic policies, in which most economists are likely to feel that subsidies should have no part at all since governments should be concerned with aggregate supply and demand and not structural matters. However, for the reason already suggested, that preference is not likely to be satisfied, at least when governments are having a difficult time. Moreover existing subsidy practices are likely to carry through abnormal as well as normal times. It seems prudent, then, to think of how subsidies might be treated in these circumstances.

Perhaps something along the following lines would cover the problem. Ordinarily, subsidies would not be used for macroeconomic purposes. In times of cyclical difficulty normal rules about subsidies should continue to apply. If the problem is general, it may be necessary to reinforce commitments of the sort described above to avoid beggar my neighbor practices. If a country with serious inflation or unemployment or both feels the need to introduce new subsidies to deal with these difficulties, it should consult other countries in the group with the aim of getting them to agree not to retaliate or seek to offset the effects of these subsidies. A process of consultation seems preferable to an effort to devise an automatic procedure, such as that a country should be free to subsidize once its unemployment or inflation hits a certain rate. Differential treatment, of countries and practices, seems likely to be the heart of the matter. In 1977, for example, Britain and Italy might be permitted to use some kinds of subsidies with impunity but not the United States or Germany. There would be a presumption in favor of subsidies that clearly held up employment but not if they did it by pushing exports into other countries' markets. Measures aimed at staving off the bankruptcy of firms or the contraction of work in whole areas would ordinarily be left mostly to the judgement of the government concerned but other countries would have the right to complain if the action damaged them.[2] When matters go back to normal, exceptional subsidy measures should be dropped.

This rough formula assumes that there is a certain amount of international agreement about subsidies. The less agreement, the less use these guidelines are. However, the prescription here is a relatively simple one since the coordination of macroeconomic policies is a process, not something that can be very well defined by a set of rules. The exchange rate regime is also involved. When governments are not willing to see the rates move, the pressures on them to use subsidies increase. Agreements about how flexible rates should be managed—or even about the processes by which agreement should be reached—will have a good bit to do with the effectiveness of efforts to coordinate macroeconomic policies. For a variety of reasons this is a sphere of action in which the question is mainly what degree of cooperation can be achieved among the industrial countries with market economies.

INVESTMENT AND THE MULTINATIONAL ENTERPRISE

There are no comprehensive international agreements about investment. The subject is dealt with piecemeal in such vehicles as bilateral treaties covering establishment, national treatment, etc; tax treaties; a few multilateral codes (OECD, Andean Pact) and occasional other instruments. By far the most important regulation of foreign investment is through the laws, policies and procedures of host countries under which specific agreements may also be worked out between companies and the government. Regulation by the home government of investors plays a certain part and may be of increasing importance.

There are proposals for more comprehensive agreements about investments and multinationals—a GATT for investment, the various conventions that may be drafted by the UN Centre and Commission on Transnational Corporations, etc. There will undoubtedly also be more modest efforts to deal with parts of the problem, probably more tax treaties, perhaps measures to increase transparency of transfer prices and maybe a code limiting what inducements governments may offer foreign corporations. Many different countries are involved. Both developing countries and highly industrialized ones often offer inducements to foreign firms to invest; the United States, Canada, Japan and most western European countries are the homes of most multinational enterprises, but the international activities of firms based in developing countries are growing.

Subsidies play an important part in the investment pattern—or at least they are believed to. Tax concessions of many sorts are often given to foreign firms; sometimes this is part of a regional development arrangement and sometimes it results from competition among jurisdictions within a country (as in the bidding among American states for the Volkswagen plant in 1976). Once established, foreign firms may benefit from still other national subsidy programs. Their activities may have been designed for that purpose; their commitments to export, provide employment, train local technicians, etc may all rest on such expectations. Taxation in the home country has to take account of all these matters and may itself be seen as a source of subsidy if, as is often the case, it gives preferred treatment to operations abroad. In both home and host countries firms may be given government financing or guarantees which in various ways may lower the firm's costs or risks and thus amount to a subsidy.

It is hard to imagine an international agreement on subsidies—at least in the foreseeable future—that will cover all these practices. Some however are almost sure to be affected and if there are agreements on principles with procedures to apply them to cases, the potential coverage is much larger. It is equally hard to imagine agreements on international investment which do not say something about many of these arrangements. It may well be, as many people think, that the area of agreement is too small and the opportunities to work out advantageous arrangements too great for any comprehensive agreement to be expected for some time to come. But there surely will be bargains and negotiations among sovereigns and between them and entrepreneurs that will have a bearing on many forms of subsidy. The question arises in one way or the other whether what is done under one approach is consistent with what is done under another, and if not, what the consequences will be.

INDUSTRIAL POLICY

Many of the difficulties in dealing with subsidies arise from the fact that they are important instruments of national industrial policies. This means they are used in many ways, usually in conjunction with other measures and in pursuit of ends that governments feel are important. These ends may be very broad-gauged and far-sighted or they may be very immediate, perhaps the result of past short-sightedness; they may be part of a large vision or plan for shaping the economy as a whole, or they may be the result of a particular set of political pressures that a government feels it has to satisfy without regard for the full impact on the rest of the economy. The aim may be to create strong new industries which will be competitive in world markets but much more often industrial policies are efforts to shore up old and weak parts of the economy or, at best, to tide them over a period of transition.

Whatever the case, the circumstances make it difficult to make general rules about subsidies as such. The same difficulty has already been encountered in dealing with tariffs and quotas where the failures to achieve liberalization often involve sectors of an economy that are for one reason or another being treated by a number of governments as the objects of industrial policies. Non-tariff barriers and related practices—the family to which subsidies belong—are often used for purposes which can no longer be pursued by imposing new tariffs or quotas. The investment policies mentioned in the last section are to a considerable extent rooted in industrial policies, whether broadly or narrowly conceived.

There is little doubt that a failure to find satisfactory means of handling industrial policy issues will be a major setback to economic cooperation. It may well lead to the undoing of past accomplishments. Unfortunately it is far from clear how this is to be done.[3] In a sense, that is the subject of much of this book. This section simply sketches several different approaches and suggests how they might affect subsidy questions.

One possible approach is to think of drawing up (at least for a few countries) some general rules about industrial policy. The trouble with this is that it is very difficult to be reasonably concrete, even as to objectives. Countries want many different things from their industrial policies and their aims change over time. One might be able to arrive at some principles which could be taken as guidance whenever a complaints procedure showed that what one country was doing for domestic purposes had a serious impact on another. The proper (or improper) use of subsidies would undoubtedly be a central issue in such an approach, but it would usually be judged according to circumstances, not just as a permitted or forbidden practice.

An alternative approach would be to say that because industrial policy is so protean, it is impossible to think of 'rules' applying to the subject in general. Therefore the thing to do would be to build on existing trade rules to improve their treatment of the kinds of problems that are especially likely to arise in connection with industrial policy. There would have to be the same kind of emphasis on dealing with new or old arrangements about investment and related matters. In short, one would make industrial policy a matter of major concern but not treat it as a subject of separate negotiation. This approach is fairly close to some of the suggestions which have been made by Harald Malmgren in this volume for new agreements about subsidies. Whatever standards one worked out for the use of subsidies, and especially any description of circumstances in which practices were permitted that would otherwise be outlawed, would themselves become major elements in an international code about action on industrial policies, whether called that or not.

The last two paragraphs suggest that either approach to industrial policy will lead to approximately the same place so far as international negotiations about subsidies are concerned. This may well be true, but there may be a significant difference in where one might get in dealing with subsidies if one approached them in the industrial policy setting rather than in the traditional way of dealing with trade barriers. The latter seeks firm, clear commitments with a minimum of escape clauses and as little discretion as possible in departing from the rule. This approach works well when there is substantial agreement among a number of important governments about the ends to be achieved (and the means as well). It is just this which is lacking about industrial policy, and one may well doubt how far one can go in dealing with subsidies by this method. To the extent that subsidies are substitutes for forbidden trade barriers one may be able to make rules that are stronger and clearer than those now in GATT; at least the principle is clear. But when the goals are more complex, the meaning of the instruments also changes. Subsidies can focus on the internal economy instead of foreign trade; they are used for a variety of purposes and sometimes purposes that governments rate higher than trade liberalization. Rules will have to allow for contingencies and may work out rather differently in different contexts.

How these contexts are determined may become the biggest single factor shaping the kinds and even amount of agreement on subsidies that become possible over the next few decades. There are a number of quite different kinds of processes at work, not all of which can be outlined with confidence, though an effort to project them is often suggestive. One of the clearest is that part of the Tokyo Round of multilateral trade negotiations that is concerned with 'safeguards'. The essential problem there is to reach agreement about when a country may check a large rise in imports without fearing retaliation from other countries, while at the same time limiting the duration of the restrictive measures and—the hardest part of all—assuring that the time is used to adjust to a situation in which the exceptional protection is no longer needed.

The adjustment can take many forms, from making the domestic industry more competitive to phasing it out altogether. Unless quite temporary conditions are involved—a momentary surplus, a disaster in major plants, etc.—the adjustment process raises the kinds of issues that national industrial policies are concerned with. In addition to what is done to reshape the industry suffering from import competition, there are major questions about other industries, at least if the government guides the adjustment. If resources are to be transferred out of textiles should they go into electronics? Or is electronics about to go through the same global shifts that made the textile issue so intense for so many old industrial countries. Would an expansion of automobile production make more sense? To some people, the only solution is to let investors make their own decisions and take the consequences. But others see a need for government help, especially if major investments are required. In either case there is some risk of moving from one case of 'market disruption' to another, perhaps in an infinite sequence. The process might be intensified if several countries moved at the same time in the same direction. The exchange of information, perhaps even some kind of international understanding about who does what, begins to suggest itself. Problems of this sort are not limited to further trade barrier reduction although that is the framework for much of the GATT debate. Market disruption can result from new investments, technological change, the rise of industry in third countries or a number of other factors that change the patterns of trade in the world.

It may require a considerable stretch of the imagination to see countries reaching international industrial agreements on any scale. Indeed, in a period of increasing eeonomic nationalism and uncertainty they may move in the other direction, so that concern over safeguards will lead to more not fewer trade barriers and less adjustment as well. But it is sufficient for our present purpose to see that whichever way the process goes, the future of subsidies is affected. They are, after all, partial substitutes for trade barriers, and sometimes improvements over them; they can be used to improve or hinder the process of adjustment. What is more important is that decisions about subsidies will be made in specific industrial contexts. While amendment of the safeguards process will lay down general rules and procedures, the working out of concrete arrangements will concern a single industry or related sets of them.

There are also other forces at work which suggest that international industrial policy developments will frequently have a sectoral focus. The main considerations are not always economic. The European Coal and Steel Community created in 1952 was in part an industrial agreement resulting largely from considerations of foreign policy and security. The Euratom Agreement of 1957 was a response to political, security and economic hopes (and satisfied none of them). In contrast the Canadian-American automotive agreement of 1965 grew out of a dispute about export subsidies and countervailing duties. It led to limited free trade in part of the automobile industry and significant shifts in patterns of production.

Probably the best illustration of sectoral problems, mixed motives, and the clash between trade liberalization and national industrial policies lies in agriculture. The special treatment given to farming throughout the industrial world for generations relies heavily on subsidies as well as trade barriers. The adoption of the Common Agricultural Policy by the European Community overcame some of the conflicts of national policies within a limited group of countries and at the same time sharpened the issues between them and the rest of the world, notably the United States. The suggestion during the Kennedy Round that negotiation should focus on the *montant de soutien* underlined the key role of subsidies, but failed partly because the pattern and methods of support and protection were also judged important.[4] Even while the Tokyo Round again entered the tortuous and not very promising process of talking about agricultural trade barriers, a broader question has arisen about the extent that old problems may be transformed by an international effort to promote food production in developing countries and to achieve a certain security of supply by a program of building up international stockpiles, especially of grain. It is hard to imagine a system of this sort that did not depend on the international acceptance of a number of subsidies, in one form or another (and probably trade barriers as well).

Energy, too, has been taken out of the sphere of normal trade negotiations. The search for security of supply and the hope of reasonable costs put net consumers of oil in a position in which subsidies may be of increasing importance domestically (and perhaps internationally as well if any degree of burden sharing is involved). Within the oil-producing countries there are subsidy issues concerning development outside the petroleum sphere, possibly some burden sharing among themselves and aid to non-oil countries with which they have political affiliations. A global agreement about the use of subsidies in energy is hardly to be expected, but quite a number of different kinds of international agreements are imaginable (among producers, among consumers, bilaterally between individual producing and consuming countries, and perhaps on a wider basis as well). As the oil-producing countries industrialize, perhaps especially in petrochemicals, they will contribute to the process (to be discussed later) by which adjustments may be required in the industrial countries thus once more bringing into question the uses of subsidies.

Subsidies are rife in shipping and aviation where complex international sectoral agreements are official and private, multilateral and bilateral. Their general aim is to mitigate competition as well as to assure service and safety. But they rarely, if ever, try to deal with the variety of sea and air subsidies that governments use. Instead they fix on rates, routes, access, what is permitted and not in service and the like. The case for an approach via *montant de soutien* has not, so far as I know, been explored. The explanation almost surely lies in the fact that it is assurance of results that governments want (often fruitlessly) and that subsidy payments to private operators for losses by government owned lines are only instruments to those ends.[5]

An allied industry which is heavily subsidized—shipbuilding—has come to occupy a great deal of attention, especially in Europe.[6] For reasons that may once have emphasized security but are now more concerned with employment and, for some countries, balance of payments needs, shipbuilding has been of special concern to many countries. Efficiency has varied from country to country in Europe and those who have lost orders have done what they could to retain capacity and, if possible, a share of current sales. Many kinds of subsidies have been involved, not least, government-backed credits. At the same time, Japan became the dominant shipbuilding country with half the world's capacity and, in 1976, some 85 per cent of the world's few new orders.

Not surprisingly, this process led to chronic overcapacity in the shipyards of the industrial nations, much exacerbated by the recession. Efforts to deal with the problem within the Community went back a long way but were not very successful in limiting subsidies and losses. This alone did not suffice since the more efficient yards sometimes did not need subsidies, while the worst off created the greatest domestic problems so that governments felt they could not abide by international rules. In 1976 a loose gentlemen's agreement was reached in the OECD by which the main shipbuilding countries' governments were to reduce capacity. National plans to do this varied considerably. Some used subsidies to encourage the contraction and to sustain the building of better quality ships. Difficult negotiations with the Japanese seemed in early 1977 to be strengthening the view that stronger protective measures should be taken in Europe. One proposal involved the idea of common financing, perhaps even Community subsidies, but the old habits of separate national competitive policies also showed themselves. Regardless of how matters work out in the short run, there is little doubt that some kind of international industrial policy agreements in ship-building will remain on the agenda of possibilities, if not always practice.[7]

Sharpened international competition also set in motion what might become significant sectoral negotiations in steel, an industry with a special position in all industrial economies that is also a symbol to developing ones. Great expansion of Japanese production and exports during the postwar period was one factor increasing competition in world markets; business cycles, the differential pace of investment and of the introduction of new technologies were others. In the late 1960s the American producers' complaints about import competition led the government to negotiate with foreign producers to hold down their shipments to the United States for several years. In the mid-1970s, competition and recession led the European Community to resist imports and propose a sharing of world markets. At about the same time, the American producers, saying they wished no part of a cartel, called for international agreements that would ensure fair competition. Their argument was that Japanese and European producers enjoyed the benefits of various kinds of favored treatment by their governments, and so had both protected markets at home and financial advantages for their exports to the disadvantage of the Americans. American producers claimed that their government gave them no help at all, except when they could win support for quotas on imports of products that threatened to disrupt the domestic market.

The American industry urged that Washington accept its case as an objective of the Tokyo Round negotiations. The position gained added weight from the fact that the Trade Act of 1974 under which the American officials were negotiating called for an appraisal of results, sector by sector. Differently interpreted by different authorities, this provision reflected two views fairly widespread in major American industries. One was that unless this kind of examination took place it would be impossible to get at hidden barriers and arrangements in foreign industries. The other was a fear that import concessions would be made affecting one industry to gain concessions on American exports from other industries and that manufacturing as a whole might be 'sacrificed' to Washington's wish to get something for the farmers. While expressing a preference for an international agreement the American steelmakers pushed ahead with measures that could lead to unilateral import restriction. An agreement on fair trade in steel would have to say something about subsidies and the financing of government owned companies. But the history of the steel industry casts doubt on the idea that an agreement on competitive conditions alone is possible unless it also gives national industries a sense of assurance about their position in their home markets. Such an arrangement among the OECD countries would implicitly or explicitly affect—and be affected by—the growth of steel production in developing countries (which may well not be involved in the negotiations). Already by the mid 1970s, producers in a number of developing countries were supplying a growing share of domestic steel needs and a few, such as South Korea, were beginning to export. Not surprisingly some of the biggest of the developing countries—Brazil, Iran, Venezuela, Mexico and Egypt—had the most ambitious steel development plans, while Saudi Arabia intended to develop an export capacity based on the direct reduction of ores by its cheap gas.[8]

It was exports from low-wage countries that led to the most elaborate international sectoral agreements, those concerning textiles. The cotton textile agreement of the early 1960s was sparked by American resistance to exports from Hong Kong and Japan. They have been to a considerable extent replaced by exports of less developed countries. However, Japan was again a key factor in bringing on the agreements covering manmade textiles and woolens in the early 1970s. In fact the agreements of all the industrial countries, both importers and exporters, looked at generally, seemed intended to permit a controlled shift of much of the textile industry from the older industrial countries to the newer ones, moderating the growth of imports so that the existing industry could adjust to it. However, the animus for the agreement was a protective one and there is little doubt that without it unilateral measures would have been imposed in many countries.[9] So it is not surprising that the implementation of the agreements and especially the bilateral arrangements through which they operate have made them quite restrictive in a number of cases. Even so, a major expansion of exports from the low-wage countries has taken place and there have been continuing complaints from industry in Europe and North America. Indeed in the Tokyo Round the European Community (but not the United States) has sought a tightening of the agreement. Only a few countries have undertaken major domestic adjustment policies. The major concern of the textile agreements is with trade barriers not subsidies, but it is easy to see that any attempt to refine the arrangements (which already provide for multilateral surveillance and consultation) might run into the question. A ban on the use of certain kinds of subsidies in exporting countries or importing countries would clearly affect the meaning of the arrangements. But at this stage the basic point is that by concentrating on trade controls, the international textile agreement leaves it to each country to decide what pattern of subsidization is in its own interest.

One common characteristic of all these sectoral arrangements is that they do not try to deal with subsidies in isolation or to rely primarily on the regulation of subsidies. This is probably significant for a consideration of the future of international agreements on subsidies if there are more sectoral experiments. It does not cope, however, with the other side of the question: whether general agreements on subsidies might have to be modified to take account of the aims of sectoral agreements on industrial policy. On the face of it one would expect that would be so if the agreements are concerned with division of the market, maintenance of production in each country, spreading adjustment over time, etc. Such agreements are not primarily aimed at freeing trade or even establishing the conditions of fair competition (with the exception of the proposal of the American steel industry, on its face).[10] Subsidies are treated as instruments rather than practices that are good or bad in themselves.

There are, however, important interrelations between trade liberalization, subsidies as instruments of national industrial policy, and sectoral agreements. The legitimization of some kinds of subsidy practices may be important as a safeguard against foreign retaliation or even simply the imposition of countervailing duties. While Canada's dependence on the United States market is exceptional, Caroline Pestieau makes an important point when she says that an increase in countervailing action by the United States can give rise in Canada to a 'feeling that its domestic policies are threatened'.[11] As Guy de Carmoy points out in his contribution to this volume, the meaning of the overlapping subsidy practices of France, Germany and Britain is that in these sectors the countries do not accept the international division of labor. But the meaning of a sectoral agreement would be that they wanted to find a division that they would accept. Even if the approach that governments took were the one called for by Richard Cooper in his paper (greater reliance on flexible rates and macroeconomic policies followed by restraint and consultation in the process of introducing change) they would, as he says, have to negotiate about sectors when they were each concerned with the same industry.[12]

The aim of this analysis has not been to suggest that sectoral arrangements are either inevitable or altogether desirable. The pressures for them are strong but the difficulties of agreeing are often great, and we may well be moving into a period of less international cooperation than before. Looked at in terms of economics, negotiating experience and the requirements of striking reciprocal balances of advantage, the sectoral approach is open to many objections. [13] It has a built-in bias towards producer domination and restraint and flirts with cartelism, even if it does not yield to that temptation. As the record shows, the agreements run to protectionism. That is at least partly explained by the fact they represent the kind of industrial policy Goran Ohlin has called 'defensive'. They are mostly found in weak industries like textiles and special cases like agriculture. Thus one question is whether on an international basis they yield better results than purely national protective practices would, a matter too complex to go into here. Another is whether they might be different if they were undertaken in advance of the worst pressures. That points directly to the next section on north-south relations, for if there is any simple prediction to be made about the next few decades it is that the expansion of exports of manufactured goods from the developing countries will increase and that in many parts of the industrial world there will be pressures for protection against the new competition.

NORTH-SOUTH NEGOTIATIONS

This large and rather miscellaneous group of negotiations overlaps most of the categories already listed and adds to them. Nevertheless, it is worth separate mention both because it is likely to continue to be a major element on the world scene for quite a few years to come and because it raises a number of fairly fundamental issues about how one goes about dealing with subsidies.

As to the first point, it is hard to believe that any 'planetary bargain' struck in the foreseeable future will bring into being a full-grown New International Economic Order with its own system of rules and procedures and the prospect of stability for a long time to come. Some aspects of international economic life may be more or less definitively reformed in that fashion. But some differences will surely remain unbridgeable for some time to come and some will yield only slightly to efforts to codify national behavior. Concepts of 'development' and the way to achieve it may remain in flux forever. As power, interests and perceptions shift, the problems and possibilities of north-south negotiations will change. Issues will evolve as concrete measures are taken to deal with them separately. New forums will be created to deal with some matters which are now rather clumsily lumped together. The north-south dichotomy is in many respects artificial and arbitrary and certainly far too crude to contain the complex reality of the world. The different kinds of problems faced by say, Taiwan, Brazil, Iran and the Sudan will sooner or later lead to differences in behavior. Nevertheless, either because it has become conventional or because it is useful to the strategy of someone in a position to shape the agendas of the world, the north-south focus is likely to be retained for many issues whatever its objective validity.

The second point, about the subsidy issue raised in north-south relations, can be reduced to the question of whether developed and developing countries are to be treated on the same footing concerning the use of subsidies. If not, what kinds of differences should there be? The same problem is familiar from discussions of trade policy generally, so a few highly oversimplified statements should suffice to trace the story from a reasonable starting point to the present unsatisfactory state of affairs.

1. General acceptance of the argument for the infant industry exception to classical free trade led to its incorporation in GATT. In the absence of a selective procedure, LDCs have been allowed to apply it across the board as if anything that seemed likely to aid development exempted a country from any obligation to reduce trade barriers. But it has become apparent that a number of countries have damaged their own development by providing unwise protection for import-substituting industries.

2. The reciprocity that is a major dynamic factor in most trade liberalization has not existed in north-south trade as LDCs have been exempted from the need to match what others do for their exports. That has probably been one of the reasons the industrialized countries have retained more barriers to imports from LDCs than from one another.

3. The acceptance of the principle of generalized preferences seems to be a major commitment by the industrialized countries to treat the LDCs better than in the past and better than they treat one another. But the preferences are in fact hedged round with many qualifications and are strictly limited in the benefits they confer.

4. Thus the developing countries encounter serious barriers in selling many of their goods to the industrial countries. Not surprisingly, the barriers are highest where the competition is sharpest. There is no doubt that the developing countries could gain substantially from further trade liberalization. But it is also true that in spite of the limited past liberalization, sales of manufactured goods from LDCs to the industrial countries have increased rapidly. With or without further liberalization, a major question is whether the industrial countries will be willing to accept increasing quantities of manufac-

tured goods from the developing countries without taking new protective measures.

One need only translate these statements into propositions about future action on subsidies to see what the key questions are. Shall rules limiting the use of subsidies apply to developing countries or should they be exempted and thus left free to take measures the developed countries have forsworn? Should the benefits of whatever arrangements on subsidies the industrial countries work out be extended to developing countries unconditionally and without reciprocity?[14]

If the answers to these questions are affirmative, will the resulting one way street inhibit the industrial countries from acting on subsidy issues in ways that would tie their hands in dealing with increasingly severe competition from the developing countries? They may have to choose between doing nothing about these matters or finding ways to limit the benefits to those who reciprocate, even if that means reaching agreements which apply only among industrialized countries. The most desirable or most feasible course may differ from case to case. There may also be good reason to treat some developing countries one way and some another.

Another line of approach would be to work out a set of rules or principles that would provide special treatment for developing countries but not complete exemption from all obligations. The subsidy issue would be part of a larger and much needed effort to work out trade rules specially geared to development problems. Subsidies might well have a major part in such work. Though they may present administrative problems, selective subsidies have many advantages over general tariff protection as a means of assuring sound development.

There are a number of conditions that might justify for developing countries even export subsidies that industrialized countries had agreed to give up. It has been suggested, for example, that devaluation might unnecessarily cheapen exports of raw materials in an effort to make manufactured goods competitive and that subsidies would be better than multiple exchange rates. The infant industry argument can be applied to the capacity of industries to export as well as to produce for the home market and that might justify certain subsidies. There are disadvantages to be offset in the developing countries. Some are imposed by the high costs of domestic production resulting from tariffs. Others are connected with disadvantageous conditions of production somewhat analogous to those that give rise to regional development subsidies in rich countries. Taxes can be important in fostering development, and shaping domestic consumption and investment; substantial rebates on exports may well be in order. One could imagine codifying these conditions so that when any one existed a developing country would be allowed to use export subsidies without encountering countervailing duties from industrial countries. Its case might be subject to international review. There might be a limit on the imports exempt from countervailing duties so as to avoid serious problems of adjustment. [15]

If this process seemed too complex one could envisage a broader code or set of rules subject to reasonable safeguards against their abuse and the ability to check imports when major and difficult dislocations threatened. Then the industrialized countries could make a positive contribution to development by agreeing that developing countries accepting these principles should receive, without reciprocity, the benefits of the subsidy agreements made among the industrial countries and perhaps other concessions as well.

Subsidies would also find a place in other agreements between developing and industrialized countries. A number of cases have been mentioned already: investment, agriculture, energy. Agreements focusing on raw materials are usually concerned with stabilization or a floor under prices or income or with access. The financing of stockpiles and arrangements for diversifying production to reduce output of some materials may involve elements of subsidy but for the most part the focus is quite different. [16]

There is however a segment of the raw material issue where subsidy rules may be very important. This concerns the tariff structures that protect processing and fabrication near the markets instead of near the sources of raw materials. Removal of these duties—which can be claimed on grounds of old fashioned trade liberalization—would not always lead to a shift in location. [17] When it did not, raw material producing countries might be tempted to induce a shift by subsidies (or export taxes), but these ought to be looked at in terms of development trade principles generally and not given blanket exceptions to subsidy rules. When a shift did occur it might cause dislocation and adjustment problems in industrial countries; these too should be treated in the same way as other forms of market disruption.

The processing example suggests a point touched on earlier with regard to sectoral agreements. Can one anticipate problems and make a better arrangement than would result from waiting until there are the difficulties which drive governments to such measures as the textile agreements? Adjustment could be spread over a longer period than usual, and subsidies could be used either to equalize conditions temporarily or to cushion the impact on those who lost in the process. Thinking along these lines leads naturally enough to the following question: Could other industrial shifts also be the subjects of agreements between the countries where production of certain products was growing and those where it might have to contract? The latter group might also be important sources of development finance or the home bases of companies responsible for the new expansion. The aspiration is ambitious and perhaps impractical. Its realization is surely not just around the corner. Such an effort would almost certainly entail the considerable use of subsidies or subsidy-like arrangements. But as in the case of most of the other examples discussed in this section, the negotiations would not be about subsidies *per se*.

AGREEMENTS AMONG WHOM?

The previous section has made very clear that subsidy issues will arise in a considerable number of settings. Different countries will have differing degrees of involvement in these matters. One can guess that often enough the question will arise whether an agreement among a few countries is better than no agreement at all or whether the failure to include certain countries will either make an agreement fail, or will make it succeed at the price of introducing damaging discrimination into the world economy. It is impossible to do justice to the subject without going into a good bit of detail about types of subsidies, patterns of production and trade and real or hypothetical countries and there is no room here for anything of that sort. As the issue is not dealt with elsewhere in the volume, the next few pages raise questions and suggest a few guidelines but they do not go very far toward solving the resulting problems.

Before getting to the particulars of subsidies it is necessary to think about international agreements on economic issues in general. In doing so, the following factors have to be taken into account:

1. The minimum grouping needed to make an agreement effective; the prospects of enlarging this to whatever might be thought the optimum size.
2. The greater prospects of getting agreement among certain countries than among others.
3. The trade-off between the firmness of the agreement, the chances of enforcing it, etc and the advantages of having a larger number of adherents. This is what Miriam Camps has called the efficiency-participation dilemma.[18]
4. The extent of the damage to outside countries and international trade as a whole of an agreement applicable to a limited number of countries only; the burden on the signatory countries of extending some or all of the benefits to others without reciprocity.
5. The dynamics of a partial agreement.
6. The cost to the international system of not getting agreement, if the result of estimating these factors is to make it seem preferable not to have an agreement than to have one among the only countries which

can, at a given moment, actually agree (and of the sort they can agree on).

These considerations can be applied to any combination of countries but the following list seems to cover the major types of agreements that need to be thought about.

1. Agreements on subsidies incorporated in a larger agreement—presumably GATT—so that they have to be accepted by all countries that want the other benefits of the broader agreement.
2. Agreements open to all and intended to cover many countries, but standing on their own feet and not applicable except to signatories. There could be a link to a broader agreement, as in the GATT anti-dumping code, but existing obligations would remain intact. Between this and the preceding arrangement there is a range of possibilities that would blur the difference. For example, the revision of GATT might only come into effect for each country when it accepted it; the rule might have exceptions for classes of countries; etc.
3. Agreements intended to be confined to countries sharing some characteristics and linked to some other arrangements among them, for example, OECD or a development code for subsidies of the sort mentioned in the previous section.
4. Agreements open only to countries which are already members of a close association (the European Community; the Andean Pact).
5. Agreements aimed at quite specific purposes and only involving countries directly involved in that activity; an example would be the possible agreements about the processing of raw materials discussed above.

In many agreements a fundamental question concerns relations with outsiders. Should they be given the same treatment as signatories even though they do not take on the same obligations? Should each signatory decide for itself how to treat others? Or should a condition of the agreement be that its benefits are not to be extended to others, though naturally the group as a whole could make exceptions? A related question is whether to treat some outsiders differently from others. Both issues come up if one considers the non-reciprocal extension of benefits to developing countries. Many people favor doing this but if the obligation made industrial countries unwilling to give up the use of certain kinds of subsidies in trade among themselves, it might be better to have the more limited agreement rather than none at all. Much depends on how serious the resulting discrimination would be. There is a good bit of logic in withholding benefits from countries otherwise similar to the signatories, if they do not take on the obligations. The ability to broaden agreements is likely to depend on giving others an incentive to join. Sometimes there are a number of countries that have no claim to special treatment, but whose adherence or not to the principles of the agreement is of no great importance. In the interest of uniformity of conditions in world trade and administrative simplicity, it may often be useful to give them equal treatment, unless they abuse it. To leave signatories free to discriminate between outsiders is a good way of coping with special problems. But it could be unwise if, as seems quite possible, industrial countries go in, increasingly, for bilateral trade and investment arrangements with the suppliers of oil or other raw materials they are dependent on.

Related issues are brought out by a comparison of three approaches to the process of extending international economic agreements. The Atlantic Council of the United States brought together a group under the chairmanship of John Leddy, who retired from the State Department after a long career specializing in, but not confined to, trade.[19] Its detailed and careful proposals aim at broadening and deepening economic cooperation among the countries that have already done most to liberalize trade among themselves, essentially the OECD group. Remaining within the framework of GATT they would continue to extend freely to developing countries the benefits covered by most-favored-nation obligations, but no signatories of the code would be treated as developing countries. Only by accepting all its obligations could one secure all its benefits which, it seems fair to say, is tantamount to joining the 'club' of industrial countries.

A set of proposals with a quite different emphasis comes from a group brought together by the American Society of International Law under the chairmanship of another former State Department specialist in economic policy, Anthony Solomon (who subsequently became Under Secretary of the Treasury for Monetary Affairs).[20] While its main proposals are not necessarily incompatible with the Atlantic Council's report, this group tries to allow for greater diversity. It concerns itself with codes and other kinds of agreements which would be open to anyone, but would frequently include only the countries with a special interest in a certain subject or those willing to agree to new rules and procedures. Favorable treatment of developing countries is called for but not made mandatory. Countries should be stimulated to adhere to agreements by a wish to get the advantages that go with obligations, but there are quite a few provisions to ensure that the interests of outsiders are taken into account. All agreements are to conform to some general principles, have similar arrangements for the settlement of disputes, and are to be to some degree linked with all other agreements in a World Trade Organization.

Miriam Camps deals with some of the same issues in a study that uses the future of the OECD as a focus for discussing the problems of differential treatment and the relation of broad if not universal agreements to those involving only a selected group of countries.[21] She gives particular attention to how the OECD countries can use their special relation to one another and the processes of that organization to the best advantage, without deepening the divisions between them and the rest of the world in pursuit of the broadest possible effective cooperation on matters of global or general international concern. Quite often this points in the direction of preparing a global approach—or an approach to developing countries—among themselves, and agreeing on how to overcome certain obstacles (sometimes a kind of burden sharing), while not simply presenting the rest of the world with a *fait accompli* or a confrontational kind of bargaining position.

To these considerations that apply to a wide range of economic arrangements we have to add points made earlier that apply specifically to subsidies. Agreements applying to subsidies generally can hardly have precise substantive rules unless they are linked to the avoidance of fairly well defined results or simply injury to other parties. The same subsidy practice if it hurts no one is legitimate. Freedom to impose countervailing duties is likely to seem insufficient in many cases, even stronger forms of trade retaliation or better international machinery may seem needed if the aim is to prevent the spread of subsidies or to preserve an important part of another nation's industrial policy.

Agreements aimed at particular kinds of subsidies can be more specific and firmer. Even so it might seem unnecessary to tamper with arrangements that were not alleged to damage others. While most efforts are likely to be specific, there is no inconsistency between seeking a loose general agreement and a tighter agreement on specific subjects. Furthermore, one can easily imagine a code of principles subscribed to by a large number of countries and a series of specific codes applying to only some countries. International industrial policy agreements of the sort mentioned earlier permit certain countries to use certain types of subsidies for certain purposes even if such practices were not in accord with the general rules. All these possibilities suggest difficulties in consistency and uniformity, but they should not be insuperable. Presumably the best result would be one in which the entitlements and complaints procedures of the broader agreement were respected but were then used to work out an arrangement under which the exceptions built into the industrial agreement were legitimized.

Any partial regulation of subsidies—and one can be reasonably sure that that is what will be achieved if anything is achieved—raises questions about the substitutability of instruments and the creation of conditions by other means. If certain practices are banned what is to be done about unbanned practices that have the same result? The principle is not hard to see—GATT has it for measures that nullify the effects of tariff reductions—but it is not easy to enforce or sometimes even to determine the facts of the case. More broadly, an effort ought to be made to think about how governments are likely to try to cope with the problems they once sought to solve by national preferences, for example in procurement policy.

If so many different factors have to be taken into account in thinking about agreements involving a few, many or potentially all countries, which are most important? Is it better to have a reasonably firm agreement among a few countries, a looser one among more, or no agreement at all? Where should one draw the line between the desirable pressure on outsiders to join so as to gain the benefits and the loss of incentive by granting the benefits freely because the main purpose of the agreement is served by committing the smaller group or because there is no reason to treat the outsiders more generously? One cannot hope to find very helpful answers in general terms but there is, in my view, a rough hierarchy of preferences. Trade rules applying to all countries have considerable advantages. Few can be universally applied, but agreed and controlled derogations from principle are better than a lack of rules. While the division of the world into north-south, rich-poor, etc. is too crude, something along those lines is sufficiently likely to be accepted for a long time to come to make it a working basis. The first key problem then will be to find better principles than exist for the treatment of the developing countries. Simple exemption from rules with no control has two main disadvantages. (1) Like anyone else the developing countries are tempted into courses of action that damage their own long-run interests. (2) An obligation to extend unreciprocated benefits to developing countries may inhibit agreement among industrial countries that would otherwise be desirable. The latter point is related to the resistance in industrial countries to increased competition in manufactured goods from developing countries. A necessary, though not sufficient, condition for change is the general use of better adjustment arrangements, with some international pressure built in for them.

These rough indications of a desirable direction for policy apply to subsidies as well as other international economic relations. Sometimes the character of subsidies makes it easier to see how the principles might be applied to cases; this is particularly true since subsidies can be targeted on sectors, firms and types of transactions and need not apply across the board as trade barriers and, usually, taxes do. This is the very characteristic that limits general agreements about the use of subsidies, conceptually, in practice and politically. Taken together with the frequency with which the significance of a subsidy depends less on its form than on the purpose for which it has been used, we are led to the conclusion that it makes little sense to consider subsidies apart from trade policy generally or industrial policy and even then one soon comes up against the need to look at cases.

That does not mean *ad hocery*, the abandonment of principle or surrender to the forces of the moment. It is simply another version of a point which has appeared frequently throughout this paper: if international economic cooperation in the future is to increase it will have to become more complex. Without that kind of development, at least some of the improvement in the international division of labor achieved in the last quarter century will be lost and there may be a marked movement toward economic nationalism, mercantilism and narrow concepts of national interest.

Notes and References

1. One subject which has not been explored in other papers in this collection is the possibility of working out rules for east-west (or intersystemic) trade. One way of reducing the absurdities in the western application of antidumping rules and countervailing duties to exports from centrally planned economies is to conflate the issues with questions about market disruption and the possibility of using multilateral instead of bilateral standards. Arrangements (or the lack of them) about export credits also raise subsidy questions but are rarely brought into the context of trade rules. This last is a field in which an effective agreement is conceivable that involves relatively few countries.

2. The issue here is no different from that of any set of rules about subsidies. Effects on foreign trade can arise even though the form and immediate purpose of the subsidy are domestic. There is no good way to define such problems in advance so there has to be room for a complaints procedure that sets in motion a process of weighing the damage.

3. I am exploring most of the questions in this section in much more detail in work for the 1980s Project of the Council on Foreign Relations.

4. The concept and the problems are authoritatively explained in Ernest H. Preeg, *Traders and Diplomats*, (Washington, D.C., The Brookings Institution, 1970) pp. 73, 144–58; and John W. Evans, *The Kennedy Round in American Trade Policy: The Twilight of the GATT?* (Massachusetts: Harvard University Press, 1971), pp. 203–17, 238–44.

5. A good account of the problems and complexities of dealing with those two fields can be found in Susan Strange's, 'Who runs World Shipping' *International Affairs*, Vol. 52, No. 3, July 1976; and Andreas F. Lowenfeld, 'A New Takeoff for International Air Transport' *Foreign Affairs*, Vol. 54, No. 1, Oct. 1975.

6. US shipbuilding subsidies are part of a system which also involves various forms of aid to the operators of American ships. Concern with competition for foreign orders is rare.

7. Were it not for the sharpness of the security issues one would be tempted to say the same thing about the aircraft industry, or at least some parts of it. Even the differences push in the same direction: the large investment needs, the large markets required, the rapidly advancing technology in the product (there are technological changes in the shipbuilding process more than in the product). The key role of government procurement makes the subsidy issue a somewhat different one but does not reduce the analogy.

8. A good survey of the situation appears in *The Economist*, 12 Feb., 1977, pp.

81–6. For a statement of the US Steel Industry's case see R. Heath Larry, *A Trade Policy for Steel: Is there a Problem, Is there an Answer?*; AISI, 84th General Meeting, Waldorf Astoria Hotel, N.Y., 27 May 1976; mimeo.

9. It is also true that parts of the textile industry in many industrial countries are quite capable of competing against low wage producers. An excellent examination of one country's problems with imports, domestic production, industrial policy and the international agreement is Caroline Pestieau, *The Canadian Textile Policy: A Sectoral Trade Adjustment Strategy?* (The Canadian Economic Policy Committee; C.D Howe Research Institute, [Montreal] 1976).

10. And in this respect these are quite far from the kind of sectoral or industry-by-industry agreements that Eric Wyndham Whyte had in mind when he first introduced the idea as a device for proceeding to free trade by eliminating tariffs in a few industries. Speech to the Deutsche Gesellschaft für Auswärtige Politik, 27 Oct 1966, 'Perspektiven des Welthandels nach der Kennedy-Runde,' *Europa-Archiv*, (Folge 22, 1966) pp. 793–802.

11. See Chapter 4 in this volume by Caroline Pestieau.

12. Which I should have thought was very frequently the case. Cooper's program, by the way, seems to me far more ambitious than his modest words suggest and would represent an important step forward.

13. These and other points are set out more fully in William Diebold, *The United States and the Industrial World*, (New York: Praeger Publishers, 1972) pp. 140–4. Other parts of the book deal with a number of issues touched on in this paper.

14. The situation with regard to subsidies is not quite the same as in providing either equal treatment or preferences in trade barriers. A subsidy agreement may be a commitment not to engage in certain practices with the result that all foreign countries benefit whether they reciprocate or not if the forbidden subsidy cannot be selectively applied. Export subsidies can vary according to destination but not production subsidies. To exceed a limit in concessions to foreign investors or on export credits damages a third party who may be a signatory of the agreement. Sometimes, as is the case of government procurement, the analogy with trade barriers is close and reciprocity, discrimination, etc. are easily applied.

15. This is essentially the proposal (worked out in more detail) of Lorenz L. Perez, 'Export Subsidies in Developing Countries and the GATT' in *Journal of World Trade Law* (Vol. 10, No. 6) November/December 1976, pp. 529–45. Perez, a US official, focuses on export subsidies and the GATT rules, but his arguments which I have found very helpful can be applied more broadly.

16. We are not here treating international aid as a subsidy.

17. There are often other trade barriers as well as tariffs. To deal with them and to provide for adjustment, the Canadian government has suggested sectoral negotiations for industries in which the processing issue is important. Caroline Pestieau, *The Sector Approach to Trade Negotiation: Canadian and U.S. Interests*, (Canadian Economic Policy Committee: C. D. Howe Research Institute [Montreal], 1976) pp. 6–9.

18. Miriam Camps, *The Management of Interdependence: A Preliminary View*, (New York: Council Papers on International Affairs published by the

Council on Foreign Relations, Inc. 1974) p. 92.

19. Atlantic Council of the United States. *GATT Plus—A Proposal for Trade Reform*, (Report of the Special Advisory Panel to the Trade Committee of the Atlantic Council. New York: Praeger, 1976).

20. American Society of International Law. *Re-Making the System of World Trade: A Proposal for Institutional Reform*, (Report of the Panel on International Trade Policy and Institutions. St. Paul, Minnesota: West Publishing Company, 1976).

21. Miriam Camps, *'First World' Relationships: The Role of the OECD*. The Atlantic Papers 2/1975 and Council Papers on International Affairs: 5. (Published by the Atlantic Institute for International Affairs and Council on Foreign Relations, Inc. (New York) 1975).

9 Measuring the International Effect of Subsidies

SEAMUS O'CLEIREACAIN

Several contributors to this volume have pointed to the difficulties in finding methods which might provide generally agreed upon estimates of the extent and effects of government subsidies. This chapter discusses some of the methods which have been developed in recent years to provide empirical estimates of both the *ex ante* and *ex post* effects of subsidies. The former involves prior evaluation of the potential implications of national legislation, and the latter is concerned with the actual effects of specific instances where a subsidy has been granted. While there is a growing flow of information on the extent to which governments subsidize the private sector, the national reporting systems need an oversight mechanism capable of identifying potential sources of conflict. Two such present sources of conflict are the inadequacies of the GATT Articles VI and XVI and the disparities between the GATT and the national legislation of contracting parties shielded by the grandfather clause.

While the growth in subsidization has its origin in political choices, an economic rationale for some subsidization has been provided by economic theorists contributing to the literature on the theory of distortions and welfare.[1] These contributions have shown that the first best policy to correct a distortion is to attack it at source through the use of direct subsidies which remove the distortion in relative prices. In an imperfect world, the policies of governments differ from the prescriptions of the theorists in two important respects. Capital subsidization is used as an employment-generating device in situations in which a direct labor subsidy would be more appropriate, and sector-specific subsidies are used where general subsidies are called for by the theorists. These divergences from the policy prescriptions of the theory of distortions add government-generated distortions to an already distortion ridden world trading system.

Those who profess to see little difference between the dumping practices of private corporations and the subsidization practices of governments miss a rather important distinction in the price effects of these two practices. Unlike dumping, domestic production subsidies do not entail dual pricing. Production subsidies reduce the price of *all* domestic output whether it is exported or not. They do not introduce a differential between domestic and export prices. The US negotiating team at the MTN professed to find the distinction between production and export subsidies more theoretical than real in the case of subsidies provided in economies where a large part of domestic output is exported.

The theoretical distinction between export and production subsidies hinges on the dual price criterion: export subsidies cause consumers in the home market to face higher prices than their counterparts in the export market, production subsidies cause no such differential. The US concern may be construed as a mercantilist attempt to obstruct free trade by preventing both specialization and dependence on the US market, and raises the difficult question as to what, in the case of production subsidies, is to be considered as an acceptable level of specialization. International trade theory has little difficulty in providing an answer to this question. Canadian concern in the MTN discussions on subsidies is focused on ensuring that the political realities which dictate a less than satisfactory answer for the trade theorist do not excessively penalize smaller, more open economies. The matter is one of limiting domestic subsidies to those which do not have significant trade effects.

The difficulty in defining a subsidy has also been alluded to at several points by other contributors. The confusion of government officials and international negotiators as to what is, and what is not, to be considered a subsidy mirrors the general confusion of economists on a matter which is more intricate than is commonly understood. Professor Alan Prest of the London School of Economics, an authority on public finance, has confessed 'I was under the delusion that I knew what a subsidy was; now I am not so sure.'[2] As Prest points out, the confusion is not confined to one side of the Atlantic. He cites a US Department of Commerce estimate of 1969 US subsidies as $4000 million and a US Congress Joint Economic Committee estimate of $63,000 million in fiscal 1970–1.[3]

The definitional confusion hinges on the different treatment accorded to cash outlays and imputed transfers. Tax concessions or 'tax expenditures' have economic effects similar to cash grants but are much more difficult to quantify. An element of subsidization is present in government loan programs which charge interest rates below those at which the loan recipient could otherwise obtain financing. This element of subsidization is extremely difficult to quantify accurately, because of doubts about what the market interest rate might have been, especially in high-risk bailing-out operations. Loans made with the expectation that they will never be repaid because of a future renegotiation of the formal loan terms are almost entirely pure grant, but attempting to label them as such invariably raises questions as to how the probability of repayment was estimated. The injection of what in the UK has been termed 'public equity', that is, the use of central government purchases of equity as a device by which cash may be provided to ailing firms is a subsidy, but again, of uncertain amount.

In addition to the definitional problems outlined above, there is also a wide range of problems in attempting to calculate the size and effects of a subsidy once it has been so categorized. Published national accounts, input-output, or budgetary data on government expenditures are inaccurate guides to the level of subsidies. While disbursements in the form of grants may readily be labelled as subsidies, disbursements on loan programs will give rise to the difficulties concerning the choice of interest rate mentioned earlier. Even if public disclosure of formal loan terms occurs, these are often quite meaningless if the loan granting agency possesses and makes use of, discretionary powers to commute, postpone or substitute equity participation on loan repayments. The use of such discretionary powers makes it extremely unlikely that the estimates of subsidy payments obtained from a program-by-program investigation of a country's policy will not differ from estimates obtained from a case-by-case investigation of recipients.

It is understandable that the difficulties listed above should lead some to seek a 'workable definition' by restricting discussion to such readily quantifiable categories as cash grants. To draft international rules with the aim of limiting the potential trade effects of *cash outlay* support systems would undoubtedly lead to a proliferation of government designed implicit subsidy systems. This danger has long been recognized by the European Community which has had some experience in policing aid programs which have a potential to influence trade flows within the Community. Regional aids have been limited to a degree of subsidization which is 20 per cent of the investment costs in well defined depressed regions. The approach of the Community recognizes the need to place some checks on implicit subsidies, and makes use of a three-way classification based on the principle of transparency, that is, subsidies are considered to be either transparent (measurable), semi-transparent (estimable), or opaque (unestimable).

Translating expenditure or disbursement data into a level of subsidy is only the first step in estimating the size and effects of subsidy programs. The level of subsidy must then be related to a base to obtain a rate of subsidization. The wide choice of bases on which subsidies may be paid, ranging from output level to usage level of a particular input, makes it difficult to determine the extent to which unit production costs of a particular product line have been reduced. In addition, before the reduction in costs may be translated into a subsidy-induced price cut, it is necessary to make some determination concerning the mechanism through which the subsidy is shifted forward on to final prices.

The international trade effects of subsidies stem from the more direct price, production, consumption, employment and investment effects of these subsidies. Efforts to quantify the international repercussions of domestic interventions have centered around three approaches: the effective protection approach, the dual-price approach, and the trade-patterns approach.

In his study of non-tariff barriers in the US and the UK, Robert Baldwin of the University of Wisconsin produced some calculations of the rate of effective protection provided by tariff and non-tariff measures.[4] The UK estimates have since been updated and considerably refined by Nicholas Oulton of the University of Lancaster.[5] Similar studies have been conducted for West Germany.[6]

The effective protection method provides estimates of the extent to which a variety of policy instruments such as tariffs, import quotas and subsidies alter the value-added of an industry. These changes in value-added may be seen as the policy-induced changes in resource allocation. In those instances in which effective protection studies have focused on non-tariff issues, they have precluded the isolation of the influence of domestic subsidies. Instead, attention has been concentrated on the effects of net indirect fiscal policy, that is, on the effects of indirect taxes minus subsidies. The theoretical reasons for combining indirect taxes and subsidies were probably originally grounded in the mistaken belief that subsidies might be defined as negative taxes.[7]

The practical reason for not isolating the influence of subsidies lies in the design of the main research tool used in calculating effective protection, the input-output table. Published input-output tables submerge the data on subsidies in a row characteristically labelled 'net indirect taxes' or 'indirect taxes less subsidies'. While it is possible to obtain the unpublished subsidy data from which this row of the table is constructed, this data will refer to disbursements which, as has been shown above, are inaccurate measures of the level of subsidization.

Effective protection is a measure of the resource-pull of particular policies. Complaints concerning the international repercussions of domestic subsidy programs are rarely couched in such esoteric terms. Rather, international complaints tend to involve the more mundane considerations of market penetration or improper pricing.

In a recent attempt to gauge the price effects of what he terms UK 'export-promoting' domestic subsidies, Melvyn Krauss of New York University makes an ingenious attempt to cut through the definitional maze of what is to be considered an export, and what a domestic, subsidy.[8] Krauss calculates a 'rate of export emphasis' from the subsidy component of the 'indirect taxes less subsidies' row of the UK input-output table. The rate of export emphasis of a domestic subsidy program is considered by Krauss to be the product of two quotients: the ratio of subsidy to export value-added, and the ratio of exported value-added to total value-added.

Krauss concludes that in the case of the UK, the rate of subsidy to exported value-added is so low as to have little distorting influence on relative prices. His estimates of the rate of subsidy payments to exported value-added in manufacturing ranged from 0.91 per cent to 3.59 per cent. Since his methodology is more operational than that employed in effective protection studies, his calculations could conceivably be used by other governments to calculate the rate of countervailing duty to impose on UK exports.

While Krauss' technique is a creative attempt to identify sectors where it may be shown that domestic subsidies have an export-promoting effect, his methodology guarantees that small open economies which provide domestic subsidies will be shown to have a higher rate of export emphasis than less open economies with an identical rate of subsidization of domestic production. This is an issue which the Canadian delegation to the Tokyo Round Multilateral Trade Negotiations sought to have discussed in negotiations on a revision of the subsidy provisions of the GATT.

The dual-price approach implicit in Krauss' study suffers from some of the weaknesses of any study which has its origins in input-output data. Just as in the case of effective protection calculations, reliance on data garnered from input-output sources will involve the use of a definition of subsidies which is limited to cash payments. While these are the easiest to quantify and the most amenable to negotiations, use of such a concept of subsidy involves the errors and omissions refered to at an earlier point in the paper. Interest rate concessions in loan programs, loan guarantees, nationalistic government procurement programs etc., are subsidy practices which are *not* included in input-output tables. To obtain an accurate estimate of the value of subsidies, there is no alternative but to dig through budgets and departmental practices, ignoring statistics which are part of a system of national accounts. The overriding objection to the use of any concept based on input-output tables will be the same objection as is raised when subsidies are defined in terms of disbursements.

The third method of calculating the effects of domestic subsidies concentrates on identifying changes in the composition of international trade which may be ascribed to the existence of subsidies. This approach first identifies the determinants of the commodity or industrial composition of trade flows and then seeks to isolate the influence of subsidies either from these determinants or on these determinants. My own estimates of UK domestic subsidies to private enterprise (reprinted above by de Carmoy in his table 2), showed the direction in which UK aid was channeled in fiscal 1970–71.[9] When the industrial pattern of UK aid was related to the pattern of a number of other indicators of domestic economic activity, no conclusive evidence was found to suggest that UK aid to private enterprise had pronounced effects on the pattern of trade. While the composition of trade flows could be shown to be related to a number of commonly accepted determinants of the commodity-composition of trade flows, there was little evidence to suggest that the pattern of subsidization was correlated with these influences, or even directly with the trade flows.[10]

The three techniques discussed above focus on different effects of domestic subsidies. The effective protection approach indicates the direction of domestic resource allocation due to subsidies while also providing a measure of the protection of domestic industries from foreign competition. The export emphasis, or implied dual-price approach attempts to measure the export-promoting effects of subsidies which would not be considered export subsidies within the definition contained in Article XVI of the GATT or the 1960 List.[11] This approach also provides a measure of what Krauss terms 'indirect dumping', estimates which a government capable of using the grandfather clause to escape the limitations of Article VI of the GATT might have recourse to, in determining the rate of countervailing duty it might see fit to impose. The third, or trade composition approach, restricts itself to discovering the impact of subsidies on international trade flows without attempting to discover a price, and hence countervailable, effect of subsidization.

Before turning to the GATT framework, what are the implications of a floating exchange rate system for determining the impact of subsidies? The presence of an automatic balance-of-payments adjustment mechanism, whether in the form of flexible exchange rates or flexible real wages and fixed exchange rates, guarantees that general subsidies, provided under either the origin or destination principle, will not affect production, consumption or trade patterns. The flexibility of either the exchange rate or real wages will ensure that movements in these variables will offset the change in relative prices caused by general subsidies and will restore balance-of-payments equilibrium. Given the limited applicability of general subsidies however, attention must be focused on the more pervasive category of selective subsidies. As Richard Cooper has pointed out, under flexible exchange rates sectoral policies which alter domestic relative price ratios and the international competitiveness of one sector will provoke an exchange rate movement which alters the international competitiveness of those tradeables which have not been affected by the domestic sectoral policies. In other words, while flexible exchange rates guarantee that sectoral subsidies have no more influence on the overall balance-of-payments than general subsidies, they do alter the commodity composition of trade flows but not in a manner which might be immediately determined by an investigation of the domestic pattern of sectoral subsidies.

There is a considerable difference between attempting to isolate the effects of a national subsidy program, and calculating the rate of subsidization received by the exports of a particular firm. In the latter case, the first and third methods outlined above are both too aggregative, and addressed to questions rather different from estimating the price effect of a subsidy once the dual price criterion has been met. Only the second of the three methods directly considers the price effect of a subsidy, and hence the level of countervailing duty should such action be appropriate.

When the GATT, and indeed the 1960 List were drafted, the degree of interdependence in the world economy was considerably less than that found today. Increased interdependence has raised the likelihood that domestic subsidies will have trade distorting effects. These effects will still, of course, be smaller than are found with an equal expenditure on export subsidization.

While the methods outlined above may provide some indication of the likely magnitude of the effect emanating from a subsidy program, these methods must be placed within an organizational structure which is capable of making use of them. The GATT provisions on notification contained in Article XVI.1 have never been adequately observed, while the unilateral nature of the countervailing duty process leaves the calculation of both the size of the subsidy and its effects in the hands of the government contemplating imposition of the duties.

Both subsidization and countervailing duty action possess an important characteristic not found in anti-dumping cases, namely two *governments* are involved. Since countervailing duty action involves one government making a judgement as to the extent to which another government is engaging in an increasingly common practice, and making a further judgement as to the extent to which this practice produces injury, it is surely time to improve the present GATT mechanisms on subsidies and countervailing duties. The introduction of a Special Body, as proposed by the European Community during the Tokyo Round MTN discussions on subsidies would be a useful addition to a process which presently seems designed to exacerbate rather than resolve international conflict. Such a body, perhaps modelled on the Anti-Dumping Committee or the Textiles Surveillance Body could serve as an agency for multilateral consultation on the classification of a particular practice, calculation of the subsidy should the practice be so classified, and calculation of the extent to which it causes injury. Such a body would, of course, have no more than consultative status in international disputes, with the present rights and obligations of Articles VI and XVI being maintained.

There are two dimensions to the reporting and control of subsidy practices. What might be termed an *ex-ante* approach would call for the vetting of proposed subsidy programs before they are introduced. The European Community's system of control on the proliferation of regional and industrial aid calls for the Commission to play an oversight role permitting it to confer not only with the government officials in member states contemplating the introduction of new programs, but also with representatives of commercial concerns in other member states who may be appraised of the proposed legislation and whose views on the likely impact of their own operations may be sought.

An *ex-post* approach invariably involves a complaint mechanism and, ultimately, resort to countervailing duty action. While the European Community's control system involves both an *ex-ante* and *ex-post* component, the US and other GATT members rely on *ex-post* control because of the present weakness of the notification requirement of Article XVI. A Special Body, charged with surveillance and compliance with Article XVI, could provide other GATT contracting parties with the type of conflict resolution mechanism presently available to members of the European Community. As Harald Malmgren points out in his contribution to this volume, governments are insufficiently concerned with discovering in advance all the likely effects of contemplated subsidy programs. A Special Body might cause an improvement in assessment techniques prior to introduction of proposed programs.

The grandfather clause released the US from some of the obligations contained in Articles VI and XVI. The US countervailing duty statute has required the Secretary of the Treasury to impose countervailing duties once it has been determined that a foreign export to the US has received a 'grant or bounty'. Prior to the 1974 Trade Act, the Treasury had considerable discretion in choosing the speed with which it sought to determine the existence and level of subsidization once a complaint had been filed. The 1974 Trade Act considerably eroded this discretion through the imposition of a strict timetable for the processing of complaints.

The secrecy surrounding administrative decisions has in the past provided the Administration with some flexibility in developing an informal injury test not required by US law while also providing little direct information as to the manner in which the level of foreign subsidization is computed.[12] This has been the source of some dispute, not only in cases involving export subsidies, but more recently in instances involving domestic subsidies. Ultimately, the subsidy must be related to the f.o.b. price of the US import to assess the rate of countervailing duty. The assessment may be viewed as a two-stage process in which the value of the subsidy is first allocated to exports in the domestic currency and then converted into the currency of the countervailing state at a chosen exchange rate. The allocation of the subsidy to exported production is quite straightforward in instances of direct export subsidies, but in cases of a subsidy granted to production or input usage where only a part of the output is exported, the complications discussed at an earlier point in this paper must be dealt with. In an attempt to minimize international controversy over the choice of a rate of countervailing duty when not constrained by an Article VI injury test, the US Treasury probably uses a conservative estimate of the extent of the complained about subsidization. While this tends to limit appeals to discussions of the legality of imposing *any* countervailing duty, there have been a number of cases in which the level of countervailing duty has been disputed.[13] The unwillingness of the Department of the Treasury to divulge the details of its calculation techniques in the interests of maintaining administrative flexibility has yet to be made the subject of a Freedom of Information Act action.[14]

In a significant departure from previous practice the US Treasury announced on 8 January 1973 its decision to impose countervailing duties against Canadian assistance granted to the Michelin Tire Corporation. This consisted of a £16 million regional development grant and an accelerated depreciation allowance from the federal government, a £50 million loan and a £7.6 million training and capital grant from the provincial government of Nova Scotia, and a reduced property tax assessment and a free site from the local government.[15] None of the aid carried a stipulation that the production be exported. The ostensible purpose of the assistance was the alleviation of severe regional unemployment. However, the US Treasury determined that the assistance constituted a 'bounty or grant' within the meaning of section 303 of the 1930 Tariff Act, and imposed a 6.6 per cent countervailing duty. In a series of complaints which bear similarities to the Michelin case, US producers have complained of regional assistance received by the float glass industry in the UK, Belgium and West Germany.

The Michelin case established the precedent that the US was prepared to countervail against practices which even the US finds necessary. All governments, including that of the US, provide some form of regional or industrial assistance. However, the Michelin case demonstrated that the US considered 75 per cent to be too high a percentage of production to export and still expect the US to view the subsidy as a domestic rather than an export subsidy. In the process, an important ambiguity has been introduced into US policy. It is left unclear how an acceptable export percentage is to be computed. This question should not be confused with the injury test issue. The distinction between domestic subsidies, which may have trade effects requiring countervailing action, and nonprimary export subsidies which are banned under the GATT, is a fundamental issue. Smaller, more open economies have a particular interest in ensuring that they are not the victims of modifications of the GATT which make use of such concepts as Krauss' rate of export emphasis.

Notes and References

1. Jagdish Bhagwati, 'The Generalized Theory of Distortions and Welfare', in Bhagwati *et al.* (eds.) *Trade, Balance of Payments and Growth: Essays in Honor of C. P. Kindleberger* (Amsterdam: North-Holland, 1971).
2. Alan Prest, *How Much Subsidy?* (London: Institute for Economic Affairs, 1975), p. 11.
3. Ibid., and Joint Economic Committee *The Economics of Federal Subsidy Programs,* parts 1—7 (Washington: U.S. Government Printing Office, 1972, 1973).
4. Robert E. Baldwin, *Nontariff Distortions of International Trade* (Washington: Brookings Institution, 1970).
5. Nicholas Oulton, *Tariffs, Taxes and Trade in the UK: The Effective Protection Approach.* Government Economic Service Occasional Paper No. 6. (London: HMSO, 1973).
6. Ulrich Hiemenz, and Kurt von Rabenau, 'Effective Protection of German Industry' in W. M. Corden and Gerhard Fels (eds.) *Public Assistance to Industry: Protection and Subsidies in Britain and Germany* (London: Macmillan for the Trade Policy Research Centre and the Institut für Weltwirtschaft, Kiel, 1976).
7. Prest, *op. cit.*
8. Melvyn Krauss, 'Export-Promoting Subsidies in the United Kingdom: Theoretical and Empirical Aspects' a paper presented at the First Annual Meetings of the UK SSRC International Economics Study Group, University of Sussex, 24—6, Sept 1976.
9. Geoffrey Denton, Seamus O'Cleireacain, and Sally Ash, *Trade Effects of Public Subsidies to Private Enterprise* (London: Macmillan for the Trade Policy Research Centre, 1975), p. 60.
10. Ibid., pp. 93—4.
11. See Appendix B.
12. Harald B. Malmgren, *International Order for Public Subsidies*, Trade Policy Research Centre, Thames Essays (London: Trade Policy Research Centre, 1977).
13. E. Bruce Butler, 'Countervailing Duties and Export Subsidization: A Re-emerging Issue in International Trade', *Virginia Journal of International Law*, vol. 9: 1 (1969), pp. 82—151.
14. Attempts at secrecy on the part of parties engaged in dumping or subsidized production may provoke the Treasury to impose a punitive anti-dumping or countervailing duty. Failure to cooperate with the Treasury in determining the dumping margin in an action involving Japanese carbon steel resulted in the imposition of an initial dumping duty bond of 32 per cent in October 1977. In the absence of data from five Japanese steel producers named in an action brought by Gilmour Steel, the Treasury found the firms to be selling in the US market at a price which was 32 per cent below a 'constructed value'. The Treasury arrived at the 'constructed value' by estimating Japanese production costs, adding a 10 per cent margin to cover overheads and a further 8 per cent for profit.
15. T.D. 73—10, 7 Cust. Bull. 11 (10 Jan, 1973).

10 Negotiation of Rules on Subsidies in a World of Economic Interventionism

HARALD B. MALMGREN

There appears to be consensus that state aids to industry are growing in scope and in effect, worldwide. These aids are sometimes general, such as in the case of investment incentives available to all industries, and at other times they are specific to a particular firm, industry, region, or area of research and development. Their effects are to distort market conditions and to reorient the pace and direction of adjustment of the industrial structure of each nation. Consequently, aids distort the conditions of international trade, affecting imports as well as exports. They can create adverse effects, giving rise to disruption or injury to particular economic interests. This brings about the potential for conflict among nations.

The international rules which should provide a framework for defining legitimate and illegitimate actions, and which should provide a system of conflict resolution, are vague. The problems in agriculture are similar, but because of the historic commitment of virtually all governments to interventionist policies in agriculture, international rules really do not apply to farm products. The previous chapters in this volume have posed some of the problems. This one discusses the issues from a negotiating perspective, with a view to the development of a new type of international order.

GROWING DISORDER IN THE INTERNATIONAL ECONOMIC SYSTEM

Whether, and under what circumstances national governments should aid specific sectors or industries within the framework of national economic and social objectives, can be argued at length. The *laissez-*

faire, non-interventionists will tend to argue in one direction, and the managerial interventionists in another. Between these positions is a spectrum of opinion and economic and institutional or managerial theory. Whatever one's intellectual or philosophic position on intervention, it is increasingly apparent that *the interactions of the various national policies among nations are creating significant disturbances in the orderly workings of the international economic system.* Jan Tumlir has described the problem as a political crisis:

> . . . governments have been accepting—avidly, unthinkingly, haphazardly—various responsibilities for the economy as a whole and for various groups in it, until they have found themselves overextended, unable to discharge all the responsibilities expected of them. Too many objectives and constraints have led to policies which only too often either cancel out each other, or produce wholly unanticipated, even undesired, results. It is not surprising that their mutual relations have been deteriorating.[1]

Since government is expected to do something—anything—the political solution may not be well thought through or economically efficient. The fact that other parts of the economy may be adversely affected by aids provided to a particular firm or industry is rarely considered by government, and since the effects are diffused, the political adverse reactions are usually minimal. Effects on other nations' economies are rarely considered at all, in official decisions to provide assistance to various sectors of the economy.

There are fundamental questions of sovereignty involved. Governments want to keep their freedom of action. Since many governments have become committed, through the process of negotiation with each other, to fewer and lower import restrictions, the ability to intervene through various forms of assistance is jealously guarded.

It is sometimes argued that subsidies need not be of great policy concern because they are in any event self-limiting, as a result of the limits on national budgets or on the manipulation of tax revenues. If all aids were explicit, and known to the public, this might be a sufficient restraint. However, most aids take forms which are relatively invisible or sufficiently complex that the public perception is not of concern in their implementation.

The growing role of government intervention, and the proliferation of complex methods of assistance, are combining to threaten the traditional ground rules of trade and the tacit restraints which limit the innate nationalism and mercantilism of politics in each nation. Put simply, the commercial system is in trouble, from types of intervention which were never fully taken into account when the international rules were originally worked out.

WHAT IS A SUBSIDY?

It is often not clear what is meant by a subsidy, and the difficulty of definition increases in the case of the more recondite methods of assisting an industry. Perhaps the most important case arises in connection with privileged or subsidized credit finance, or where the government is the lender of last resort. Complexities abound in this field. Institutions which lend at preferential rates should in theory operate at a loss, and this should be visible, but in practice these same institutions often borrow at special rates from central banks rather than receive direct support from treasuries. The case of the Italian holding companies (for example, IRI) is even more complex. These entities receive an annual official investment contribution (*fondi di dotazione*) which is like injection of equity capital, interest-free, and this in turn allows the entities to offer market rates of return on other borrowings even though the overall rate of return on their investments is subnormal. Indeed, the newer holding companies have received such endowments on a scale which allows them even to ignore the need to cover current costs with current revenue.[2] The evolution of this complex system in the 1970s is even more interesting, as private firms were increasingly 'bought' by the holding companies. In this period, Italian monetary policy became quite restrictive, which forced many private firms into financial difficulties. The government then gave additional support to the public holding companies to permit them to rescue private firms by buying part or all of their equity. Instead of seeking financial autonomy, the holding companies learned to expand their own deficits in order to argue the case for additional public funds.

The use of public funds for equity participation has not been limited to Italy, of course. Even in the Federal Republic of Germany, where the illusion of nonintervention prevails, the Bund and the Laender own shareholdings in a wide variety of companies. Some of these holdings are minority positions, but large, while in others (for example, a major steel firm and the dominant shipbuilding group) the government's position is a majority holding.

The orientation of official assistance to investment and financial flows has other twists and turns in Japan. For example, when the fast-growing computer firms began to have difficulties with cash flow, the government organized a leasing company to buy up computers and handle the leasing, thus providing a fast injection of cash and reducing the ongoing capital burden. Government-assisted merger activity, government purchasing policies, and favorable loan terms were among the various techniques used by the Japanese government to bring about the spectacular success of the Japanese computer industry. The complex ways in which 'guidance' of Japanese firms and industries results in transformation of the economic structure must be admired. But for purposes of analysis, what is due to subsidy, and what to direct intervention, and what due to a 'cooperative spirit' between government and business, and what due to the stability of expectations in the private sector which is generated in this environment (no one is really allowed to fail), is difficult to separate.

The interaction of the financial or banking system and the industrial sectors is another area of ambiguity. If banks extend finance under more lenient conditions during periods of weakness, or for the weaker firms, and are in turn administered more leniently by central banks and other national authorities (write-offs are not pressed, for example), and are treated especially leniently as regards taxes on their income, then where does commercial banking end and subsidy begin? The 'banking relationship' to its industrial customers is intimate and interactive—as longer lines of credit and lower interest rates automatically improve the security or risk position of the industrial firms in question. The banks may indeed exert profound influence and even control over the client. So what then is the difference as compared with an official, state-sponsored holding company? It could be said that ' . . . a holding company is often just a slightly more formal version of a banking relationship.'[3] As parts of the financial market are carved out and handled by government directly or through government guarantees or equity participation, other parts of the financial market may bear less burden from the risks which have been removed or isolated, and the commercial competition factors could in theory at least operate with more vigor. The problem, of course, is that discipline is removed by virtue of the ability to slip from the 'market forces' sector to the government-assisted sector when things go badly.

Subsidized lending rates, guarantees, public participation in lending or equity, lenient administration of troubled lending situations—all such distortions of the market in the final analysis involve government aids to industry. Complex insurance schemes based on low premiums which insure against cost escalation in fulfilment of big-project contracts (such as shipbuilding), particularly for export, are subsidies too.

All of this we see as common practice—and often we separate that which is financial and intricate from policy discussion of explicit subsidies to industry.

Another type of subsidy occurs in fiscal policy. Taxes are often the means of manipulation. Investment incentives through tax treatment, including treatment of depreciation, is a major method of assistance in many countries, but the precise effects, in terms of revenue *not* collected, are usually obscure. Manipulation. especially for external trade effects, is often possible by converting from one form of taxation to another. Thus, if a direct tax or payroll tax (for example, social security or employment tax) is dropped and an indirect tax (increment in VAT, for example) put in its place which raises the same amount of revenue, the new tax is adjustable at the border (the tax does not have to be applied to exported products since it is a consumption tax).

As an example of just how complex these questions can become, consider the introduction of a payroll tax in September, 1966, in the United Kingdom. This selective employment tax was paid by all industries, but manufacturing industries received a refund of 130 per cent of the tax. Public sector and transport industries were paid a refund of 100 per cent. It was collected with the existing National Insurance contributions system. Discrimination in this case in favor of manufacturing and against service industries was based on three main considerations: First, the existing tax structure excluded services from the general purchase tax, so that the refund for manufacturing helped offset the imbalance. Second, there was a belief that overall economic growth was directly linked to growth of the manufacturing sector. Third, a high proportion of manufacturing output was exported, and it was believed that by aiding the manufacturing sector as a whole, tax policy could provide an aid to exports without overtly acting inconsistently with the GATT strictures on export subsidies for manufactures.[4]

Indeed, it is precisely in the area of taxation, and in particular in the amount of taxation which might legitimately be adjustable at the border, that international controversy on subsidies began—in the mid-nineteenth century. The earliest known government efforts to limit subsidization were contained in national pledges not to grant export bounties, commonly found in commercial treaties negotiated by European countries in the latter half of the nineteenth century.[5] These initial pledges focused on refunds or drawbacks of excise or import duties in excess of the amount of such taxes or duties which had been collected in connection with the manufacture or sale of a product. (In spite of the pledges, excessive drawbacks and fiscal remissions were common in this period.) This led to formulation of national laws, including especially the US countervailing duty law (based on the Tariff Act of 1890 and the Tariff Act of 1897).

THE NEED TO CONTROL THE POLITICIZATION OF MARKETS

From the various papers prepared for this book, and from the preceding examples, it should be evident that we are confronted by a significant and growing problem in the world trade order. The growing intervention of governments in the workings of national economies is a force which must be reckoned with. The variety of techniques used, their complexity, and relative invisibility in many cases, pose very difficult problems in the formulation of basic principles which might be brought into the picture to bring order out of chaos. *The gradual extension of the public sector in the workings of most of the world's economies requires change in the nature of the inter-governmental rules.* Yet we find a tendency to try hard to fit all these interventionist practices into the old framework of rules, a framework which assumes a modest government role, declining trade protection, and maximum operability of market forces in economic transactions among nations.

State owned or managed enterprises are considered aberrations, and the international trading rules are not really geared to handling them. In the case of economic relations between the Western industrialized countries and the Soviet Union–Eastern Europe group, *ad hoc* solutions are employed for problems, and the problems are defined in *ad hoc* ways. That is, special judgements are made as to what conditions might be considered as 'disruptive,' and special methods of protection are devised for dealing with them—primarily on a bilateral basis. This may suffice for the dealings between the industrialized market economies and the command-economies of Eastern Europe (I think even here changes in the rules are needed), but what do we do about relations with state owned or operated enterprises in other nations (in India, the UK, Italy, or wherever)? The problem is not hypothetical. The iron and steel industry of the US in the mid-1970s is complaining strongly about competition from British steel, which is produced and sold under conditions which the US industry describes as subsidized by the British Treasury, since the producers in question are nationalized.

The very real trade policy questions raised in the trade in iron and steel include other forms of government guidance and intervention. In Sweden, the government wants steel producers to keep production up in slack times, in order to keep employment up. The inventory accumulations are therefore subsidized as a matter of policy. This in turn leads to periodic rounds of forced selling at unusually low prices (is this really a trade subsidy?). In 1976, the problems of the European producers within the Common Market led to formulation of the Simonet plan, which put limitations on intra-EEC shipments, but not on EEC production. (Governments did not want to limit production because of the adverse employment effects.) This in turn obviously generated new trade pressures, artificially. In the 1975–6 period the European Community also worked out an 'understanding' on an industry-to-industry basis with Japanese iron and steel exporters, and the 'understanding' was officially endorsed by MITI. This gave Community producers added insulation from external competition, and gave rise to formal complaints by American producers concerning 'unfair trade practices' and possibly even conspiracy (within the meaning of the anti-trust laws of the US). The interaction of these various forms of industry aids and government control, together with world overcapacity and low rates of world construction and investment activity in the mid-1970s, provides highly distorted conditions of competition. (The simultaneous crisis in world shipbuilding, with its heavily subsidized conditions of competition, adds yet another dimension to the interaction.)

First and foremost is the fact that many of the decisions in the marketplace are becoming *politicized*. Once there is intervention, in however circuitous a fashion, there is a political dimension—and of course a political uncertainty. Unfortunately, as soon as an aid is perceived as remaining for a long period, it tends to become capitalized in the value of a producing entity—which in turn builds in a force of resistance to removal of the aid at a later date.

The *political* decisions will normally be based upon a different time horizon as well as a different set of objectives, from the decisions which would otherwise be taken in the marketplace. Moreover, the political decisions may relate to a specific sector of the economy, or a specific location, without regard to the effects on other elements or sectors of the economy. There can consequently be inconsistency, and even direct conflict, between the various measures taken within a national economy. Internationally, this is also true, except that the problems are sometimes more intense, because of the strong incentive politically within any one nation to push significant adjustment costs outwards onto industry in other nations (which do not have 'votes').

There are often *trade effects*. The trade effects may be a direct consequence of the use of internal policy instruments—that is, the trade effects may be intended. On the other hand, the trade effects may arise unintentionally, as a consequence of the differences in national policies and implementing techniques.

The interventions of governments take many forms, ranging from taxes and subsidies to regulation, administrative guidance, law enforcement, and public ownership. All of the forces at work at the interface of government and the private sector can, at one level of generalization, be considered relevant.

It is particularly important to be aware of the broader context, because the purpose of particular aids is often to achieve some end which other nations achieve through regulation or competition policy. Thus, in the Federal Republic of Germany one might reasonably describe the objective of intervention, where it occurs, as a means of increasing competition rather than reducing it (strengthening some firms so they can better compete with others). Competition policy in the US is more directly addressed through the combination of regulatory practice and anti-trust law, with a condemnation of conspiracy as such, while the European practice is to look at the effects of collusion or conspiracy, and then address the problem directly or indirectly. Subsidies or government participation in equity in the FRG thus can be compared with US competition policy, and to limit consideration to trade policy might be misleading.

The *trade effects of aids to industry may not be undesirable in the long run.* It all depends on where and how the aids are applied. A strong argument could be made that aids which accelerated the adjustment of industrial structure or its transformation to knowledge-intensive activities in the face of growing imports of labor-intensive manufactures from developing countries, would be constructive in terms of global economic development, or global equity in income distribution.

THE INHERENT AMBIGUITY OF ECONOMICS

Economics should provide guidance as to when and under what circumstances aids are allowable, and perhaps even desirable, at least from the point of view of economic efficiency. That, at least, is a view expressed by many economists. However, murky analytical questions are raised when intervention takes place to achieve social objectives which are different from private market objectives. This is the realm of what economists call 'external economies.' The theory of external economies is clear enough in an unchanging, nonevolutionary world, but in a growing economy which is undergoing continuous transformation the theory is less precise. The economists would argue that subsidies are permissible where it is desired (1) to correct a discrepancy between private costs and social costs (or benefits); or (2) to bring about a redistribution of income as decided through the appropriate political mechanisms, reflecting the broad interests of the public.

This line of reasoning has been developed elsewhere,[6] and does not need repeating here. However, the real political problem, and therefore the real analytical problem, is that perceptions of private and social costs and benefits vary. A firm in trouble and requesting assistance to tide it over a difficult period, keeping its workers employed, will tend to see its troubles as temporary and abnormal. The government may see the problem as chronic. The consumer may see the problem as one of inadequate competition. The firm in trouble therefore provides one economic case, the government another, and consumers yet another, in the policy argument over whether to assist the firm. Who is right? What is the 'social cost' or 'social benefit' and who determines it (unanimous agreement is highly unlikely)?

This raises an even more basic question: *what is it that governments know, when they intervene?* Governments operate politically, balancing opinions and differing perspectives and perceptions. Governments are not omniscient. *If we formulate criteria for judging efficiency which require divine knowledge* we are evading the problem. Since governments intervene where it is believed business is wrong, and since the form and timing of intervention is politically determined, efficiency criteria based on perfect knowledge, including knowledge of how the future comes out, are scarcely worth having.

Governments also intervene for a variety of different reasons: they may wish to facilitate or expedite adjustment to new circumstances; or slow down adjustment so as to minimize disturbance of particular regions or groups of workers; or moderate cyclic peaks and valleys in economic activity; or redistribute income; or to achieve innumerable other objectives. One of the problems with government assistance to industry is that it often tends to be aimed at *adjustment resistance* as opposed to *adjustment assistance*.

The *time horizon* is a crucial part of this puzzle. The difference between a temporary problem which time will correct and a problem of fundamental disequilibrium which requires some degree of assistance may depend upon how much time you have, politically. Aids to industry make sense only in connection with long-term assessments of social value versus private value, so that incentives and penalties applied today can bring about changes later which, on balance, are believed to be socially desirable. Since the results cannot be fully known in advance, but have their justification in *future gains believed to exist*, there must be some kind of framework of long range planning or policy assessment. But it is no secret that national plans do not work very well, and that details become rapidly more hazy as the time horizon exceeds two or three years (some might say one or two quarters).

The time horizon is often the focus of policy attention. The market anticipates change at a certain rate, and the politicians decide it is too slow, or too fast. Thus, the time period for full adjustment is compressed, or stretched out. But the period or rate of adjustment is not an agreed matter. On the contrary, opinions will differ strongly.

So we have differing perceptions of the nature of current problems, differing perceptions of where we are going and where we ought to be, and differing perceptions of the time involved in achieving change.

Since there is no overall planning framework, or at least no broadbased consensus on the future pattern or structure of the economy, the differing perceptions and concepts are bargained out, usually with reference to a specific micro-economic objective, but occasionally with reference to contra-cyclical economic policy. Since micro-economic adjustment tends to be the focus, techniques of intervention tend to be tailored to the particular characteristics of the problems in specific sectors or regions. The *ad hoc* character of intervention becomes an inevitable consequence. Politically, those assisted prefer that assistance to be indirect and obscure. The result is complexity and inconsistency. Without consistency or an underlying planning logic, it is most difficult to establish the legitimacy of any international negotiating position.

SUBSIDIES AS NEGOTIATING CONCEPTS

Since intervention is both direct and indirect, and takes so many forms, the question comes up of where to begin to carve out specific parts of the problem for inter-governmental action. Are all government policies affecting national economies to be made subject to new international principles? How do we determine which policies have undesirable implications which should be dealt with internationally? Or do we limit our objectives to more narrow concerns?

The attention of this volume is on aids to industry, and for that purpose it may seem reasonable to focus more specifically on subsidies. However, the existence of a policy which affects the evolution of an industry, whether regionally, technologically, or otherwise oriented, must itself 'aid' the industry. Moreover, one country may use a financial aid for the same purpose that another country employs competition policy.

Suppose we do nonetheless focus on subsidies. What is a subsidy? From a fiscal point of view, a subsidy could be looked at as a negative tax. This does not, however, comprehend government actions which have the effect of giving a more favorable or more preferred position as a result of restraints or conditions placed upon behavior of enterprises. For working purposes, we might instead consider a subsidy to be any government action which causes a firm's, or a particular industry's, total net private costs of production to be below the level of costs that would have been incurred in the course of producing that same level of output in the absence of the government action.[7] This is not a fully satisfactory definition, because it includes government enforcement of contracts, anti-monopoly regulations, and other general government services financed out of general revenues and deemed to be necessary to the functioning of the market economy. Yet this observation simply demonstrates that the role of the government is pervasive, and where subsidy begins and socially desired legislative and administrative conditions end, will never be entirely clear. On the other hand, this working definition does call attention to the specificity or discretionary nature of a subsidy which benefits particular firms, industries, sectors, or regions.

This definition does *not* depend upon the existence of international trade in the products or services affected. It is a definition which holds irrespective of whether there is a significant foreign trade impact. The definition can be further broken down into two basic categories: 'export subsidies' and 'production subsidies.' Subsidies which are granted irrespective of the destination of the output of a producing entity, whether domestic or foreign, and where volume of assistance is solely determined by volume of production, can be called production subsidies. On the other hand, subsidies which are contingent on the product being exported, with the size of aid determined by the volume of overseas sales, may be referred to as export subsidies.

Economists will argue that wherever a subsidy is used, a production subsidy is more efficient than an export subsidy.[8] Since export subsidies distort the conditions of competition, and therefore cause adjustment problems for other nations, without commensurate domestic adjustment in the subsidizing country, some governments have suggested that export subsidies be *prohibited.* The present GATT rules, for example, are aimed at severely limiting the use of export subsidies for trade in manufactures, and the US Government has in the mid-1970s suggested broadening the coverage and making more precise the ban on export subsidies.

However, the trade effects of subsidies are often more unclear than this neat division of production subsidies and export subsidies would suggest. Production subsidies can be received by firms producing import substitutes, which certainly affects trade. And production subsidies may also have trade effects by enhancing the relative competitive position of certain enterprises compared with their position without the aids. Indeed, private producers can become concerned with several potential effects of aids: (a) artificial import pressure in competition with domestic products in domestic markets; (b) distorted conditions of competition in selling to 'third markets'; (c) deterrence of entry to foreign markets resulting from aids for import substitution; and (d) diversion effects of distorted conditions of competition in other markets (such as those resulting from import substitution) which result in 'abnormal' competition in one's own market.

Governments worry about the effects on producers more than on consumers, because the benefits to consumers are of uncertain duration, and are diffused broadly, while the distortions faced by producers are specific in effect, and may even force a change in the structure of industry and employment.

From the point of view of a trading partner, a subsidy's impact on trade (on their imports, on their exports, or on conditions of trade competition in world markets generally) is the relevant policy consideration. If this is substantial, particularly if it appears to 'frustrate benefits' that the trading partners had been expecting to reap from liberalization measures agreed to in negotiations, then it is likely to be considered equivalent to an export subsidy, whatever its status or description according to other criteria. The European Community's agricultural support mechanisms are not aimed at trade effects (the export restitution payments are theoretically designed to offset high domestic prices by bringing exports down to the equivalent world market prices, but no more). Yet the internal support system, by stimulating domestic production, exports, and import substitution, has had a greater impact on world trade than have many more strictly defined export subsidies.

In the final analysis, any official aid or distortion-creating measure will have some trade impact. The difference for trade policy is therefore a matter of degree, rather than of kind. The *intent* may therefore come into question between governments—and yet intent may not be a factor in many cases, as aids are introduced without much thought as to their external effects.

DEVELOPMENT OF MULTILATERAL GROUNDRULES

Some governments believe that the only way around these complexities is to focus on whether the degree of 'danger' is significant, or that is to say, whether there is *injury*. The GATT rules specify that countervailing duty action can only be taken where injury has been found. The US is not covered by this GATT provision, because US law predated the drafting of the relevant GATT rules, and is consequently 'grandfathered' in a protocol of provisional application. The US law calls for mandatory countervailing action against subsidies embodied on imports into the US, without regard to injury. Therefore, some governments believe the simplest solution to global negotiating problems is to bring the US into conformity with the present rules. It is then argued that most subsidies will turn out to have trade effects which are relatively minor, and which therefore will only rarely give rise to injury. The US position in recent years has been rather tending in the opposite direction, with the question raised whether an injury test should be required for any nation (that is, should private producers ever have to compete with official treasuries of other nations?).

Thus, governments might reasonably agree that all export subsidies should be *prohibited*. But this suggestion does not by itself generate much controversy, and it scarcely touches the underlying problems. The real problems lie in defining what is to be considered as a subsidy, and determining whether any injury has been done by the subsidy. Smaller countries believe that larger countries should never be able to act unilaterally, to subsidize or to countervail against subsidies, regardless of the principles agreed to, *and* that no one should be allowed to act against another without some reasonable evidence that harm (injury) has been done.

These preoccupations confuse the problems of overt export subsidies and internal production subsidies which may have a trade effect. Therefore, a reasonable international rule would be that action against production subsidies could only be taken within a framework of multilateral procedures, and only if substantial adjustment problems (disruption, injury) had been incurred in the complaining country. By moving in this direction, attention might be shifted to the effects on other national economies of national actions.

In effect, this would provide a foundation for development of a new 'common law' or a new 'case law' based on a principle of fairness: you may carry out such incentive and penalty programs as you wish internally, so long as you do not force me to undertake costly adjustments to accommodate your actions; and if there are disruptive problems for me then you are obliged to work them out with me or allow me the freedom to take offsetting action. This is simply a variant of the principle of avoiding 'beggar-thy-neighbor' policies.

The suggestion here that case law may be entailed is based on the judgement that inter-governmental discussion of national industry assistance policies will be both technically intricate and politically delicate. A regional aid, for example, which resulted in establishment of a new producing facility, might help employment—while the output may be primarily destined for third markets although this was not the intention of the regional aid. Questions of damage need to be looked at, and the degree of damage which is 'acceptable' or 'tolerable' without counteraction would have to be explored. (Even if nations acted on the basis of their own assessment of disruption or injury, multilateral surveillance of counteractions taken would be desirable.)

To get a preliminary description of what is in and what is out of consideration, as among government policy instruments, it would be desirable to develop a 'complaints list' much like the inventory of nontariff barriers which was developed under the GATT framework in recent years. (It will be recalled that the GATT list of NTB's was built up from complaints by each country concerning the trade practices of other countries.) This kind of notification procedure could then lead to a framework of categories and sub-categories of national assistance measures.

Now it should not be presumed that aids are simply substitutes for traditional forms of protectionism, to be subsumed by the same kinds of trade rules. That would be too narrow a concept. As Ohlin points out in his chapter 'Governments had also assumed very much greater responsibilities and the changing character of economic policy may reflect the rise of new objectives requiring new instruments.' Indeed, it is the likelihood that governments will continuously intervene innovatively that creates a special problem, namely that the specific character of intervention, and its timing, cannot be anticipated in every case, nor can it be known in advance whether there will even be trade effects worth considering. The governments will often not even have trade in mind when taking action.

Damage to another nation, in terms of impact on its enterprises, derives from the spilling-over of the effects of a government subsidy in one nation into the private sector in the other nation. New government actions may be involved which are not linked to purposeful changes in international commitments negotiated with other governments in the past. But the suddenness of official actions, and the fact that they cannot easily be anticipated, being political more than economic in character, create a problem of adjustment for competitors in other markets. It would therefore seem fair to provide a looser set of criteria for damage in relation to official aids than in relation to specific trade restrictions of the 'safeguard' type. Some form of 'market disruption' concept might be devised for this purpose. However, the GATT as it is already written offers a logical solution. Article VI refers to 'material injury,' which can be construed as a lesser degree of injury than 'serious injury' (this latter concept employed in connection with the imposition of Article XIX safeguards to restrict imports).

A multilateral look at the questions, either in the form of a surveillance system, or in the form of a dispute settlements procedure, should *not* entail a decision whether or not the production subsidy of industrial aid is 'justified' from the domestic point of view, within the country implementing the aid. To ask for multilateral judgements on the soundness of domestic economic, social, and political actions of a particular nation would be totally unrealistic at this stage in the history of multilateral cooperation.

Other elements of the GATT framework can also be utilized, in spite of the ambiguities. Article XVI and the 1960 Declaration which interprets it for a number of signatories, provide a reasonable foundation for dealing with export subsidies (as against production subsidies).

But this is not enough. The example of iron and steel illustrates the complex interaction of subsidies in one place, public enterprise activity operating at a loss in another, cartel-like trade agreements superimposed, and a variety of other 'aids' operating to distort the world market. As developing countries come on stream with their own iron and steel production for export, it may be assumed that heavy subsidization will be involved in those countries as well. The European Community approach (the Simonet plan) to solving the problems internally and fencing off the Common Market from the world is not acceptable. It is apparent that an overall international discussion of the iron and steel sector is needed. (At the time of this writing the problems are being multiplied rapidly by various formal procedures set in motion in the US by the American iron and steel producers, both in the Executive Branch and in the US courts, to bring about counteractions against the iron and steel producers of the EEC, Japan, Sweden, and other countries, including complaints against 'unfair trading practices', dumping, tax remissions or rebates, public enterprise operations which may be characterized as benefiting from subsidies, and cartel-like understandings.)

Since the distortions in any world industry arising from government intervention may be consequent upon a variety of different types of government aids and restrictions, and these distortions are often interactive among the various national economies, a good case can be made for examining the problems of major world industries on a sector by sector basis. The US Trade Act of 1974 *requires* sectoral evaluation of the results of the Multilateral Trade Negotiations, and US officials have therefore suggested that at least some of the key sectors be looked at independently. The Canadian government also favors sector negotiations, because of its keen interest in the problems and possibilities of restructuring resource industries as a matter of government policy. The EEC, Japan, and other nations have resisted this approach—primarily because they perceive no real need for multilateral discipline of their own national (or Communitywide) industrial policies.

The sector approach does involve the danger that industries might wish to insulate themselves from the broader process of trade liberalization, or might even wish to work out cartel-like arrangements to restrict trade and new entrants (as in the case of the international textile agreements). However, the sector approach could be used with profit, in supporting the broader negotiations on tariffs, subsidies, and NTBs, if used *in conjunction with* general negotiations. Thus, if a subsidy code were developed which contained principles of general applicability, the sectoral difficulties could be attacked within a *given framework of liberal trade principles*.

The sector approach might also be developed in a different manner, with a view to 'harmonizing' national industrial policies, in a framework such as the Industry Committees of the OECD. Such an exercise could run in *parallel* with the multilateral procedures for dispute settlement which might be developed in the GATT framework. (The present situation of worldwide excess capacity in shipbuilding, with discussions of possible sharing of markets and of cutbacks in production, would be better dealt with in this way—especially since governments are not thus far really talking to each other about the uncontrolled, widespread subsidies used in all countries.)

As world economic interdependence grows, and the developing economies intensify their participation in world production and trade activity, there will inevitably be some restructuring of the pattern and location of world production. Some countries will wish to process their own raw materials, before sale to other countries. Some countries will wish to develop exports of labor intensive manufactures. As noted earlier, it is desirable that the more industrialized countries move up the industrial ladder to develop knowledge intensive industries—and subsidies which truly assisted such change might well be justified.

It is inevitable that there will be a global shift in the pattern of industrial activity, which is related to changing world population densities, and changing age profiles of populations in the developed nations. More and more countries will be reaching the stage of industrial organization at which they are competitive in world markets in a wide, and widening, range of manufactures. This structural change, and industrial growth, is limited only by the capacity of the richer countries to absorb imports and adjust their economies to take account of shifting competitiveness.

The efforts of each country to assist adjustment, or forestall it, on an *ad hoc* basis, must inevitably hinder this more fundamental process of restructuring, if national measures are in conflict with one another. Simply relying on low tariffs to reconcile the various policies of national economies will not be adequate. The same can be said for counter-cyclical policies (such as inventory subsidization in Sweden, or purchases of equity by public holding companies in Italy). Variation in national approach must be brought into some framework of harmonization.

In the Warnecke chapter a number of ways are described in which the European Community has dealt with such problems. The European economies are characterized by more *conscious* intervention than the American economy, and it is obvious that rules and procedures had to be established to prevent governments from 'frustrating the benefits' of the internal liberalization of the Common Market (just as the EFTA countries had to develop an elaborate section of their agreement, on competition policy, which was designed to prevent 'frustration of benefits'[9]).

The Commission, in order to accomplish this end, had to determine how the Community perspective differed from a national perspective, and ensure that aids of the member states took the interests of their partners into account. Towards this end, Warnecke points out that aids were categorized into three groups: regional, sectoral, and general. In the case of regional aids, certain principles were established: (a) There should be *specificity* in regional aids, so that the nation's regions or zones to be assisted would be precisely defined. (b) The aids should be *transparent*, involving open and prior knowledge of the geographical and sectoral locations of aids, and their quantitative significance. (c) The *intensity* of aids must be tailored to the nature, seriousness, and urgency of the problem. (d) Various programs in the Community should be *coordinated and harmonized*, to permit a 'Community attitude'. Prior review is inherently difficult because the effects or incidence of aid measures are hard to determine in advance of their implementation. As Warnecke points out:

> In addition to determining whether a subsidy will distort competition the Commission is also faced with making an entrepreneurial judgment concerning the viability of a firm or a sector. But this not only requires an analysis of a firm's efficiency in the national context, but also in reference to the Common Market, and when necessary in reference to the global economy.

The Commission cannot readily decide each issue on an *ad hoc* basis, and needs guidelines—but the nine member states do not really agree with each other on proper sectoral or regional policies, or on the distribution of industries among them, or on the proper contra-cyclical policies each should pursue. All of this is consequently still in an early stage of development.

What lessons can be drawn from the Community's limited experience? Clearly, the notions of *specificity* and *transparency* as described by Warnecke could be made part of a multilateral code of conduct (perhaps in the GATT framework). The tailoring of aids, and their coordination or harmonization, could then be addressed in industrial sector committees (perhaps in the OECD, with the multilateral code of conduct as a frame of reference).

Thus, a multi-pronged approach may be the most sensible way of introducing order to what is becoming an increasingly disorderly process of national action:

I. GENERAL PRINCIPLES (embodied in a negotiated code of conduct which became part of the GATT system of rules)

A. Prohibiting *export* subsidies (within the meaning of this chapter) *except*

1. In the case of agricultural products covered by price support programs, which will have to be dealt with in connection with the whole range of agricultural policy issues

2. 'Infant exporter' situations, in which case the exceptions would be temporary, subject to multilateral review, and tailored to the problem (for example possible special treatment of market promotion and distribution incentives for developing country exporters not selling through multinational enterprise channels).

3. Specific allowable subsidies for developing countries which qualify, with stipulation of economic conditions (exchange rate and balance of payments situation reviewed by IMF, employment, per capita income, reliance on primary products, fiscal structure, budget, etc.) so that only certain types of developing countries qualify (a large number, but not all)

B. Providing for multilateral consultation, dispute settlement, and surveillance of 'production' subsidies, subject to

1. the subsidy having a trade effect, *and*

2. there being a market disruption effect, either in the complainants' own market or in a third market where the subsidized exports and the complainants' exports are in competition.

C. Allowing for countervailing action

D. Avoiding 'beggar thy neighbor' policies

E. Favoring actions which enhance rather than frustrate the effects of liberalization of trade policies

F. Requiring specificity and transparency of aid measures of all types

II. PROCEDURAL MECHANISMS (to be established within one or more institutions)

A. For building 'case law' in connection with consultation, dispute settlement, and surveillance in a multilateral (GATT?) framework

B. For harmonizing interventionist policies within key sectors, in a framework of industry committees (OECD?)

C. For providing international reports on measures taken and their apparent significance (GATT list of 'complaints' and OECD industry commentaries?)

D. For general examination of the relationship of industrial aids, industrial policies, and 'competition policy' (OECD?)

In regard to point IIA if a multilateral body were established within the GATT to evaluate complaints and settle disputes, it should be able to:

A. Request the termination of subsidies, without reference to injury or dual pricing

B. Notify other trading partners of their right to countervail if the subsidy is not withdrawn

C. Approve retaliatory action or compensation if the subsidy is not withdrawn and other nations do not countervail, leaving a third country competition problem

D. Review the extent of market disruption in the case of production subsidies subject to complaint

E. Develop interpretive guidelines for production subsidies percentage of output exported, *de minimis* export effects, import substitution and its 'frustration of benefits' effect.

DEVELOPING COUNTRIES

We have not yet covered the special problems posed by the developing countries—or at least those developing countries which have become successful exporters of manufactures and which are in a rapid industrialization phase of their growth. Such countries want 'special and differential treatment' when it comes to writing down new rules on aids to industry. They want freedom to subsidize.

An argument can be made for 'infant industry' aids in such cases—but differential permission to engage in more aggressive subsidization should not be permanent for situations of infants or new starters. Rather, special dispensation could be granted for a temporary period, subject to 'graduation' of the successful developing countries, making way then for the weaker developing countries to have their 'turn'.

However, such dispensation, even where granted, should be subject to multilateral scrutiny, bearing in mind the fiscal position of the country in question to sustain prolonged subsidization (of consumption in the rich countries, for that is what is involved) as well as the balance of payments needs of the country concerned.

A warning about the problem posed by freedom to subsidize should be made. The extent of possible subsidization for any country is limited by tax collection and other revenue considerations as well as by budget requirements. Rich countries will always be potentially freer than poorer countries to subsidize. Therefore a major long-term problem for the developing nations will be the relative freedom and capacity to subsidize on the part of the richer nations, in competition in world trade with exports of poorer nations, in manufactures as well as in some primary products. The developing nations have given virtually no thought to this problem, but instead focused exclusively on how to implement special and differential treatment for them (greater freedom of action) in this area.

Are developing countries doomed to trade stagnation if they do not have freedom to subsidize? Exports of developing countries have been growing roughly one-third faster than exports of developed countries in the period 1962–73. To the extent that this growth in exports of manufactures was not evenly distributed among the developing countries, it is likely to have been concentrated in the more advanced developing countries—which also means that it is likely to have been concentrated in those developing countries with the most advanced tax systems. This means, in turn, that those developing countries which have the greatest need for speeding up their exports of manufactures—the less advanced among the developing countries—would be the ones least capable of taking advantage of special treatment of export subsidy practices.

If the problem for the developing country is learning how to conduct export business (finding markets, meeting standards and delivery dates, learning how to penetrate through trade barriers, etc.), which it may well be, then a trade subsidy for marketing and distribution activities would be the 'first best' solution. This is one of the most plausible justifications. In effect, the multinational enterprises do not have the same difficulties, because their internal transactions comprehend many of these activities, and they have institutional experience and long standing international relationships for dealing with such problems. The use of subsidies in a developing country in such cases would in a way be an offset to the 'multinational enterprise advantage'.

Reverting to the warning made at the outset of this section on developing nations, the more important problem for many of them at the low end of the development ladder is the greater flexibility and capacity of the relatively more developed countries (including the more developed among the developing nations) to out-compete them by out-subsidizing them as and when necessary in world competition. The uncertainties implicit in government actions, either to subsidize or to countervail, are themselves a deterrent to development of export activities. Stabilizing and making predictable the rules of the game by which the more developed countries are guided should be the principal concern of nations which are not now vigorous exporters of processed products and manufactures, with the issue of special derogations a secondary priority in terms of its economic value to them.

THE FUNDAMENTAL CHOICE: A NEW ORDER, OR GROWING DISARRAY

In conclusion, we have seen that the issues in this field of industrial policy and official aids to industry are highly complex. The aids are often relatively diffuse, or invisible or recondite. The boundary between general guidance or intervention and specific aids or subventions is unclear. The financial side of the economy is particularly ambiguous, and many of the aids are focused in their effects on the location and type of capital formation which takes place in the economy. Where the public sector leaves off and the private begins, in banking and finance, is unclear.

We also know that official activism is on the rise. Structural changes are becoming politicized in many nations—which in turn creates a situation of instability and unpredictability. This is even more true in the developing countries than in the developed. This in turn raises risks, and therefore investment costs, for both domestic producers and foreign exporters.

When governments act, they often are reacting to specific circumstances in a micro-economic context. Hence actions are often inconsistent one with another, and even conflict. The government's judgement typically differs from that of the private industry interests, and both from the assessments of consumers and other interests in the economy. When a government acts, it assumes that some finite period is entailed to provide correction or eliminate a maladjustment of some given size. However, it has to be constantly remembered that the government cannot really know in advance, any more than others, what the real magnitude of the structural problem is. As Tumlir has put it, 'The extent of the maladjustment can only be revealed or ascertained in the process of adjustment: it can only be measured by the extent of labor transfers and capital write-downs through which equilibrium is re-established.'[10]

The question then of who knows what is critical—because, in a period of growing official activism, we do not want intervention to *intensify* structural problems, or *prolong* them, or simply *escalate public expenditures* as numerous policies become mutually cancelling. This then suggests that it should be in the interests of governments to find international rules by which they can bind themselves, as well as each other, and which require them to act in transparent, measurable ways with specifically tailored measures, thus limiting the micro-economic pressures, and the related political pressures, from dominating national policy.

We thus do not want greater order or harmony just for trade policy reasons—we need order because otherwise the role of governments, acting in the dark, will dominate the structural adjustment processes of our respective economies, creating massive investment uncertainties, and consequently stagnation.

The government-business interface, in its broadest sense, is in question. This is not so much a question of who owns the capital (the means of production), as how decisions are made—whether primarily in light of narrow political pressures or in light of reasonably active market forces, and within a framework in which various actions can be compared in the light of day.

The approach of this paper, in conclusion, is to design (a) a system of discipline which is evolutionary; (b) a system which catches in its filter those interventions which are most readily perceived, and which give rise to political friction, so that 'major problems' are resolved as the rules are developed over time. Thus, it is not so much a complete rewriting of present rules that is recommended, as starting a process of development of rules through interpretation, conflict-settlement procedures, adjudication, and accretion of case law.

Notes and References

1. J. Tumlir, 'Adjustment Cost and Policies to Reduce It', for the MIT Workshop on Specific Proposals and Desirable DC Response to LDC Demands Regarding the New International Economic Order, 17–20 May, 1976.
2. See John B. Sheahan, 'Experience with Public Enterprise in France and Italy', Chap. 7 in W. G. Shepherd, ed., *Public Enterprise: Economic Analysis of Theory and Practice*, (Lexington, 1976) pp. 142–4.
3. W. G. Shepherd, 'Public Enterprise in Financial Sectors', Chap. 8 in W. G. Shepherd, *Public Enterprise*, p. 187.
4. See Chap. 2, 'Industrial Policy in the United Kingdom', in G. Denton, S. O'Cleireacain, & S. Ash, *Trade Effects of Public Subsidies to Private Enterprise*, (Macmillan, London, 1975) pp. 32–4.
5. See Jacob Viner's history in his *Dumping: A Problem in International Trade*, (reprinted, Augustus M. Kelley, N.Y., 1966) Chap. 10.
6. For a survey of the state of thinking, see my monograph *International Order for Public Subsidies*, (Thames Essay, London, 1977).

7. This concept of a subsidy is used as the basis of my analysis in my Thames Essay.

8. The economics are rather complex, but the most common way of looking at the efficiency of an aid is that if there is a problem to be corrected, that problem is a result of *domestic* relationships of factor prices among workers and firms throughout the economy. To correct the basic relationship, and at the same time benefit from economies of scale whatever the destination of the product, is more efficient than simply assisting that part of overall production aimed at export. My monograph, *ibid.*, goes into the arguments somewhat, and from there the curious reader can pursue further a number of more intricate and somewhat esoteric papers listed in the bibliography in that monograph.

9. See R. Middleton, *Negotiating on Non-Tariff Distortions of Trade: The EFTA Precedents*, (Macmillan, London, 1975) esp. pp. 42–54.

10. Ibid.

PART 3

Appendix A

GENERAL AGREEMENT ON TARIFFS AND TRADE*

ARTICLE VI

ANTI-DUMPING AND COUNTERVAILING DUTIES

*From: General Agreement on Tariffs and Trade, Basic Instruments and Selected Documents, Ninth Supplement, Geneva, February 1961.

1. The contracting parties recognize that dumping, by which products of one country are introduced into the crmmerce of another country at less than the normal value of products, is to be condemned if it causes or threatens material injury to an established industry in the territory of a contracting party or materially retards the establishment of a domestic industry. For the purposes of this Article, a product is to be considered as being introduced into the commerce of an importing country at less than its normal value, if the price of the product exported from one country to another

(a) is less than the comparable price, in the ordinary course of trade, for the like product when destined for consumption in the exporting country, or,

(b) in the absence of such domestic price, is less than either

(i) the highest comparable price for the like product for export to any third country in the ordinary course of trade, or   (ii) the cost of production of the product in the country of origin plus a reasonable addition for selling cost and profit.

Due allowance shall be made in each case for differences in conditions and terms of sale, for differences in taxation, and for other differences affecting price comparability.

2. In order to offset or prevent dumping, a contracting party may levy on any dumped product an anti-dumping duty not greater in amount than the margin of dumping in respect of such product. For the purposes of this Article, the margin of dumping is the price difference determined in accordance with the provisions of paragraph 1.

3. No countervailing duty shall be levied on any product of the territory of any contracting party imported into the territory of another contracting party in excess of an amount equal to the estimated bounty or subsidy determined to have been granted, directly or indirectly, on the manufacture, production or export of such product in the country of origin or exportation, including any

special subsidy to the transportation of a particular product. The term 'countervailing duty' shall be understood to mean a special duty levied for the purpose of offsetting any bounty or subsidy bestowed, directly or indirectly, upon the manufacture, production or export of any merchandise.

4. No product of the territory of any contracting party imported into the territory of any other contracting party shall be subject to anti-dumping or countervailing duty by reason of the exemption of such product from duties or taxes born by the like product when destined for consumption in the country of origin or exportation, or by reason of the refund of such duties or taxes.

5. No product of the territory of any contracting party imported into the territory of any other contracting party shall be subject to both anti-dumping and countervailing duties to compensate for the same situation of dumping or export subsidization.

6. (a) No contracting party shall levy any anti-dumping or countervailing duty on the importation of any product of the territory of another contracting party unless it determines that the effect of the dumping or subsidization, as the case may be, is such as to cause or threaten material injury to an established domestic industry, or is such as to retard materially the establishment of a domestic industry.

(b) The Contracting Parties may waive the requirement of sub-paragraph (a) of this paragraph so as to permit a contracting party to levy an anti-dumping or countervailing duty on the importation of any product for the purpose of offsetting dumping or subsidization which causes or threatens material injury to an industry in the territory of another contracting party exporting the product concerned to the territory of the importing contracting party. The Contracting Parties shall waive the requirement of sub-paragraph (a) of this paragraph, so as to permit the levying of a countervailing duty, in cases in which they find that a subsidy is causing or threatening material injury to an industry in the territory of another contracting party exporting the product concerned to the territory of the importing contracting party.

(c) In exceptional circumstances, however, where delay might cause damage which would be difficult to repair, a contracting party may levy a countervailing duty for the purpose referred to in sub-paragraph (b) of this paragraph without the prior approval of the Contracting Parties; Provided that such action be reported immediately to the Contracting Parties and that the countervailing duty shall be withdrawn promptly if the Contracting Parties disapprove.

7. A system for the stabilization of the domestic price or of the return to domestic producers of a primary commodity, independently of the movements of export prices, which results at times in the sale of the commodity for export at a price lower than the comparable price charged for the like commodity to buyers in the domestic market, shall be presumed not to result in material injury within the meaning of paragraph 6 if it is determined by consultation among the contracting parties substantially interested in the commodity concerned that:

(a) the system has also resulted in the sale of the commodity for export at a price higher than the comparable price charged for the like commodity to buyers in the domestic market, and

(b) the system is so operated, either because of the effective regulation of production, or otherwise, as not to stimulate exports unduly or otherwise seriously prejudice the interests of other contracting parties.

ARTICLE XVI

SUBSIDIES

Section A—Subsidies in General
1. If any contracting party grants or maintains any subsidy, including any form of income or price support, which operates directly or indirectly to increase exports of any product from, or to reduce imports of any product into its territory, it shall notify the Contracting Parties in writing of the extent and nature of the subsidization, of the estimated effect of the subsidization on the quantity of the affected product or products imported into or exported from its territory and of the circumstances making the subsidization necessary. In any case in which it is determined that serious prejudice to the interests of any other contracting party is caused or threatened by any such subsidization, the contracting party granting the subsidy shall, upon request, discuss with the other contracting party or parties concerned, or with the Contracting Parties, the possibility of limiting the subsidization.

Section B—Additional Provisions on Exports Subsidies
2. The contracting parties recognize that the granting by a contracting party of a subsidy on the export of any product may have harmful effects for other contracting parties, both importing and exporting, may cause undue disturbance to their normal commercial interests, and may hinder the achievement of the objectives of this Agreement.
3. Accordingly, contracting parties should seek to avoid the use of subsidies on the export of primary products. If, however, a contracting party grants directly or indirectly any form of subsidy which operates to increase the export of any primary product from its territory, such subsidy shall not be applied in a manner which results in that contracting party having more than an equitable share of world export trade in that product, account being taken of the shares of the contracting parties in such trade in the product during a previous representative period, and any special factors which may have affected or may be affecting such trade in the product.
4. Further, as from 1 January 1958 or the earliest practicable date thereafter, contracting parties shall cease to grant either directly or indirectly any form of subsidy on the export of any product other than a primary product which subsidy results in the sale of such product for export at a price lower than the comparable price charged for the like product to buyers in the domestic market. Until 31 December 1957 no contracting party shall extend the scope of any such subsidization beyond that existing on 1 January 1955 by the introduction of new, or the extension of existing, subsidies.
5. The Contracting Parties shall review the operation of the provisions of this Article from time to time with a view to examining its effectiveness, in the light of actual experience, in promoting the objectives of this Agreement and avoiding subsidization seriously prejudicial to the trade or interests of contracting parties.

Appendix B

MEASURES CONSIDERED SUBSIDIES UNDER GATT ARTICLE XVI:4

(Adopted 19 November 1960)

The following detailed list of measures which are considered as forms of export subsidies by a number of contracting parties was referred to in the proposal submitted by the Government of France, and the question was raised whether it was clear that these measures could not be maintained if the provisions of the first sentence of paragraph 4 of Article XVI were to become fully operative:

(a) Currency retention schemes or any similar practices which involve a bonus on exports or re-exports;

(b) The provision by governments of direct subsidies to exporters;

(c) The remission, calculated in relation to exports, of direct taxes or social welfare charges on industrial or commercial enterprises;

(d) The exemption, in respect of exported goods, of charges or taxes, other than charges in connexion with importation or indirect taxes levied at one or several stages on the same goods if sold for internal consumption; or the payment, in respect of exported goods, of amounts exceeding those effectively levied at one or several stages on these goods in the form of indirect taxes or of charges in connexion with importation or in both forms;

(e) In respect of deliveries by governments or governmental agencies of imported raw materials for export business on different terms than for domestic business, the charging of prices below world prices;

(f) In respect of government export credit guarantees, the charging of premiums at rates which are manifestly inadequate to cover the long-term operating costs and losses of the credit insurance institutions;

(g) The grant by governments (or special institutions controlled by governments) of export credits at rates below those which they have to pay in order to obtain the funds so employed;

(h) The government bearing all or part of the costs incurred by exporters in obtaining credit.

The Working party agreed that this list should not be considered exhaustive or to limit in any way the generality of the provisions of paragraph 4 of Article XVI. It noted that the governments prepared to accept the declaration contained in Annex A agreed that, for the purpose of that declaration, these practices generally are to be considered as subsidies in the sense of Article XVI: 4 or are covered by the Articles of Agreement of the International Monetary Fund. The representatives of governments which were not prepared to accept that declaration were not able to subscribe at this juncture to a precise interpretation of the term 'subsidies', but had no objection to the above interpretation being accepted by the future parties to that declaration for the purposes of its application.

Appendix C

SUGGESTED EXPANSION OF LIST OF MEASURES CONSIDERED SUBSIDIES UNDER GATT ARTICLE XVI:4

The following is the list of prohibited practices as examined by Working Group 1 at its last meeting (Spec [73]44, paragraph 6) it being understood that this list did not commit any delegation and that the 1960 list of prohibited practices remained as it stood:

(a) The provision by governments of direct subsidies to exporters.

(b) Internal transport and freight subsidies on export shipments on terms more favourable than for domestic shipments.

(c) The government bearing directly or indirectly all or part of the transport or freight charges incurred on export shipments beyond national frontiers.

(d) The government bearing all or part of the costs incurred by exporters in obtaining transport and freight insurance cover.

(e) The government bearing all or part of the costs incurred by exporters in obtaining credit for financing export shipments.

(f) Government loans to exporters on concessional terms for working capital purposes, where such loans enable the exporter to offer concessional sales terms, including financing.

(g) The grant by governments (or special institutions controlled by governments) of export credits at rates below those which they have to pay in order to obtain the funds so employed.

(h) The provision by governments (or special institutions controlled by governments) of export credit insurance and guarantees, or insurance against increases in the costs of products at premium rates which are manifestly inadequate to cover the long-term operating costs and losses of the insurance institutions.

(i) The accordance by governments of preferred treatment to certain exporters based on their export performance, such as the extension of time for the more favourable terms in export insurance programmes.

(j) Loans that minimize the risk involved in developing new markets abroad, (i.e. the obligation to repay the loan is forgiven if the firm is not successful in developing a substantial market abroad).

(k) Currency retention schemes or any similar practices which involve a bonus on exports or re-exports.

(l) Special government measures to offset, in whole or in part, the price disadvantages on exports that result from its own or other countries' exchange rate adjustments.

(m) the remission (including credit allowances) or deferral of direct taxes or social welfare charges paid or payable by industrial or commercial enterprises when the criterion for remission or deferral is related to the export performance.

(n) The exemption, in respect of exported goods, of charges or taxes, other than charges in connexion with importation or indirect taxes levied at one or several stages on the same goods if sold for internal consumption.

(o) The allowance of special deductions related to exports, over and above those granted in respect to production for domestic consumption, in the calculation of the base on which direct taxes are charged (e.g. accelerated depreciation allowances on capital goods used in the production of exports; deduction of special reserves set aside to cover risks connected with export sales).

(p) Tax rebate allowed beyond that of actual costs incurred, in calculating income payable for expenses incurred in developing markets abroad.

(q) Rebate of indirect taxes or charges on exports or components thereof, in excess of accrued indirect taxes or charges on the exported products.

(r) Remission calculated in relation to exports of taxes not borne by the products (taxes occultes).

(s) The reduction of the direct tax burden on producers and exporters of a product accompanied by an increase in the indirect taxes borne by the same product.

(t) In respect of deliveries by governments or governmental agencies of imported raw materials for export business on different terms than for domestic business, the charging of prices below world prices; and for such deliveries of raw materials of domestic origin, the charging of prices for such materials destined for processing for export sales, below those charged for materials destined for processing for domestic sales.

(u) Government payments to producers or exporters that vary with the value of domestic materials used in the manufacture of goods for export.

Appendix D

TREATY ESTABLISHING THE EUROPEAN ECONOMIC
COMMUNITY

SECTION 3

AIDS GRANTED BY STATES

Article 92

1. Except where otherwise provided for in this Treaty, any aid granted by a Member State or through State resources, in any form whatsoever, which distorts or threatens to distort competition by favoring certain enterprises or the production of certain goods shall, to the extent to which it affects trade between Member States, be deemed to be incompatible with the Common Market.

2. The following shall be compatible with the Common Market:

   a) aid of a social character granted to individual consumers, provided that such aid is granted without discrimination based on the origin of the products concerned;

   b) aid intended to remedy damage caused by natural calamities or other extraordinary events;

   c) aid granted to the economy of certain regions of the Federal Republic of Germany affected by the division of Germany, to the extent that such aid is necessary in order to compensate for the economic disadvantages caused by such division.

3. The following may be deemed to be compatible with the Common Market:

   a) aid intended to promote the economic development of regions where the standard of living is abnormally low or where there exists serious underemployment;

   b) aid intended to promote the execution of important projects of common European interest or to remedy a serious disturbance in the economy of a Member State;

   c) aid intended to facilitate the development of certain activities or of certain economic regions, provided that such aid does not change trading conditions to such an extent as would be contrary to the common interest. Any aid to shipbuilding existing on 1 January 1957 shall, to the extent that such aid merely offsets the absence of customs protection, be gradually reduced under the same conditions as apply to the abolition of customs duties, subject to the provisions of this Treaty relating to the common commercial policy in regard to third countries;

   d) such other types of aid as may be specified by decision of the Council acting by a qualified majority vote on a proposal of the Commission.

Article 93

1. The Commission shall, in conjunction with Member States, constantly examine all systems of aid existing in those States. It shall propose to the latter any appropriate measure required by the gradual development or by the functioning of the Common Market.

2. If, after having given notice to the parties concerned to submit their comments, the Commission finds that aid granted by a State or through State resources is not compatible with the Common Market within the meaning of Article 92, or that such aid is applied in an abusive manner, it shall decide that the State concerned shall abolish or modify such aid within the time-limit prescribed by the Commission.

If the State concerned does not comply with this decision within the prescribed time-limit, the Commission or any other interested State may, notwithstanding the provision of Articles 169 and 170, refer the matter to the Court of Justice directly.

At the request of any Member State, the Council, acting by unanimous vote, may, if such a decision is justified by exceptional circumstances, decide that any aid granted or planned by that State shall be deemed to be compatible with the Common Market, notwithstanding the provisions of Article 92 or the regulations provided for in Article 94. If the Commission has, in respect of the aid in question, already initiated the procedure provided for, in the first sub-paragraph of this paragraph, the request made to the Council by the State concerned shall cause such procedure to be suspended until the Council has made its attitude known.

If, however, the Council has not made its attitude known within a period of three months from the making of such a request, the Commission shall render its decision.

3. The Commission shall be informed, in sufficient time to enable it to submit its comments, of any plans to grant or to modify any aid. If it considers that any such plan is not compatible with the Common Market within the meaning of Article 92, it shall without delay initiate the procedure provided for in the preceding paragraph. The Member State concerned may not put its proposed measures into effect until such procedure has resulted in a final decision.

Article 94

The Council, acting by a qualified majority vote on a proposal of the Commission, may make any appropriate regulations for carrying out Articles 92 and 93 and may, in particular, determine the conditions for carrying out Article 93(3), and the types of aid which are exempt from this procedure.

Index